Blackfoot Physics

Blackfoot Physics

A Journey into the Native American Worldview

F. David Peat

PHANES PRESS
AN ALEXANDRIA BOOK

An Alexandria Book
Alexandria Books explore intersections —
the meeting points between cosmology,
philosophy, myth, culture, and the creative spirit.
www.cosmopolis.com

PHANES PRESS, INC.
PO Box 6114
Grand Rapids, MI 49516
www.phanes.com

9 8 7 6 5 4 3 2 1
Printed in the United States of America
∞ This edition is printed on acid-free paper that meets the
American National Standards Institute Z39.48 Standard.

Library of Congress Cataloging-in-Publication Data
Peat, F. David 1938–
[Lighting the seventh fire]
Blackfoot physics: a journey into the native american universe /
F. David Peat
p. cm.
Originally published: Lighting the seventh fire. Secaucus, N.J.:
Carol Pub. Group, ©1994. With new afterword.
"An Alexandria book."
Includes bibliographical references and index.
ISBN 1-890482-83-8 (alkaline paper)
1. Indian philosophy—North America. 2. Science—Philosophy.
3. Space and time. 4. Indians of North America—Medicine.
6. Indians of North America—Mathematics. I. Title.

E98.P5 .P43 1994
191'.089'97–de21   2002073251

This book is dedicated to the First People of Turtle Island in the hope that the Circle of Four Races will grow. I hope that there will be something in this book that pleases and in some way reflects what I have experienced and been told. At best I can say with Geoffrey Chaucer, "And if ther be anythyng that displese hem, I preye hem also that they arrette is to defaute of myn unknonnynge, and nat to my wyl, that wolde ful fayn have seyd bettre if I hadde had konnynge."

Contents

Acknowledgment

I would like to thank the many Native American people who offered me their friendship and hospitality and who freely shared their knowledge and wisdom with me. Some of them are specifically mentioned by name in the text. If I were to attempt to mention everyone here I would run the risk of inadvertently leaving out the name of a friend or someone who helped me. I would, however, like to mention three people who have been particularly important to me and ask them to stand as representatives for all—they are Leroy Little Bear, Ernie Benedict, and Sa'ke'j Henderson.

Author to Reader:
A Different Worldview

Within the chapters of this book can be found discussions of metaphysics and philosophy; the nature of space and time; the connection between language, thought, and perception; mathematics and its relationship to time; the ultimate nature of reality; causality and interconnection; astronomy and the movements of time; healing; the inner nature of animals, rocks, and plants; powers of animation; the importance of maintaining a balanced exchange of energy; of agriculture; of genetics; of considerations of ecology; of the connection of the human being to the cosmos; and of the nature of processes of knowing. In addition, there are references to technologies such as the Clovis spear point, ocean-going vessels and birchbark canoes, tepees and longhouses, the development of corn and other plants, farming methods, observational astronomy and record keeping, and the preparation of medicines from various sources.

All of these topics have been gathered together under the general rubric of Indigenous science, a term I have used following the lead of Pam Colorado, Leroy Little Bear, and others. While I am comfortable with this term *Indigenous science*, I am also a part of the Western science tribe and I can already sense the kind of objections that its members could make: "Why do you use the term *science?* Native Americans don't have any science in the real sense of the word. They don't have an ordered system of investigation or rational theories of the universe as we do. Science is a specific and disciplined approach that was developed in the West. Indigenous people have traditions, folklore, and mythology."

There might also be the objection that I have confused science with technology, that while, critics may say, Native people have indeed developed their crafts and artifacts to a fine art, this has nothing to do with real science. Moreover, the various innovations I have mentioned are simply the result of trial and error combined with patient observation.

These sorts of criticisms are generally presented when Indigenous peoples all over the world are discussed. It is still possible to find words like *primitive, superstitious, undeveloped* and even *pagan* in books and museum exhibitions referring to Native peoples. One tends to hear the word *civilization* used only in the context of the Incas, Mayans, and Aztecs.

Civilization, it is held, comes about when people have advanced to the point where they become centralized into cities, where crafts become specialized, and artisans and merchants appear. Civilization is the feature of a society that has sufficient leisure for the perfection of arts, as opposed to crafts and decoration; science, as opposed to superstitions and trial-and-error technologies; literature, as opposed to folktales and oral traditions; organized religion, as opposed to animism and polytheism. Thus, it is argued, the societies of Turtle Island (the American continents)* never developed to the extent that they could enjoy that degree of complexity and sophistication that provides the fertile ground in which true science can grow.

Texts on psychiatry speak of Indigenous peoples as representing "earlier" and "more primitive" forms of mental and

---

*The Aboriginal people of North America refer to this continent as Turtle Island. This name is sometimes also used to encompass the entire North and South American land mass.

social development. The study of "primitive peoples" is of interest to the psychologist and psychiatrist more for the light it casts on hypothetical stages in the development of the human mind and human societies than for the intrinsic values that Indigenous metaphysics may hold. The spirituality of The People is considered to belong to the supposed earlier animistic or polytheistic stages in the development of world religions. Each of the Indigenous groups or nations refers to itself by a name that can generally be translated as meaning "the people," "the true people," "the real people," etc. On the evolutionary ladder of religions, the spirituality and traditional ways of the Lakoda, Hopi, and Haida stand in relation to Judaism, Islam, and Christianity as the lower primates do to human beings. Learned papers discuss the question of whether certain Native American groups had "advanced" to the early stages of monotheism, or if their talk of the Creator was merely a parroting of what the first missionaries had told them.

While many medical professionals would agree that certain traditional curing ceremonies appear to help in activating the patient's natural processes of healing, they would argue that there exists no proper "medicine" in the sense of an integrated approach to sickness that involves a comprehensive theory of the origin of disease and the biochemistry of the body; a range of diagnostic tools; well defined surgical interventions; and a broad base of drugs, immunization techniques, and so on. Scientific medicine, it is claimed, only exists within the West and what Indigenous Americans practice is a mixture of old wives' tales, folk remedies, and the sorts of superstition and self-hypnotism that are associated with faith healing.

I believe the verdict of most "hard-nosed" scientists would, be that while Indigenous metaphysics and philosophy is certainly fascinating and, to the extent that it brings people close to nature, attractive; nevertheless, it should not be called a science. This is the inevitable conclusion within a worldview whose values are dominated by the need for progress, development, improvement, evolution, and the linear unfolding of time. Within such a world it stands to reason that things evolve, that automobile engines become more efficient, that new computers are faster, and that some societies are more highly developed than others.

Our Western concept of nature is based on an evolutionary model. Left to the natural forces around them, things will "progress," getting better and better. Going along with this worldview is the need, when faced with alternatives, to decide which one is "better" than the others. It goes without saying that when it comes to other people's cultures we are generally the ones who are doing the measuring, and are supplying the yardstick as well! If two systems exist, both of which claim to be sciences, our natural tendency is to compare them, like the latest model autos, and see which one comes out on top.

This desire to compare, to measure, and to categorize in terms of better and worse does not seem to be the natural way of doing things within the Indigenous world. As my friend Clem Ford has observed, in Labrador there was a traditional Indigenous way to hunt beaver and one that the European trappers used. Today both methods are used by Native people, and there is no sense that one method is "better" than the other, or that one should replace the other. Rather, both methods are used, side by side.

Blackfoot Physics

Spirits of Renewal

It is mid-January and, as I write these pages, the snow in Ottawa is thick on the ground and the temperature well below –20°C. East of me in Quebec the Huron people are celebrating their New Year, while an hour's drive to the south, at Akwesasne, the Mohawks are in the midst of their midwinter festival. My Akwesasne friends, Kim Hathaway-Carr, Brenda La France and the Elder Ernie Benedict, are Mohawks of the Iroquois Confederation, or, more properly, the Haudenosaunee people. (At the end of this introduction you will find a note on all the sorts of problems that crop up when one group of people tries to pin a name on another.)

Following the Akwesasne midwinter festival, in which the ashes of the dying year's fire are stirred and thrown over the participants, comes the Tapping of the Maple Trees and the maple sugar festival. The year's round continues with corn planting; strawberry, bean and green-corn festivals; and, finally, the thanksgiving dances that celebrate the gathering of the corn. As the Haudenosaunee move through their calendar year, they participate in ceremonies that celebrate the annual cycle of nature—the great rotation of time that begins and ends with death and renewal.

To the west, friends who are members of the Blackfoot Confederacy have their own cycle of ceremonies. One summer I was privileged to be present at the opening days of the Sun

Dance carried out at the Blood Reserve near Standoff, Alberta. There I sat and dreamed late into the night with the northern lights playing in the sky above me. There, listening to the singing and drumming as it moved around the camp, I tried to come to some understanding of the great mystery that surrounded me.

This mystery of renewal is celebrated by the First People all over Turtle Island—the name that many Indigenous nations give to the continent on which they live. It is a mystery that stretches far back to the times of the Ohio Mound Builders, the Olmecs, the Mayans, the Incas, and deep, deep into the origin of the human race and even beyond into the cycles of the cosmos itself. Just as the sacred tree at the center of the Sun Dance ground acts to connect Mother Earth to the powers and beings of the Sky World, so, too, all over the Americas can be found that same power of rotation and return; the same axis around which the cosmos and the people, time, history, and the cycles of ceremonies and renewal turn in their rotation.

As these ceremonies metamorphose one into the other, so, too, do they lead us into a profoundly different reality from that which we encounter in our everyday Western world. To enter into this domain is to question what we mean by space and time, by the distinctions between the living and the nonliving, by the individual and society, by dreams and visions, by perception and reality, by causality and synchronicity, by time and eternity.

Thunder Birds

Take, for example, the cycle of life among the Mohawk people. In the spring of each year life is renewed as the sap begins to rise in the trees, as seeds germinate under the blanket of snow, as air from the Gulf of Mexico moves north to meet the colder Arctic air over Lake Ontario. This is the season when electrical charges build up between these two currents of air, tension is felt in the atmosphere, and the first thunder is heard grumbling in the distance. In Akwesasne a number of people, as they go around their daily tasks, take responsibility to listen for this first roll of thunder. As soon as it is heard, sacred tobacco is burned in offering and the rest of the people are told of the return of thunder.

The sound of the thunder means the return of the Thunder Birds, and this notion, I suppose, raises some of those questions that flood the Western mind when it first encounters the Native American world. People may have heard mention of Thunder Birds; they may have seen depictions of Thunder Birds on the great carved cedar poles, often called totem poles, which tell the history of the peoples of the northwest coast of North America; they may even have read stories in which the Lakoda (Sioux) peoples refer to *wakinyan* or Thunderbeings.

Our Western minds desire to sort things out, to arrange knowledge in a logical fashion and order the world into categories. Observation shows us that birds return to Lake Ontario and to the south shore of the St. Lawrence River at about the same time as the first thunder is heard. Just as the birds fly south before the first snows fall, so, too, they reappear with the first sound of thunder. Our linear, logical minds ask: Are these Thunder Birds actual birds; a particular ornithological species? Are they mythic beings or are they forces of nature?; Do the Mohawk people believe the thunder brings the Thunder Birds, or that the birds bring the thunder?

Searching for answers to questions like these, one begins to wonder if they are the right questions to ask in the first place; indeed, if such questions make any sense at all! Pretty soon the realization comes that it is not so much the questions themselves that are the problem, but the whole persistent desire to obtain knowledge through a particular analytical route. While this approach may be the norm within Western society, it does not seem appropriate when sitting with Native American people. In that act of simply being with another culture there comes the realization of a need for balance, the understanding that there are times when it is better to listen than to ask, better to feel than to think, more appropriate to stay with a silence than to seek answers in speech.

Western education predisposes us to think of knowledge in terms of factual information, information that can be structured and passed on through books, lectures, and programmed courses. Knowledge is seen as something that can be acquired and accumulated, rather like stocks and bonds. By contrast, within the Indigenous world the act of coming to know something involves a personal transformation. The knower and the known are indissolubly linked and changed in a fundamental way. Indigenous science can never be reduced to a catalogue of facts or a database in a supercomputer, for it is a dynamic and living process, an aspect of the ever-changing, ever-renewing processes of nature.

Visions From Two Worlds

It is at this point that a tantalizing paradox presents itself. On one hand it seems that the very activity and busy-ness of our analytic, linear Western minds would obstruct us from entering into Indigenous coming-to-knowing, yet, on the other, scientists who have been struggling at the cutting edges of their fields have come up with concepts that resonate with those of Indigenous science. For example:

- Quantum theory stresses the irreducible link between observer and observed and the basic holism of all phenomena. Indigenous science also holds that there is no separation between individual and society, between matter and spirit, between each one of us and the whole of nature.

- The physicist David Bohm has spoken of what he calls the implicate, or enfolded, order (an order in which the whole is enfolded within each part) as being a deeper physical reality than the surface, or explicate, order that is immediately perceived by our senses. In a similar way, members of the Gourd Society wear a necklace of mescal beads in which each bead symbolizes the cosmos and reminds them that within each object is enfolded the whole.

    In writing this down I am immediately aware that the word *symbolize* simply does not capture what I would like to say. Today a symbol is generally understood to stand for something else and is not seen as possessing a numinous power of its own.

The mescal bead, however, is no mere symbol. For those who wear it, it really does enfold the universe and bring them in direct contact with all of creation.

- In modern physics the essential stuff of the universe cannot be reduced to billiard-ball atoms, but exists as relationships and fluctuations at the boundary of what we call matter and energy. Indigenous science teaches that all that exists is an expression of relationships, alliances, and balances between what, for lack of better words, we could call energies, powers, or spirits.

- Several leading-edge thinkers in physics suggest that nature is not a collection of objects in interaction but is a flux of processes. The whole notion of flux and process is fundamental to the Indigenous sciences of Turtle Island. Algonkian-speaking peoples, such as the Cheyenne, Cree, Ojibwaj, Mic Maq, and Blackfoot, all share a strongly verb-based family of languages that reflects this direct experience.

- Some physicians question our current medical models and suggest that healing involves the whole person—body, mind and spirit. Native healers have never fragmented their vision of health, for it is regarded as emerging out of the whole of nature and is one with the processes of renewal.

- Ecologists stress that we must attend to the basic interconnectedness of nature and to the sensitivity and complexity of natural systems. This has always been the approach of Indigenous peoples. The traditional Thanksgiving Address of the Iroquois people, for example, specifically acknowledges the wholeness that is inherent within all of life.

- Scientists are alerting us to the fragility and sensitivity of our planet. It is the tradition of the Iroquois people that in arriving at a decision they consider its implications right down to the seventh generation that comes after them.

The Heart of Knowledge

Indigenous knowing is a vision of the world that encompasses both the heart and the head, the soul and the spirit. It could no more deal with matter in isolation than the theory of relativity could fragment space from time. It is a vision in which rock and tree, bird and fish, human being and caribou are all alive and partakers of the gifts of Mother Earth. Indigenous science does not seek to found its knowledge, as we do, at the level of some most ultimate elementary particle or theory, rather it is a science of harmony and compassion, of dream and vision, of earth and cosmos, of hunting and growing, of technology and spirit, of song and dance, of color and number, of cycle and balance, of death and renewal.

We can all, I believe, learn something of great importance from this vision, from this way of coming-to-knowing of the First Peoples of Turtle Island. In many ways our cultures and values seem so profoundly different that it would appear to be almost impossible to have a dialogue between these two ways of knowing. However, the striking similarities between traditional teachings and some of the insights that are emerging from modern science suggest that a coming together is indeed possible.

It is not so much that a particular physicist may have hit upon a theory that echoes images or connections with a traditional piece of teaching—that would be far too trivial to be of importance. No, it is more that the whole way the Western mind works is beginning to open itself to new possibilities, and that from within this openness a dialogue may be possible. This is certainly something I have learned from my Native friends who are excited about some of the new ideas in science they are hearing and have pointed out to me the resonances with their own tradition.

A Dialogue Between Worlds

It is in such a spirit, and with such an aim, that this book is written. This is not a book "about" Native American society, or "about" Indigenous knowledge. It is certainly not the result of objective academic study. Rather, it is an exploration of two different ways of knowing, two different worlds of consciousness, and a discovery of the ways that peoples can begin to have dialogues with each other, enter into relationships, and offer each other the respect and courtesy that is the hallmark of humanity.

In beginning this dialogue, however, it is wise to be aware of the difficulties we may encounter along the way. No matter what our color, religion, social status, or racial origins may be, those of us who have grown up within a North American or European school system, playing with other children, watching television, reading newspapers and books, going to college, and eventually entering the work force have learned to participate in a worldview that is common to the Western industrial nations. Although we may begin to acknowledge the importance of other cultures, races, and worldviews, North American culture is still, to a great extent, based upon the traditions of European civilization, that stream of culture that began with the Greeks and Romans and underwent a partial transformation first during the Renaissance and again with the rise of science and technology. In particular, modern science, which emerged through the efforts of Bacon, Galileo, Newton, and others, has created an intellectual mechanism that dominates much of the world.

Today many people have begun to question the more materialistic aspects of this worldview. There is an interest in the meditative practices of the East, in various therapies that deal with personal growth and transformation.

Change can come from dialogues between different cultures and forms of spirituality. The ancient Mayan peoples spoke of the end of our present world and the appearance of a new sun. This fifth sun was said to herald the World of Consciousness and it may well be that the wisdom that can be found here on Turtle Island* will help to catalyze a change in global culture.

---

*Many Indigenous peoples refer to living on Turtle Island. There are stories that a giant turtle rose out of the ocean and allowed the plants, animals, birds, and people to live on its back. Some people suggest that Florida and Baja California are the turtle's back flippers with Labrador and Alaska as the front. While I have heard some Native people associate Turtle Island with the North American continent, others suggest that both the Americas are one land.

Five hundred years ago a major contact was made between the peoples of Europe and Turtle Island. At that time Indigenous knowledge was freely given and in many cases this led to the survival of a people who were new to this continent. Yet, in light of the centuries of repression and bloodshed that followed, it is clear the deeper meaning of this teaching was never really understood by the first guests who set foot on Turtle Island. There are Native Elders who believe that today the time has come for them to speak again, that now the White Man is now willing to listen. Their prophecies also tell of a time of purification. To some this means a period of devastation when Mother Earth cleanses herself and renews the processes of life across the planet. Others interpret this as an opportunity for transformation, for global devastation can be prevented provided that the races cooperate, hand in hand toward a renewal of our relationship with all of nature and with each other.

But how is such a dialogue to commence? Many of the world's spiritual traditions speak of the impossibility of the rational mind alone ever approaching a deep understanding of another way of being. Some of them refer to particular religious experiences as having a flavor or a taste that is impossible to appreciate without direct experience. The same thing applies, I believe, to cultures that lie outside our own. One can no more understand them from the outside than one can describe the taste of an orange to someone who has never eaten such a fruit, nor a sunset to a blind person. How then can we grasp the flavor, the odor, the spirit of a profoundly different worldview, one that cannot be approached by reason, analysis, description, and the accumulation of facts alone?

Changing Consciousness

The answer, I believe, is that we can come to some form of knowing, albeit in a strictly limited way, through an actual change in consciousness. If we remain as observers, objective scholars of another society, we will never enter into its essence. However, if we approach it in a spirit of humility, respect, enquiry, and openness it becomes possible for a change of consciousness to occur.

As you sit with Native people, walk in nature, and spend time at sacred sites an actual transformation of consciousness takes place. For a time, at least, you can begin to hear, see, feel, touch, and taste the world in a profoundly different way: You can think and perceive with a different mind so that your ego can, temporarily at least, blend into that of other people.

If you happen to hold that human consciousness is no more than the epiphenomenon, or secretion, of our individual brains then you are more or less trapped in your own skull. But if consciousness is open, if it can partake in a more global form of being, if it can merge with the natural world and with other beings, then, indeed, it may be possible to drop, for a time, the constraints of one's personal worldview and see reality through the eyes of others.

The poet Robert Graves, for example, believed that he was possessed by the spirit of one of the Caesars when he wrote *I, Claudius*. On several occasions the historian Arnold Toynbee was projected across time and space to become a participator in another historical era. One time he found himself in the Italy of 80 B.C. witnessing a suicide. Another time, while walking near Victoria Station in London he had the experience of being plunged not into a particular historical period but into the entire passage of history and time.

Thus it may be that, for a few moments, or hours, or even days, we can enter into the heart and head and body of another culture. We will always return to our own world, for that is where our roots lie. Nevertheless, on our reentry we may be changed in some subtle yet important way. And, sometimes, when we spend time living within that other culture, we are able to look back upon our own world and see it through alien eyes, appreciate its limitations as well as its beauty and attraction.

It is my belief that, at its deepest level, the dialogue between Western and Indigenous science will engender an increasing flexibility in human consciousness, an ability to leave the boundaries of our own egos and worldview and temporarily enter into those of another. It goes without saying that the more we do this the easier it will become. In time we will no longer attempt to understand another culture from the outside or think in terms of analysis and description. Rather, we will enter in, partake, and absorb. And, in so doing we will engage in a new relationship; we will both give and receive; we will create alliances and become one with a much greater spectrum of consciousness, one that involves not only humans but other beings, forces, and powers of the natural world.

In writing this book I have kept this approach in mind, that of moving between the worlds of Indigenous and Western science and attempting to convey their respective flavors. In particular, chapter 2 attempts to give the feel of my own experiences at a Sun Dance as my own perceptions flickered back and forth between those two worlds.

This is a book about two worlds, two ways of knowing and being, and of the traffic that can take place between them. It is based upon my own experiences and encounters, experiences that were built on the foundation of puzzling over the nature of reality and Western science for more than thirty years. Within the Native American worldview I discovered a vision that was staggeringly subtle, yet perfectly natural, a vision that was sophisticated in its philosophical engagements, yet never strayed from the human heart and the warmth of relationships. Since no other encounter has affected me in such a personal way, let me begin with the story of my first contact with Native science.

The First Encounter

I arrived in North America in the late 1960s after completing my Ph.D. in Liverpool, England. At the time I had hoped to learn more about the First Peoples of Turtle Island, yet I discovered few good books existed about the First Nations, and I couldn't find anyone who had had firsthand contact with their culture. Indeed, it almost seemed to me, back in the 1960s, that the First People of this continent had been hidden away and North America was a dark continent whose ancient mysteries and achievements had remained concealed for the last five hundred years.

Sometimes, as I walked through the woods or camped beside a lake, I sensed that I was intruding upon an ancient land, that I was an uninvited visitor who moved noisily and disrespectfully into what had once been the home the First People shared with trees and plants and birds and animals. I longed to be given permission by the guardians of the land to stay awhile. Sometimes there was the faint hint of voices from the bush, a movement across the face of the water that may have told me, had I been sensitive enough, that somewhere a spirit was watching and assessing me.

During my first years in North America I worked as a scientist engaged in theoretical research, studying the way atoms, molecules, and solids are formed at the quantum level of matter. As time went on I began to ask more fundamental questions about the nature of space-time and quantum reality. I was struck by the way our society had become separated and abstracted from nature and how good intentions concerning the integration of body and mind so often stayed within the conference hall and laboratory. Indeed, much of the new holistic thinking remained no more than abstractions without balance or grounding in the much wider world.

By the 1980s I had begun to explore these questions in a series of books, and it happened that one day I began to sense the need for some new idea, a fresh approach perhaps, something that would integrate with my felt sense that all nature, indeed, the entire universe, is alive and vibrant. I wandered around the house pulling out books from the bookcases, turning their pages and putting them back again. A feeling of undefined frustration and a sense of unease came over me until, by pure chance, I came to a book my wife had bought. It was called *Touch the Earth* (edited by T. C. McLuhan) and contained nineteenth century photographs of Native American Elders and leaders together with some of the speeches they had made.

As I turned the pages I was struck by the serene power of the faces that stared back at me from across the century. These were faces with the character of a rock, or the bark of an ancient tree. I returned to my desk and, as I began to read the first of the leaders' speeches, the telephone rang. Still looking at the book, I picked up the receiver and heard someone asking for David Peat and announcing that his name was Leroy Little Bear. For an instant it was as if one of those images had sprung to life and was actually speaking to me. For over twenty years I had unconsciously sought contact with a subtle and ancient culture, and now it was actually reaching me by telephone!

As it turned out, Leroy was inviting me to a conference that was to be held on the land of the Stoney Indians at Nakoda Lodge in Alberta. For several days Native Elders and Indigenous scientists would meet with a few Western scientists to explore their different visions of reality. Leroy was not only a philosopher within his Blackfoot tradition but was also well acquainted with the writings of David Bohm and the new ideas of quantum reality. A few days later I received a follow-up call, this time from Pam Colorado, an Oneida of the Iroquois Six Nations Confederacy, who has written papers on the nature of Indigenous science and is one of the first Canadian Native women to obtain a Ph.D. Pam has since devoted more and more of her time to exploring the worldwide connections of Indigenous science.

These two phone calls represented my first contact with Indigenous science—and the whole thing almost ended there. A couple of days before I was due to fly to Calgary I was stressed-out by writing deadlines and felt I was coming down with a heavy cold. At least that was what I was telling myself, but a deeper part of me knew that I was simply resisting the invitation to enter another world because I realized that once that door had been opened it could never be closed.

As a result, I was still packing some time after the aircraft had departed! I came to the conclusion that I would never see Nakoda Lodge and that my contact with Indigenous science had been stillborn. But I had not counted on Leroy and his influential friends. He called late that night to say that I had a seat on the first flight out next morning and that someone would pick me up at Calgary Airport.

That someone proved to be Kim Hathaway-Carr, a Mohawk woman from Akwesasne, who became a good friend and taught me about the integrity of the heart within Indigenous knowing. Thus, after a false start, I arrived at Nakoda Lodge and was exposed to a different way of seeing the world. At that meeting there were Iroquois, Blackfoot, Cree, Haida, Navaho, Hopi, and Creek people present as well as a fellow physicist, a linguist, a few other Western scientists, and two Aboriginal women from Australia.

On the first day we began conventionally enough, sitting in a room and listening to presentations. But on the following day we moved out to a nearby tepee where we talked around the fire until late at night. Very gently, those of us we from the West were led into another way of being, dreaming, and conversing together. A high point of our time together was a visit to an ancient Blackfoot medicine wheel* where ceremonies were performed and my Western scientific mind was opened to an alternative way of experiencing the world. An account of what happened that day is given later in this book.

From that day on I was drawn to the richness, power, and subtlety of the Indigenous approach to knowing and being. As a physicist I became impressed by its ideas of time, causality, and reality; its view of number; its interest in astronomical observations; and its painstaking attention to the details of the natural world. I was struck by the depth of its metaphysics and by the way in which Indigenous knowledge permeates every aspect of life, from education to healing, from sacred ceremony to an effective legal system and the daily care for the environment. Above all, I was struck by the way in which all aspects of life are based upon relationship and renewal, upon the balance of heart and head, upon the courtesies and dignities of daily life, upon harmony and balance, and upon the acknowledgment of the powers that animate the world around us.

---

*The term *medicine wheel* has many meanings, or rather many different manifestations. In this case its outward appearance took the form of a circular pattern of rocks located on a hilltop in southern Alberta. Medicine wheels may have an obvious correspondence to patterns of stars and planets in the sky, but they may also be the expression of a person's dream or vision. But it is important to note that the medicine wheel is more than a pattern of rocks, it is the relationship between the earth and cosmos, it is a circular movement, a process of healing, a ceremony, and a teaching.

Cultural Appropriation

Yet today, as I look out over the midwinter landscape, I must also acknowledge that a lifetime of experience would never be long enough for me to fully enter into the subtleties of the Native mind. For I was not born to this way of life; part of my soul's body belongs to the Lancashire plains, the British seacoasts, and the mountains of North Wales and the Lake District, and until recently all my education had been within the traditions and paradigms of the West.

Again and again I delayed writing this book, for I knew that my understanding of Indigenous science was fragmentary and that my exposure to the First People had been minimal. On the other hand, for over thirty years I had been talking and working with people who were at the forefront of scientific thinking; together we had speculated upon the limits of the Western mind, the confines of the scientific approach and the possibilities for a new science. Thus, while others may know far more about the Indigenous world, at least I am in the position of being able to have a dialogue between two different worldviews in such a way that I can understand something of those areas in which new ideas in the sciences can bridge themselves toward traditional Indigenous knowledge.

Yet, each time I sat down to write my mind was filled with doubts. I was well aware of the debate about cultural appropriation, the ways in which our Western society has used, without permission, the artifacts and stories of The People. In the past, Indigenous people were displaced from their traditional lands, their sacred sites were excavated, their dead exhumed, and their sacred objects were removed to museums. Today their art, which was never separated from their culture, history, and spirituality, is commercially reproduced or modified for Western taste. Traditional ceremonies are depicted in movies and novels, and Native American culture and spirituality is analyzed and interpreted by academic institutions.

Cultural appropriation is not simply the act of taking something away from a people, it is also using something in a way that is inappropriate, disrespectful, or distorted. How easy it is for a well-meaning outsider to interpret what he has seen and experienced, and in the process, misrepresent the knowledge and worldview of Indigenous people. How easy it is to study a ceremony, story, or area of knowledge out of its context, employing Western critical paradigms and values. In doing so one creates a profound distortion of its original meaning. In this way, after five hundred years of misunderstanding, the First People continue to suffer the denigration of their most sacred practices and the disruption of their ways of life.

Yet another of my concerns was with the very limitations of the English language in which I write. Language is intimately tied to the way we think and see the world around us. Over many centuries the languages of Europe have evolved within a particular society and general view of reality to the point where they have become inseparable from it. The English language, as well as German, French, Italian, Spanish, and so on, predisposes us to say things in certain ways and, in doing so, to lose the flavor of those subtleties that are better expressed in other languages. An almost universal factor in Native American languages is their holistic and process-view of the cosmos. Thus, Mohawk expresses the complex relationships that exist within nature and society. Mic Maq explores a reality that is based upon sound. Blackfoot and other Indigenous languages manifest a world of animation. Yet, as soon as one attempts to express these ideas in English they seem to disappear from the page.

To write a book that would explore the dialogue between Western and Native American realities seemed an impossible task, despite the fact that some of my Native friends suggested that I should attempt to articulate my experiences. In the end, my decision to begin the book grew out of something that was said to me that moved me deeply. I had been visiting with Betty Bastien on the Blood Reserve. I had first met Betty when, visiting Ottawa, she had stayed with us. As a result, I received an invitation to visit her family on the Blood Reserve during its Sun Dance. One day we began to talk about conditions on the reservation to problems that Native children faced at school. Betty also touched on the meaning of the Sun Dance that was then taking place, on the significance of the Blackfoot medicine wheels and on the connection between the cosmos and society. I can remember becoming excited by what she was saying and pointing out how closely that Blackfoot vision related to the way I had begun to see the world through science. I told Betty that there were times when we both seemed to be seeing reality from the same side.

Betty replied in words something like these:

> For so long our culture has been ignored, dismissed, and laughed at; our beliefs have been called superstitions and we have been referred to as primitive people. In most schools our children are never taught about their own history, and for them the only truth about the world is that given by Western science. As a result, the young people don't listen to the words of our Elders, they simply laugh at them. But now a physicist comes along and says that he respects the way we look at the world, that he can begin to understand the reasons for some of the things we do and that he can see connections with things from the frontiers of his own science. I think that it is important that other people should know this.

What follows is the result. This is certainly not a book that attempts to explain traditional knowledge in the light of Western science. Rather, it is an acknowledgment of another way of knowing and an attempt at dialogue between two worlds. It is only a first step, one that looks forward to other books, works written by Indigenous philosophers, metaphysicians and scientists who will present their own authentic visions and reflect upon Western science and culture from the perspective of their own traditions.

Calling Each Other Names

Every schoolchild knows that name-calling is a powerful way of humiliating one's opponents. In the last few decades North Americans have been made aware of the political implications inherent in the names that were earlier used to denote African

Americans and other ethnic groups. Similar difficulties arise in this book of how to describe people belonging to different groups and nations.

This is a particularly pertinent problem because it is not really within the Native American worldview to group things together into abstract categories of thought such as "fish" or "trees"—and particularly not the different nations of Turtle Island.

The Mohawk, Hopi, Navaho, Haida, Miwok, Blood, and other peoples have, within their own languages, names that distinguish them from others. Generally these words can be translated into English along the lines of "the people," "the true people," " real people," "the two-legged creatures, as opposed to the four-legged," or "the people who live in this place." There are also the names, often humorous or insulting, that the peoples use to describe their neighbors. Finally, there are the names that English speakers have used to describe The First People.

To take a specific example, my friend Leroy Little Bear has a Blackfoot name that refers nothing to bears. In fact, the English translation "little bear" is based upon a mishearing of a Blackfoot term that refers to part of a buffalo. Leroy is a member of the Blood Nation, the term *Blood* being an English mistranslation of the Blackfoot term *Kainah* meaning "many chiefs."

The Kainah themselves are one of four divisions of what has come to be called the Blackfoot Confederacy—although more properly the name *Blackfeet* is used by only one of these divisions, the Siksikah. Maps, treaties, textbooks, and documents even show a degree of ambiguity over naming the people Blackfoot or Blackfeet.

The other two members of the confederacy are divisions of the Pikunni people comprising the Northern Peigans in Alberta, Canada, and the Southern Piegans, or Blackfeet Tribe, in Montana. Again, note the different spelling—Peigans for the Canadian group and Piegans for the group in the United States.

The language spoken by the confederacy, called Blackfoot in English, is part of a much larger family called Algonkian which stretches across Canada and parts of the U.S. and includes the languages spoken by the Cree, Huron, Ojibwaj, Cheyenne, and Mic Maq as well as many other peoples. And when one speaks of a family of languages one should bear in mind that while certain words in Blackfoot, Cheyenne, and Mic Maq may be mutually comprehensible, as a whole these languages are as different from each other as are English, Italian, and Russian within the Indo-European family.

Thus, the many different nations and linguistic families of The First People all have their own names and designations, many of which have been mistranslated into English. What the orderly Western mind would like is a generic term that could be used to refer to each of The People as a whole—as some sort of generic unity. Such generalizations are alien to what I (and now I immediately fall into the trap of generalization!) have heard referred to as the Native Mind, or Indigenous way of seeing things. Each people has a place to live, a set of special relationships with the land and the powers around them; they simply cannot be lumped together into a single generic category. The Bloods of the Blackfoot Confederacy are not therefore "Indians"—a term redolent of past racism and considerable global geographic confusion—nor would many of them wish to be grouped into the newer category "people of color."

Yet the realities of modern politics have forced leaders of the First Nations to negotiate with governments and seek ways of advancing their people. Therefore, a variety of compromise terms have evolved in order to cope with Western thought patterns and fulfill the need to refer to the many Indigenous nations within one generic term. One of these terms is *Indigenous*—as used in the expression "Indigenous science." This conveys the sense of the people who belong to a particular region, but it also has a more global usage that extends outside the Americas.

The term *Native*, or *Native American*, is often used in general conversation and several Indigenous people have told me that it is quite acceptable to them—although, to someone brought up in England, it smacks of the unsavory associations of the British Empire in which earnest young men sought to bring law and order to "the natives." By the way, I use the terms

America and *American* to cover the entire northern continent and not simply the United States. *First Nations* is becoming a working alternative when dealing with politicians, as is *Aboriginal*—meaning the first people to occupy the land. Another approach is simply to use the direct English translation of the names many groups use and say "The People." In the end, I have followed my ear and tried to use terminology in ways that are similar to what I have heard from my Native friends.

This brings up another problem: What should I call the non-Native inhabitants of Turtle Island? Traditional people, in their early contacts, used the terms (I am only aware of the polite ones) *white man, white race, white brother,* and *European.* In some cases an African American would be referred to as "a black white man."

A few hundred years ago these designations reflected the political realities of The People's first encounters with a very different world. Today, however, North America holds people of a wide diversity of racial origins, many of whom would be offended to be described as *white, European,* or *Western,* or in terms of the masculine inclusive.

So I apologize to my readers when these terms are used in a historical context. They are a reflection of the fact that the first disruptive contacts were with people, generally men, who had "white" faces and subscribed to a fairly uniform set of beliefs about society, property, government, and religion. We should not forget, however, that they were accompanied by black slaves and servants, and that later blacks occupied positions in the U.S. Army and many worked as cowboys. Black people who escaped from their European oppressors were welcomed into Native American societies as full members.

The term *Western* is also used in this book. This refers to a certain worldview that has come to dominate the globe, both economically and through science and technology. Western sets of values are often adopted by people of other races who have grown up in North America, passed though its school system, and entered the work force. The other term, *European,* is used to denote the historical origins of a scientific, philosophical, and political worldview that evolved within Europe. *European* is also used for the family of languages that expresses that particular worldview. James Youngblood (Sa'ke'j) Henderson has also suggested the term *Mediterranean* to describe the worldview and attitude of mind that emerged out of the Greek and Roman culture and spread into Europe and across America.

So again let me apologize to readers who are neither "white" nor of European ancestry, as well as to those of European ancestry who do not choose to subscribe to the worldviews and value systems that I have called Western. In the long run I feel that, as we enter into dialogues together and learn to shift our consciousness between different ways of being and seeing, language itself will reflect an increase in flexibility and sensitivity.

At the Sun Dance:
When Paradigms Collide

At the Sun Dance

This book is about the movement of consciousness, the metamorphosis of meaning between one world and another. What better place to begin than with the movements and transformations of my own feelings and thinking as, one summer, I visited the Blood People at the time of their Sun Dance?

To reach the Sun Dance I first flew to Calgary, Alberta, and then took a bus south to Lethbridge. From the righthand side of the bus I could already see in the distance the snowcapped peaks of the Rockies and was aware of the special quality of the air. Although I was still in the plains, Calgary is already thirty-five hundred feet above sea level. The air there has a clarity and the land offers that immense sense of space that is not present in the east—a region of deep winter snows and humid summers, of lakes and woodlands, an area where the First People traveled vast distances by canoe.

Each time I see the plains I am surprised anew, for, rather than being flat, they roll and undulate. Indeed, from the window of the bus, I experienced the same sensations I have had when in a boat; that continual movement of sweeping water and sudden, thrilling dips. In a bizarre way, being out in the plains almost reminds me of my own home, of Liverpool, and the many boat trips I took out into the estuary of the river Mersey and beyond into the Irish Sea.

This, I know, is the land that Napi created. It is the land that was given to the Blackfoot people, a land they cared for until the arrival of roads and cities and railways. It is a land watched over by the Blackfoot medicine wheel, still renewed each day and each season by the ceremonies of the Blackfoot people. On the Blood Reserve I was to meet people who begin each day before dawn and, facing the rising sun, pray for their people and the world. And I have been told that Napi is that faint white light that appears in the eastern sky at dawn and draws the sun up into the sky. For, from the beginning The People have known that light itself is more powerful than the sun and is part of the great mysteries of the cosmos.

Napi created this land, his body is to be found imprinted upon it, and his name is found in its many features—here is his belly, over there his chin, elsewhere his elbow, and flowing through the land are his rivers. The Oldman River is a contemporary geographer's corruption of the Old Man's river, for Napi is also called the Old Man.

At night, and at certain of their ceremonies, the Blackfoot people relate the many stories about Napi. How easy it is for those of us with our Western minds to speak of these as "Napi legends" or mythic accounts of creation. But Napi is not a myth, he is not a legend, and his exploits are not to be equated with those of fictional characters in Western literature. Rather, when Napi is spoken of, these are sacred matters. An understanding of Napi's powers and transformations can also take us to the heart of Blackfoot science and metaphysics.

Napi is the creator, the one who brought the land into being, the one who gave it its shape and form. Napi created the animals and gave the Blackfoot their home. Napi also allowed The People to choose death over continual life and in this way provided for balance on earth. But Napi is also the Trickster, the Clown, the Old Man who transcends the laws of nature, who turns things upside down, who carries out foolish actions. Napi is metamorphosis; he is constantly changing form. Yet in no way is Napi a mythic person or an anthropological hero figure. As an actual being he walked across the earth teaching the Blackfoot and then traveled north to spend time with the Cree and Ojibwaj where his name, like his person, became metamorphosized into Nanabush and Nannabozo. Napi even found his way to the far northeast of Labrador where his exploits were witnessed by the Naskapi people—try rolling that name, Naskapi, around in your mouth and you will be creating echoes of the sounds and vibrations that the Old Man made when he created the land and lived with the Blackfoot.

Napi, who brought wisdom to the Blackfoot and insight into their own nature, is the first light of dawn and the dawning light of consciousness. Napi taught The People how to hunt and gave them the means to do so by placing certain features like cliffs and shallow pools in their landscape. Napi was a wondrous being but he was also a fool, someone whose stupidity can still make children laugh and teach them powerful lessons about the importance of rules in a well-ordered society, about the nature of the heart and mind and of the powers that inhabit the universe.

One day Napi saw a woman with beautiful breasts, so beautiful that he wanted to touch them and desired to place his lips against them. While she was sleeping, the Old Man entered the young woman's tepee and transformed himself into a tiny baby. The woman awoke and took the baby to her breast to feed it. Napi enjoyed this so much that, forgetting himself, he changed back to his usual form. The young woman reacted in horror to discover an old man sucking at her breast and began to beat him. Hearing her cries young men entered, beat Napi, and threw him out of the camp. How difficult it is for our Western minds to incorporate a Creator and teacher who is also a lecherous fool.

The bus rolls south toward Lethbridge and I think of how Napi's land has changed. Once herds of buffalo roamed from the Eastern Woodlands to the foothills of the Rocky Mountains, but today vast areas have been transformed into a wheat bowl. The buffalo fed on the buffalo grass that was fertilized by their droppings. This grass had deep roots that bound the earth and was resistant to drought. But when farmers came the grass was plowed under and replaced by wheat and other crops, crops whose roots do not go sufficiently deep into the earth to bind it. The result is that the plains have slowly become eroded as the topsoil has blown away. Intensive farming is now practiced on a thin layer of soil with the continual addition of chemical fertilizers and other additives. Some Native people have told me that this sort of intensive farming cannot last much longer. They speak of Mother Earth rejecting the pollution of her skin and purifying herself.

As you travel from Calgary to Lethbridge it is not difficult to imagine a time when the buffalo were present. A century ago, as every schoolchild knows, the buffalo were wiped out. Their massacre was not simply a matter of providing meat for railway crews who were pushing across the continent, but was a carefully planned exercise in which chartered trains slowly moved across the plains. Each coach was packed with sharp-shooters who, from the comfort of their compartments, could shoot out of the windows at the buffalo. As far as the eye could see the plains were filled with carcasses that were not even butchered for meat but were left to rot in the sun.

Have Napi's buffalo vanished forever? Once, while I was driving with Leroy Little Bear he tried to explain to me that sense of movement within time that most Native American societies share. Within this metaphysics of time and reality the buffalo are still present. It is as if, to use images from our own Western view of science, other spaces and times interpenetrate and coexist with our own. To traditional people this is no mere metaphor or poetic image but the reality in which they live, and since to The People time is a great circle, the time of the buffalo will return again. Indeed, a number of Native ranchers have started to breed herds of buffalo in preparation for this return.

If you read books on North American history and anthropology you will be told that the Plains Indians "followed" the buffalo. But I have never really believed this, not in the Western sense of hunting that implies seeking for something that we cannot currently see, or following a trail that an animal has made. Buffalo were certainly hunted, and the people of the plains knew all about their habits as well as the trails that different animals made. But it has always seemed to me that the Blackfoot did not so much "chase" or "follow" the buffalo as that they were partners in a mutual movement, one aspect of a relationship of time and motion in which the transformations of life and death, increase and depletion, light and dark, and the cycle of the seasons all had their part to play.

I have been told that the secret of hunting does not lie solely at the level of following animal tracks in the bush. Rather, it is carried out in dreams, ceremonies, and rituals, in the sweats of the purification lodge and the relationships between the People and the Keepers of the animals.

So it is that humans and animals are locked together in a cooperative movement, in a complex dance of time and season. The hunter and the animal both have an obligation to fulfill and each must honor and renew the contracts that have been entered into. One aspect of this agreement is that they should arrive at the right place at the right time. Another is that proper respect should be offered to that which offers itself for sacrifice and that mutual obligations should be reaffirmed in ceremonies of renewal. To attempt to understand the deeper meaning of hunting, and the link between the buffalo and the Blackfoot would require leaving our comfortable Western confines concerning the meaning of reality and entering a totally different paradigm of science and metaphysics—an alternative view of space, time, and causality.

As the bus traveled south, my mind, still trapped in its Western way of thinking, was continuously asking questions, attempting to make connections, and seeking some explanation for the work I was entering. I suppose that the very movement and freshness of it all excited me; the constant movement of the landscape, and those times when I caught a view of one of Napi's rivers. The rivers meander, creating wide, flat bottomlands that are rich in vegetation, small trees, and many different animals. Eroding their way into the plains until they are well protected from the winter winds by high escarpments on either sides, these fertile river bottomlands made an ideal location for the Blackfoot's more permanent winter lodges. When spring returned, however, the Blackfoot chose the more portable dwelling called the tepee. And what a marvelous invention the tepee is. Old people have spoken of the bygone days when a good fire of buffalo chips (dried dung) kept the tepee warm while stories were told long into the night. And, with its openings at top and bottom to allow for the circulation of air, the tepee is cool even during the hottest day. Although canvas is used today, in traditional times the tepee was built of the materials provided by Napi, larch poles and buffalo skins.

Napi's river runs through Lethbridge, and here it was that the bus stopped and I was picked up by my host, Betty Bastien. Betty is of the Piegan Nation of the Blackfoot Confederacy, but, having married a member of the Blood Tribe, now lives on that reservation. I had met Betty through Pam Colorado, and once, while visiting Ottawa, she had stayed with my family. Now I was taking advantage of a return invitation and was visiting the Blood Reserve to see the Sun Dance.

Betty picked me up at the bus station. But before taking me to her home on the Blood Reserve she wanted me to see the contrast between her own Piegan reservation and Head Smashed In Buffalo Jump. The buffalo jump itself has been designated by the United Nations to be a site of special historical significance and is now serviced by a beautifully designed museum staffed by Blackfoot people. It is an important attraction for visitors to this region of Alberta since it enables them to gain an impression of life on the plains before the coming of the white man.

Yet how many tourists who visit the buffalo jump also drive through the little town of Brocket and see the way the Blackfoot live today? With a culture and way of life that have been so badly dislocated, many Native American communities suffer the tensions of poverty, suicide, unemployment, alcoholism, drug abuse, and family violence. There are communities that, through the development of new businesses and the leasing of mineral rights or as the result of land claims settlements, have become relatively prosperous. There are also communities with strong leaders; spiritual men and women who are rooted in their traditions and who have foresworn drugs and alcohol. Yet many other individuals and communities are so divided and torn apart with the demands of two worlds that they are overpowered by a depression that is only relieved by occasional eruptions of violence. Too often one hears of shootings, houses that have been burned down, despair leading to suicide, wrongful arrests and convictions, all of which foments the anger that burns in many hearts.

All this seems far away when one visits Head Smashed In Buffalo Jump, for here a deliberate attempt has been made to create the atmosphere of the past, of the time when Napi taught his people how to hunt the buffalo and, in response, they carried out their ceremonies of celebration and reconnection.

The Blackfoot are famed as great horsepeople, yet, in historical time at least, it was only around 1730 that they first made contact with the horse. Horses certainly existed in North America in prehistoric times, and who knows if the remote ancestors of the Blackfoot did not once tame the wild horse and ride it? Only Napi knows. But certainly horses were re-introduced into the Americas by the Spaniards and slowly found their way north where they were taken up by the Shoshone, among other groups, and from there passed on to the Blackfoot in 1730. Before that time dogs were harnessed to travois and used to transport goods when the camp moved. A travois is made from three tree trunks lashed into the shape of an A. Originally dragged by dogs and later by horses, it is a more convenient means of transporting goods on uneven ground than a wheeled vehicle.

In ancient times the Blackfoot had no need of horses in order to hunt the buffalo. Sometimes people would cover themselves in buffalo skins and make their way into a herd to kill. Another method was to lead the buffalo into muddy territory, a buffalo wallow, where they became stuck and could be more easily killed. A more spectacular approach was to drive a herd off the edge of a cliff—the famous buffalo jump.

Head Smashed In is a prehistoric site and some have identified it as the very first buffalo jump given to the people by Napi. However, I have also been told that this aboriginal jump is in fact some distance away. Today you can visit the museum to learn about Napi and his people. You can walk along the top of the buffalo jump and see a few tepees beneath you where Blackfoot people carry out ceremonies and instruct visitors.

In the past it was always non-Native scientists who excavated a site, took away sacred objects for exhibition in museums, and published their findings in learned journals. But today a new generation of Native Americans is growing up, people who are both rooted in their own tradition and have been trained in the methodology of Western science. Stanley Knowlton, a Blood who is making a study of medicine wheels and other sacred sites once showed us a rock that he held in one hand, while he held a computer disc in the other.

The computer disc contained a program for Blackfoot pictograms and other linguistic characters. The rock also contained Blackfoot pictograms. As Stanley pointed out, he held the past in one hand and the future in the other, yet both contained the same information. He also gave us the image of how he, as a Blackfoot, was walking into the future by keeping his eyes on the past.

The buffalo jumps and wallows were created in the land where Napi walked and slept. I had also been told how the relationship between the Blackfoot and the buffalo that enabled them to engage in hunting was not inherent but had been given to them by the Sioux.

Our Western minds need something to cling to when they first venture into this new universe. The more we engage in its activities the easier it becomes and the more able we are to do without familiar images and metaphors. But it was certainly helpful to me in my first encounters to use mental props and to make a comparison between the way in which many Indigenous peoples picture the world and the images that are beginning to emerge from contemporary physics.

Today we do not so much picture the universe in terms of Newtonian billiard-ball particles but in terms of quantum mechanical fluxes and transformations of energy. In this sense, at least, although our Western science has isolated itself from its spiritual origins, the metaphysical ground of our modern view is strikingly similar to that taught by traditional people all over Turtle Island—that behind the surface reality of everyday life are energies, spirits, and powers.

Quantum physics pictures the material world as being the outward manifestation of patterns, forms, balances, and relations of energy. Likewise, the First People speak of relationships among the powers and spirits that surround them. The various alliances, compacts, and relationships that the People have entered into with these powers form an important aspect of this Indigenous world. These relationships carry with them obligations and the necessity of carrying out periodic ceremonies of renewal, of which one of the most important is the Sun Dance.

This was the way I was beginning to answer my own questions as I walked along the Head Smashed In Buffalo Jump. These were the stories and accounts that came into my mind as we drove toward the Blood Reserve. They were very much the thoughts of an outsider, of someone who was learning things secondhand; someone whose consciousness was not yet sufficiently flexible to enter another world and, for a time at least, participate in its flux and movement.

I had been told that the Blackfoot people could not hunt the buffalo until they had entered into a relationship with the powers, or Keepers, who manifest themselves in the form of that animal. This relationship was entered into through the power of the Sioux.

I had seen those sepia photographs, taken over a century ago, showing the lives of the plains people, and I knew about the appearance of Buffalo Calf Woman to the Sioux and how she had brought the sacred ceremonies. One of these ceremonies was the Sun Dance.

I had learned that long ago two young men hunting on the plains had seen a young woman dressed in white buckskin who sang as she approached them. Struck by her beauty, one of the young men had lustful thoughts. A cloud descended over his body, and when it lifted only a skeleton remained.

Buffalo Calf Woman told the other hunter that he must return to his people and prepare them for her coming. Later, the young woman appeared to the Sioux people and handed them a sacred bundle containing the first pipe. In song she instructed The People in the use of the pipe and told them of other sacred ceremonies that she would bring. Today that pipe is used by many of The First People of Turtle Island and has become a symbol of peace between them.

Buffalo Calf Woman left The People, transforming into a white buffalo calf. But the sacred bundle stayed with them as an eternal reminder of their contract and relationship with the powers of the universe. It was through Buffalo Calf Woman that the Seven Ceremonies were brought to the Sioux people: Keeping of the Soul, the purification lodge (sweat lodge), Crying for a Vision, the Sun Dance, the Naming of Relations, Preparing for Womanhood, and the Throwing the Ball ritual.

As keepers of the sacred compact with Buffalo Calf Woman, the Sioux people entered into a relationship with the Blackfoot and gave them permission to hunt the buffalo. This was symbolized by giving the Blackfoot buffalo horns. Today the Horn Society is one of the central societies of the Blackfoot people and is responsible for the proper conduct of ceremonies, such as the Sun Dance, and for the passing down of traditional teachings.

When I had learned all of this I also learned of how the federal governments in Canada and the United States had outlawed the religions of The First People, how sacred ceremonies were forbidden, and I had heard stories of how, even after World War II, Catholic priests would enter the sacred Sun Dance ground and disrupt what was taking place.

Betty Bastien lived not far from the Sun Dance ground in a beautiful house with some land and two horses in the paddock. Or at least there were supposed to be two horses outside, but somehow they were missing. Betty's young son Peter and his friend loved horse riding and would take off at any time of the day. Yet, somehow, each morning when the two boys went out into the field those horses would have vanished. A lot of the boys' time was spent riding around in a pickup truck trying to locate them. The horses seemed to have minds of their own and preferred freedom to the comfort of their field.

That afternoon we drove up to the Sun Dance ground. It was raining hard and there was a wind blowing at our backs. In fact, it looked so miserable that I did not even feel like getting out of Betty's pickup truck. I had been told that Sun Dances had been held on this part of the Belly Buttes from as far back as anyone could remember. Already that day there was a great circle of lodges and, inside the circle and off to one side, the lodge of the Women's Society had been erected. Yet nothing much seemed to be happening. There were a few dogs loping around in the rain. Occasionally someone would leave a tepee and walk across the Sun Dance ground and go into the women's lodge. Pickup trucks arrived and left. The track that led across the ground from the highway was getting muddy and for several minutes a car was stuck. Later someone pointed out the tepee used by the Crazy Dog Society to me. It was painted with lightning symbols and some people warned that it could attract lightning and storms.

I got out and walked around for awhile. Then, thoroughly wet, I got back into the truck and talked to Betty. Did she know when the Sun Dance would start? Well, the Women's Society was meeting and that was a good sign.

"When will it start?" That had been the sort of question I had been asking for the last month, ever since I had received my invitation to visit the Blood Reserve. At that time I had known the rough date on which the Sun Dance takes place each year and, wishing to take advantage of a fourteen-day advance payment in order to buy a cheaper air ticket, I had phoned Betty to find out the exact date. It appeared that I still had a great deal to learn.

Every few days I would call and ask if the date had been set. Betty would tell me that many people had arrived and that tepees were being set up on the ancient Sun Dance ground. She told me when the Sun Dance had been celebrated in previous years, she also believed that members of the Women's Society would be meeting soon. But as to an actual calendar date...

In the end I simply purchased the next advance air ticket I could and trusted to luck. Now that I had arrived I was still not too clear about when things would begin. But it was good news that the women had begun to meet.

Unlike most Western organizations, which have European origins, within Turtle Island it is the women who bring together the conditions and necessary energy for a ceremony to commence. During the Sun Dance itself, one of the most important lodges would be that of the holy woman who had called the dance that year. Nothing would happen until the Women's Society had finished their meetings. Only then would it be the turn of the men.

Betty explained that the previous year a number of sacred bundles had been exchanged and, with new owners to take part in the ceremonies, more time was needed for preparation. Some of these bundles are very ancient. They are retained within a family until they are handed over to some other keeper in a special ceremony. The bundles themselves contain sacred objects and are only unwrapped once a year during a special ceremony. It is a great honor and a considerable responsibility to become the keeper of one of these bundles and, in light of the exchanges that had been made the previous year, there was much business to be attended to and much instruction to be imparted.

In the days that followed, the Women's Society continued to meet inside their lodge. Ironically, while I was staying in her house, Betty had to travel to my hometown, Ottawa, to attend a meeting, but she left me with an old pickup truck so that I could drive to the Sun Dance ground or take a few side trips if I wanted.

It was fun to talk to the two boys at Betty's and to see how each morning they would ride off on their horses only to return and say that the horses had "gone missing" again. Each time I drove to the Sun Dance ground there seemed to be kids in need of a lift who would hop on the back of the truck. Eventually we would be crowded, and I was reminded of the old joke Leroy had told me of the Native person who was visiting the United States with his friends. After he had driven through customs he passed his first U.S. traffic sign. It was in miles per hour, not kilometers as in Canada, and read MAX-IMUM 30. "O.K.," said the driver, "twenty of you guys'd better get off."

Peter and his friend were spending a lot of time up at the Sun Dance circle. One evening they decided to return home and jumped onto the back of the truck. It was really late at night and when I got back to the house I turned into the driveway, got out of the truck, and called to the two boys. No reply!

Oh, no, I thought, What am I going to do? Losing the horses was bad enough, but now I've gone and lost her sons! I wondered if they'd been thrown off at one of those potholes and were lying injured on the roadside. Or had they not got on in the first place?

Betty returned home later that night, and when I explained what had happed she took it very well. Of course, the two boys turned up a couple of hours later with stories of great adventures; of having seen their horses and having had to get off the truck, or something like that. It sounded just like the elaborate excuses I used to give my mother when I'd gone off fishing with a friend and forgot to arrive home on time.

Each day I would drive up to the Sun Dance ground but, as far as I could see, nothing was really happening. In the end, I took off to go camping near Waterton Lake in the Rockies. I pitched my tent beside a stream and watched the sun behind one of the peaks and, as dusk came, followed the deer as they moved toward the lake.

A couple of days later word reached me that the women had left their lodge and, after a day's rest, the Horn Society would begin to meet. And so I drove back to Standoff and the Blood Reservation; maybe the dancing would begin on the following day.

By now the circle was filled with tepees and more lodges. Sweat lodges had been set up some distance away. Peter had found a gap in the circle for his pup tent and with a pile of blankets and the mattress from his bed on the back of the truck, he was ready to camp out for the duration of the Sun Dance. While Betty was gone I did not really know anyone at the Sun Dance ground. Indeed, in those days before things really got going, I suspected that I was the only non-Native around. Certainly I was enough of a curiosity to be visited by a succession of children who would stare at me and ask if I had any chewing tobacco.

I must have looked pretty lost standing there, but with characteristic Blackfoot generosity the family in one of the lodges temporarily adopted me. By now cars and pickup trucks were arriving hourly, bringing Blackfoot people from all over Montana and Alberta. Throughout the day trucks would be driving around the outer perimeter visiting, young people would be racing their horses or just hanging out with each other, and members of the Men's Society were ensuring that no drugs or alcohol were carried onto the Sun Dance ground and that no photographs were being taken. As young people talked together, I was reminded that in the old days coming together, in annual ceremonies was the primary way in which young men and women were able to choose partners so that they could marry outside their clans and family groups.

The family in the lodge next to me offered me a supper of boiled cow and potatoes, bannock smothered in jam, and plenty of strong, cold black tea to drink. With the smell of cooking in the air, stray dogs came to beg for food and would carry away the tiniest scraps, keeping the camp clean. The men seemed amused by my sense of not quite knowing what to do, but I enjoyed their jokes and gentle ribbing. Their behavior reminded me of the humor of my Liverpool home where people are always warmly welcomed, but the pompous and self-important are reduced by sharp, but witty, remarks.

One evening, as the last of the day faded, the northern lights were particularly brilliant as they played in the sky. The mosquitoes had been biting, so the family next door had invited me into an enclosure of mosquito netting, offered me a chair, and explained what was going on in the camp. We drank mint tea and they told me that it was possible that the dancing would begin that night. But as the twilight faded into total darkness, the camp began to settle down.

Groups of singers were moving from lodge to lodge, offering their late night songs. Dogs barked in the distance, horses whinnied in the corral, and half-asleep babies cried fitfully. All over the camp there was the murmur of quiet conversation and the exchange of stories. At the other side of the Sun Dance ground I could see the lodge of the Horn Society—two tepees that had been joined together. Periodically, as more wood was thrown on the fire inside, the flames would flare up and I could see a pattern of shadows on the sides of the tepee—clearly the men would be talking long into the night.

Earlier that day rich offerings had been exchanged of horses, blankets, and money—offerings that would have taken many years for a family to earn. From time to time a sacred bundle was taken across the center of the Sun Dance ground from one lodge to another. The procession was very slow. Three people, one walking ahead, the second carrying the bundle, and a third making up the rear would ceremonially walk across the sacred ground. Mothers silenced their children and would point out what was happening, whispering to them about the Holy Woman. Periodically the bundle carriers would stop in silence, then walk on again. I sensed I was in the presence of something truly ancient, a movement that connected The People with the enfoldings and unfoldings of the entire cosmos.

I had come to the Sun Dance with my head full of stories and presuppositions, with all the baggage that was inherent to my Western way of thinking. I had seen faded photographs of Sun Dances at the end of the century, of the sacred cottonwood tree that is erected in the center, and of the sacred objects that are attached to it. I knew of the sacrifices that people made, of dancing in the hot sun, of days without food and water. I knew that, in the traditions of some plains people, although not the Blackfoot, a piercing takes place and some of the dancers will drag buffalo skulls from skewers in their backs and offer pieces of flesh from their chests.

I had known of these things, and in coming to the Sun Dance my eyes had always been focused upon that empty space in the center of the ground, waiting for it to be filled. But as I sat under the northern lights, listening into that deep night, I realized I was gradually being drawn into a very different sense of time and space. I began to understand how, without my realizing it, the whole ceremony had been taking place all the time I had been there. It had begun for me the moment I stepped off the plane at Calgary and had begun my journey to the Blood Reserve.

Tired in body and mind, I simply sat and listened to the sounds of the night, to the cries of sleepy children, and to the singers in the lodge across from me. I ceased to worry if the dance would begin tomorrow. The hours passed and then the camp crier was going from lodge to lodge indicating that the

Horn Society wanted silence for the night. Somehow I was beginning to come to another way of knowing, entering into a new feeling about time. For the dance was all around me, it was stretching back in time and reaching far into the future.

The Sun Dance is meant for the whole world; it is an act of sacrifice, an acknowledgment, a coming together of the whole people to renew their relationship with the powers, or spirits, or energies, or laws that animate the cosmos. The meaning of the Sun Dance brings us to the heart of Indigenous science, to the meaning of time and reality; to the nature of life, matter, and process; and to the deeper meaning of sacred mathematics.

A Clash of Paradigms

Half dreaming in the night, I wondered by what curious path of life I had come to be sitting in a circle of tepees; for under the stars and with the sounds of drumming horses in my ears it seemed as if time had been put back and that the Great Plains could still be thundering with mighty herds of buffalo. What role had a Western scientist in all this? Why had I been chosen to have this experience? How was it that the Western scientific part of my upbringing could rest perfectly content in this so very different context?

But did I really think such things, or were these questions only created in retrospect, filled in by the imagination? Looking back on that evening, on the peace of mind that comes with great tiredness of the body, on the inner sense of warmth that tells that you are surrounded by friends, I cannot say that my mind was troubled with questions, or, indeed, that it thought of anything at all.

At that moment, on the Sun Dance ground, I was moving between two worlds. How could it be possible for a Western scientist to see the same world as a traditional Blackfoot? How could two such people ever have a dialogue together?

Ever since my connection with Indigenous science had begun I had been aware of the difficulties that it had caused my Western friends and acquaintances, the realization of what they felt to be basic incompatibilities between Western and

Indigenous visions of reality. Questions like: How can a ceremony held at a medicine wheel have any effect upon the earth's rotation around the sun? How could a dance in the middle of a circle have anything to do with the harmony of the cosmos?

After all, they would argue, Isaac Newton had taught that the dynamics of the solar system are totally determined by the inexorable laws of motion and the force of gravity. The movements of matter have nothing to do with the desires of the human soul. How could any authentic contact be possible between the peoples of the new world and those of the old?

In this, one faces a great danger of believing that the only way of understanding Indigenous science would be to explain it in terms of the truths of Western science. Thus, other cultures and ways of knowing are given their authenticity and validity, not from within the roots of their own tradition, but by using the yardstick of the economically dominant West.

In some ways this reminded me of the inhabitants of the Emerald City in *The Wizard of Oz*. When Dorothy and her companions reach the city they realize that its inhabitants see everything as a beautiful shade of green—the sky, the people, and even the horses. Even Dorothy begins to see a green world once she is inside the city, for everyone is given a pair of green-tinted spectacles. Seeing the world through green-colored glass the whole city agrees upon its greenness.

I wonder, however, if the Wizard of Oz ever had considered the problem that the inhabitants of the Emerald City could one day have to face. Suppose that a group of people from a distant land refused to wear these glasses. In such a case it would be difficult for the visitors and citizens of Oz to come to any agreement about appearances.

All of us see the world through the spectacles of our worldviews, through our particular ways of seeing and thinking about reality and society. Moreover, we hold these worldviews in a largely unconscious way. We are not normally aware that we experience the world through their transforming, or distorting, power. Since much of our worldview is culturally shared, we simply talk about "the way the world is," "the very nature of reality," "the inevitable way any society must function," "an inalienable right," and our "basic human condition."

As with the unbespectacled visitors to the Emerald City, the problem arises when we encounter people who do not share our worldview—they may appear to us as being uneducated, uncivilized, superstitious, primitive, bizarre, or untrustworthy.

This clash of worldviews, or paradigms, as they are sometimes called, is exactly what happened when Europeans began to encounter the Indigenous people of North America. Indigenous people did not behave in a "civilized" way; they had no concept of private property or ownership of land, their religion seemed a mass of superstitions, their legal system did not make sense, neither did they appear to have any proper idea of leadership, making it difficult to negotiate and sign treaties with them.

In the face of such obscurantism, the visitors to the New World administered strict doses of religion and education and, when this failed, attempted the more drastic curative measures of extermination, termination, and assimilation.

But clashes of worldviews do not only happen between Europeans and Turtle Islanders. Chief Brian David is a Mohawk from Akwesasne and tells the following story about the time that his people put on a reception for a visiting team of Cree people after a sports event.

The Mohawk people have traditionally been farmers, a people who rely upon the Three Sisters—beans, squash, and corn. They supplement their diet by fishing and hunting, but being mainly an agricultural people it is their tradition to mount lavish feasts in which the fruits of Mother Earth are displayed in abundance. These displays are meant to far exceed the ability of their guests to consume.

The Cree people, however, live farther north where farming is not such a practical proposition and they are by tradition a hunting people. When a kill has been made it is customary to organize a feast at which, according to certain rules, the meat is distributed. In such a feast no one would refuse to eat what is put before them, for it would be considered disrespectful, not only to the host, but also to the spirits that have provided the game.

Here we have two peoples who, when it comes to putting on a feast, have very different customs, but customs that flow very naturally from their particular lives and worldviews. Moreover, these worldviews go very deeply into the ways their societies have functioned for hundreds and thousands of years. And so the Cree sat down to this stupendous feast and, being well-bred, ate everything in sight. For their part, the Mohawks were a little shocked, but willingly worked in the kitchen to prepare more food, which was brought out to the tables. By then the Cree were somewhat overwhelmed but continued to eat.

With a second round of eating the Mohawks muttered among themselves that the Crees must be very ill-mannered to test their hospitality to such an extent but, nevertheless, they continued to bring out yet more food. The Crees, for their part, wondered if maybe they were being killed by eating, but continued to show their good manners by forcing the food down—even to the point that some of the older people became quite seriously ill!

In the context of a meal two peoples, each attempting to accommodate the other with a show of goodwill and politeness, end up totally at odds. Each sees the world in a way that seems perfectly natural and inevitable and so it never occurs to them that the other does not do things in a similar manner.

Are Western scientists likewise trapped within their paradigms and worldviews? It would be naive to suppose not, to believe that no amount of cultural bias can change the temperature of the sun or the velocity of light. Thoughtful scientists and philosophers have always been sensitive to the biases inherent in the way they look at the world. In his book *The Structure of Scientific Revolutions,* Thomas Kuhn, the science historian, points out that every scientist serves an apprenticeship, at school, university, and during graduate research, during which he or she picks up, in a largely unconscious way, certain ways of thinking and approaching knowledge.

A scientist, therefore, carries out research and asks questions from within the limits defined by a paradigm that is normally never questioned. It is only when a worldview has been stretched to its limits that it breaks down in what Kuhn calls a scientific revolution. In the aftermath, a new paradigm rapidly evolves and then, for the generations of scientists that follow, it becomes the inevitable way of seeing things and doing research.

The real problem with a paradigm or worldview is when it is held by a society that wields considerable economic and political power; for then a particular way of seeing begins to dominate other cultures and forces on them a single, uniform way of seeing where formerly there had been flexibility and diversity.

During the first contact, Europeans were confident that they were the bearers of truth, truth about religion and government, truth about science and law. But today that confidence has been shaken. For some people, the truths of institutional religions are no longer self-evident, or even credible. And science, which has been through two great revolutions—quantum theory and relativity—is much less confident about the nature of objective truth.

Nevertheless, there are those who still hold that Western science can achieve objective knowledge and is in a unique position to teach the truths about the world. The astronomer Carl Sagan, for instance, claims that for the first time in human history we know the truth about the creation of the universe. It has also been argued that for the first time in history children all over the world are being taught the same truths about nature.

When Western science claims to be speaking the truth then, by implication, other peoples' truths become myths, legends, superstitions, and fairy stories. A dominant society denies the authenticity of other peoples' systems of knowledge and in this way strikes at the very heart of their cultures.

Our world has become smaller, and everything we do has the potential of affecting people all over the globe. As never before it is essential that we should all learn to talk and listen together without prejudgment, learn to suspend our prejudices, and allow our consciousness to flow along new lines.

Clearly it is only in this way that the Elders of both Western and Native American science will be able to learn from each other.

Views From Two Worlds

Not long ago I sat around a table with Native and Western thinkers at the Fetzer Institute.* This was one of the first times that Western scientists, linguists, and psychologists had engaged in dialogue with Native American Elders, philosophers, and scientists in a spirit of openness and equality. At one point the discussion came around to the Mic Maq worldview and the question was asked, "Why does ice heal?" When a hole has been made in the ice for fishing, sometime later the ice will be found to have healed over, but when a hole is made in the earth it will not heal—in fact, holes in the road are often observed to get bigger. So why does ice heal?

Within their own framework Western scientists have their own idea of the answer. The problem begins when they try to "interpret" what the Mic Maq scientist may mean. The natural tendency is to jump to our own science, think up the "correct" explanation, and then attempt to fit the Mic Maq concept to our own template.

But those of us who engaged in that dialogue discovered that when faced with the question of the ice that heals we had to begin to let go of everything we had read and been taught about Western physics. For my part, I had to discover a way of entering another space. I had to allow my mind to move into another world, a world with totally different approaches and insights. It was only then, as I began to relax into that world and slowly move around within its territory, testing my way, and never attempting to judge it or compare it with what I had learned from the West, that I began to feel comfortable with a new way of seeing and understanding. Only then could I

---

*The Fetzer Institute had supported some of my work and the work of a colleague, David Bohm. The institute believed that providing an environment in which Western/Native American dialogues could take place was particularly valuable.

respect how complete and meaningful it was, how intellectually satisfying its explanation.

Having gained this new insight I could then move back, for a time, into my more familiar Western way of thinking. Gradually it became possible to develop this ability to move between worldviews, to engage in a sort of exchange or trade between them, not measuring one in terms of the other, or attempting to explain one approach using the yardstick of the other. The experience is a little like moving between different languages, each being complete in itself, each describing the world in a subtly different way, each containing ideas and concepts that are virtually inexpressible in the other.

Something similar happens when you become totally engaged in a film or novel; for a time you enter that other world, you begin to think and feel like its protagonist and accept the world as he or she experiences it. Then, when the book is set down, you move back into your own world and see it in a new and fresh way. The difference, of course, between novels and Native science is that the latter is a living, ongoing way of seeing the world, one that is completely consistent in its own right and has lasted for thousands of years.

Heisenberg's Uncertainty

Shifting consciousness may seem to be something novel to us in the West, to a culture that has assumed the truth of its position and the objectivity of its science. But transformations of being and consciousness are totally natural to Indigenous cultures in which a bear can transform into a man, or in which a mask can become imbued with animating power. For Western thinkers a normal personality is a personality that is fixed and is continuous with us from our early childhood until death. But many Native people can move between personalities. Their existence is more fluid and their ability to enter into other worlds of being is more highly adapted.

Where Western science has always sought fixed laws and ultimate levels, Indigenous science deals in flux, change, and transformation. Just how difficult it can be to shift a viewpoint and to leave one position for another can be seen in the case of

Werner Heisenberg and his struggle to interpret the new quantum theory that he had discovered. Let us follow his train of thought and see how he was forced to battle with the limits of a "commonsense" view of the world. In doing so, we will, in effect, limber up our own mental muscles for some of the shifts in understanding we must make in this book. We will also begin to see how, as Western science frees itself from many of its presuppositions, it approaches certain ways of thinking that are not dissimilar to those of Indigenous science.

In the first decades of the century scientists were puzzling over the newly discovered atomic structure of matter and attempting to integrate this with the discoveries of Albert Einstein and Max Planck that energy has a discrete, or quantum, nature. But these early approaches suffered from the problem of attempting to graft old and new ideas together in an artificial way—for example, introducing new notions of quantized energy into old-fashioned models involving electrons orbiting around a nucleus, like planets around the sun. Scientists simply were not able to go deep enough into their own paradigms and free themselves of habits of thinking. They were approaching the atomic world like visitors in a foreign city who cling to their maps and guidebooks and only walk along the most traveled paths. They would have done better to have plunged fully into the heart of the city and attempted, in all their confusion and excitement, to have captured something of its spirit.

In 1925 Heisenberg attempted to do just this. He made a break with earlier, classical physics and set down his new quantum theory. Yet, even so, it turned out that Heisenberg, himself, was still being trapped in old ways of thinking. The clue to this comes from his famous uncertainty principle. The details of his theory told him that whenever a scientist tried to measure the position of an electron, its speed would immediately become uncertain. On the other hand, when the speed was measured the position became uncertain. It was as if quantum theory were placing a barrier on ever obtaining complete knowledge of the quantum world. (In the large-scale world these quantum effects average out so that uncertainties become vanishingly small. Thus we can measure the velocity and the position of a rocket and work out its future path. The return of a comet, or the eclipse of the sun can be predicted for centuries ahead.)

Believing that he had fully entered into the new quantum thinking, Heisenberg interpreted his uncertainty principle in the following commonsense fashion: Somehow the process of measuring a quantum particle produces an uncontrollable disturbance. When a scientist measures the position of an electron, the intervention of the experiment acts to change the electron's speed in an unpredictable way. Likewise, from when speed is measured the electron's position is perturbed. Somehow the very delicacy of the quantum world prevents us from ever gaining complete knowledge about the electron's quantum reality.

At this point Heisenberg's former teacher, Niels Bohr, stepped in. "You are still clinging to classical ideas," Bohr was in effect arguing. "It's obvious in the very language you speak. When you say that the electron *has* a position and a speed which is disturbed by the act of measurement, you mean that in some way the electron *possesses* a position and speed, that it has a reality of its own that is independent of any observer."

But this idea that electrons and other quantum objects "possess" intrinsic properties, Bohr argued, is really a hangover from old ways of thinking. What Heisenberg's uncertainty principle is really telling us, Bohr explained, is that quantum reality is basically ambiguous. At the level of the atom concepts like "position" and "speed" are inherently ambiguous. Bohr went on to show that the quantum world appeared strange because "classical thinking" is so ingrained in us; indeed, it is part of the very language we speak. Immediately upon opening our mouths we cannot help but talk about individual objects, for our European languages are rich in nouns and adapted to talking about objective realities. When we come to look deeper into Indigenous science, however we shall discover the radically different way its languages work and the ways in which those languages, and the sounds they make, mirror the world of flux and change.

Indigenous science is a consistent way of being within the world; a way of binding people together and giving a meaning to their lives; a technology for relating to the powers and spirits of the world. Moreover, Indigenous science implies a whole structure to knowledge and to ways of "coming-to-knowing."

In the West we have fragmented and specialized our knowledge into a variety of different compartments. For The People, however, knowledge forms a complete whole and includes those areas that we in the West call medicine, agriculture, history, geography, spirituality, law, economics—indeed, Indigenous science encompasses a whole culture and a whole way of life.

The way people see the world around them has a profound effect upon the manner in which their society functions. Western society, for example, is based upon the notion of the primacy of the individual. This is profoundly different from an Indigenous society where each person is first and foremost a part of the group, and the group itself is an aspect of the natural world. Rather than people insisting upon individual rights and freedoms, they acknowledge their obligations and relationship to society and to the earth.

The importance of the group underlies the traditional justice system of many Native peoples. To a great extent the North American court system is based upon British common law with its principles of proof, of establishing guilt or innocence, and of assigning appropriate punishment to the guilty.

Within our courts, prosecution and defense attorneys take up adversarial positions, questioning witnesses, disputing facts surrounding a crime, and arguing over the whole issue of proof. If the accused is found guilty, then a punishment is determined.

In many ways this whole approach flows out of our particular conceptions of the way the universe works. The idea that through verbal disputation a court can reconstruct a certain sequence of events in the past is based upon assumptions about linear time, causality, objective reality, and the power of language to capture the world. The concepts of guilt and innocence reflect not only a particular religious tradition, but our desire to divide the world into fixed categories—a faith in the power of a binary, Aristotelian logic.

Even the idea of law itself grows out of some of the most fundamental notions within our Western way of thinking. It seems inconceivable to us that a society a could function in the absence of law, and it is no coincidence that this word *law*—originally meaning the body of rules that are considered as binding upon a community—should later have also come to be used in the sense of the "laws" of nature. Not only are human beings bound by the rule of law, but also by the behavior of rocks and planets.

The rule of law along with its notions of proof, innocence, guilt, and punishment seems so perfectly natural and inevitable that one of the first things European colonialists did in any new country was to set up police forces and courts of law. It is so easy to forget that European legal systems are based upon assumptions about the nature of human beings, thought, language, and the way the cosmos works. Yet not everyone sees the same world, and the traditional justice systems of Turtle Island are not so much concerned with establishing proof and administering justice as with ensuring balance and harmony within the whole group.

If a person's horses go missing, or a relative is killed, this disrupts the stability of the whole group and thus the society as a whole must seek a way of reestablishing balance. In some societies, Elders meet with the various parties involved to talk things over. The idea is not to reconstruct what happened in the past, indeed the events themselves may only be referred to obliquely or hypothetically. The emphasis, rather, is on how people are to live their lives at the present moment, the nature of their needs, and how the harmony of the whole group has been disrupted.

In some hunting societies a whole family may hunt together, men and women joining equally in the tasks involved. In others men take on this role, the women being responsible for other tasks. Suppose in this latter kind of society that a husband is killed. Someone must be willing to provide game for the dead man's wife and children. And so, in the case of a murder, the Elders may ask the person who did this act to suggest a way in which he or she could restore balance within the family and the whole society. That person may give away his horses, agree to provide food for the dead man's family, or in some other way seek to renew the balance.

Finally, when all the various parties to the dispute seem satisfied, the society will meet as a whole so that, while sitting in a circle, the issue can be publicly resolved.

On rare occasions a person may offend repeatedly and prove intractable to all attempts at reason and dialogue. In this case a form of social ostracism is practiced. And, if this does no good, then the ultimate punishment may be to physically banish the person from the tribe.

From within a worldview that is based upon relationship, the threat of banishment is far more serious than life imprisonment or the death penalty, for it means cutting a person off from the whole society, and even from the opportunity to hear and speak his own language. In other words, it removes the very context that gives a person's life meaning and identity.

The extreme seriousness of what it means for a Native person to be separated from his or her group is given in this story about a man who was at such odds with his people that, as a last resort, he decided to leave them. Even though this caused everyone great distress, nonetheless, one morning he rode away with his wife and his belongings.

On the following day a party of young men from the tribe followed his tracks and took his wife back to the camp with them. In spite of this, the man traveled on, putting more distance between himself and his people. The next day the young men appeared again and this time took all his belongings back to the camp. On the third day they took his horse, but, nevertheless, the man continued on foot. On the following day they cut off his arms, but still he kept moving. On their final visit, they cut off his legs!

Maybe one of the things this story is asking us is: Is it even possible, within an Indigenous worldview, for an individual to exist without the context of his or her society?

Just as our own Western justice system is based upon a worldview and belief system, so traditional Native American justice is rooted in notions of relationship and dialogue rather than adversarial dispute; harmony and balance rather than proof and guilt; and renewal rather than punishment. Each system of justice is indissolubly linked to the paradigm that underlies the respective society.

Back at the Sun Dance

Born into one society, steeped in its language, its paradigms, and its ways of thinking, I had begun to realize that no one can really ever "understand" another culture in the sense that true insights cannot come though processes of observation and analysis. The best one can hope for is for one's consciousness to dip in and out of other ways of seeing, for human reason to increase its flexibility and free itself from rigidities and fixed patterns of response. And so I sat at the Sun Dance ground and, although I really had no idea of what was going on, I felt myself drawn into the cycle of its deeper meaning.

One night, as I had half dozed under the northern lights, the activity within the camp had changed. By the afternoon men of the Horn Society, the sacred society concerned with the running of the Sun Dance, had cut poles and, hand over hand, were carefully measuring their lengths and smoothing away the bark. The men went back into their lodge and later another group sat outside smoking and talking.

A woman from a nearby tepee asked me inside. The previous day the Horns had brought in meat for the camp, going from lodge to lodge. She had cut the meat into thin strips and it was now hanging in the tepee, smoking in the fire. That year her son had joined the Horn Society and while the society was meeting she was responsible for feeding him. She showed me his favorite teapot and other treasures that were assembled in their tepee.

There was a tension in the air and people were silent, focused upon the twinned tepees of the Horn Society that had been set up in the middle of the Sun Dance ground. Everything was stilled, and then in the distance I heard the sound of a wind gathering and moving across the plains toward the Sun Dance ground. It was a whooshing that aroused and circled the ground, and yet it was not a wind that arrived from outside, but a sound that was being generated from within the central lodge. The sound stopped and the men began their singing and drumming. Now I could hear the sound of yelping, crying dogs and thought to myself that this must be the song of the Crazy Dogs.

The silence returned until the wind, the yelping of dogs, the drumming, and the singing began again. Four times the singing took place and then four men emerged from the entrance to the central double tepee. They wore headdresses with long yellow curls that hung down so that the man resembled dogs. Then more people emerged, all dressed in particular ways. I now saw that the poles that had been cut earlier in the day had been dressed. Some looked like images I had seen in wall paintings of the ancient Egyptians, yet others were made into crosses, and I wondered what the first Christian missionaries must have thought seeing crosses carried in a sacred ceremony by those who had not yet heard of the religions of the European world. Some of the men emerged dancing and crying like dogs and immediately all the stray dogs that had surrounded the camp swept in barking and ran out again.

The people then arranged themselves into small groups. Holes were dug in the ground to support the poles and crosses and the men of the Horn Society sat down to smoke the sacred pipe and to pray. Prayer is a constant aspect of all Native American gatherings. Everything is begun with prayer, from an important religious ceremony to negotiations with government representatives. And every circle usually begins with "smudging," an anointing of the head and body with sacred smoke from sweetgrass, sage, or cedar.

Following the prayers several of the Horns appeared with big cauldrons of soup and distributed it to the crowds. Everyone seemed to have brought some sort of container, I was handed a jam jar, but in the crush was passed by. An old woman cried out in Blackfoot, "This man wants some soup." I thanked her and only later realized that I did not understand a word of that language. The berry soup was warm and sweet, and each person was given a piece of bannock to eat with it. Even in the heat of summer a cool wind can rise on the plains when evening comes down. I was tired and cold and the soup was so good to eat, and how right it seemed for us all to be sitting so close together, partaking in the one meal.

With the meal completed the dancing began. Supporters

came out of the crowd to stand behind the dancers. The dog yelps of the singers could be heard again. The singers danced facing one way, then turned fully around and danced again. Dancing, turning, and as the dancing continued it seemed that the cycle of time had turned back on itself in an eternal renewal. I was enclosed within the circle of time, the circle of those who sat around the Sun Dance ground, the circle of the tepees, the movement of the seasons, the waxing and waning of the moon.

The circle stretched back and turned in on itself, completing and renewing, and as I looked up into the night sky I was connected to my other self, to that boy who had grown up in Liverpool, England, and once stood with his friends under a street lamp and wondered if its light reached ever upward to the stars; who asked if the universe had an end and wondered if we were all somehow connected to the farthest points of space and time. Time circulated back on itself, time was past and time was future, and within that curvature of time all the paradoxes that had passed through my mind were resolved.

I was enfolded into myself and returned to that hot afternoon of my childhood when my friend Bill Mulligan and I had gone fishing in Ainsdale Lake, a few miles from our home. It had been a lazy day of swimming and eating sandwiches and drinking soda pop, when suddenly the fish began to bite and in just a few totally memorable hours we caught an amazing fifty fish—or was it sixty, or even seventy? Each time we caught one Bill would cry out "God bless Ainsdale Lake" and we would carefully return the living fish to the water. I can't remember how our little ceremonyhad started, but we had always thanked the river that had given us fish. One time before, when we had been fishing in Wales, an old man had asked us for fresh trout, as his daughter was ill in bed. We fished all morning, without any luck, and then one of us took the first fish on the fly. After some discussion we placed it back in the river and after that our luck seemed to change and we pulled out several more sweet trout, each weighing around three-quarters of a pound.

And so we fished Ainsdale Lake until the sun began to set and its red disc shone in our eyes. Bill hooked an enormous eel and, and as he ran screaming from the lake, the eel, in its thrashing, wound itself around his line and seemed to pursue him out of the water!

I return to that lake and I am connected to those other evenings of fishing by the canal while the birds sweep low over the water as the last light fades. And later, as a student I am climbing in the Cumbrian mountains, and walking in the mysterious Welsh woods. It is a time when everything seems totally alive, when eyes and ears and mouth drink in the world; a time when, lying on my back and looking up into the stars, I feel a sudden immediate connection to those far distant worlds; a time when peering down a microscope at tiny plants and animals, or dropping bits of copper into nitric acid in my boyhood coalshed laboratory, it seems as if everything, right down to the very chemical elements themselves, is alive. That copper, zinc, iron, sulfur, and chlorine each has its own personality and I am engaged in a dialogue with their inner chemical lives.

In those far-off days everything was truly alive for me and vibrating with power. There were some places so saturated with energy that I was afraid to approach them too closely for fear that my whole being would be overwhelmed. And now as I sat in that Sun Dance ground I entered that world of power yet again and was surrounded by people for whom the numinous sense of nature had never dimmed.

At that moment paradoxes and paradigms slipped away and I realized that we had all, as children, seen the world in that way. And, moreover, that it may still be possible to touch that sense of numinous animation and direct connection of the cosmos that is hidden deep within us. It is that door into the immediacy of nature that is opened to visionaries and mystics. It was known to Wordsworth when he wrote:

> There was a time when meadow, grove, and stream,
> The earth, and every common sight,
>   To me did seem
>   Appareled in celestial light.
> The glory and the freshness of a dream.

It was known to all the great poets and painters and, I believe, to the greatest scientists, such as Newton and Einstein, who were in direct and vibrant contact with nature.

Today this vision has dimmed for so many of us. Our contact with the natural world has been lost and the power of our science seems to deny that rocks and winds could be alive, or that ceremonies can really matter. But on the Sun Dance ground I was sitting with The People, for whom the sense of intimacy and directness of nature had never dimmed. Gradually Indigenous science came alive for me. It was no longer a story, concept, or idea. It was a way of life.

3

Coming-to-Knowing

Preface

Science is about understanding; it is one of the ways we attempt to answer the perennial questions about the nature of existence. The goal of science is, in part, the gaining of knowledge, and, in many cultures, the acquisition of knowledge is associated with the possession of power. Thus, the Elizabethan philosopher Francis Bacon equated knowledge with power—"Knowledge and human power come to the same thing, for nature cannot be conquered except by obeying her." Knowledge, therefore, is something to be possessed and accumulated. In so many ways this approach to knowledge and to power is very different from that within Indigenous societies.

Knowledge, to a Native person, cannot be accumulated like money stored in a bank, rather it is an ongoing process better represented by the activity of coming-to-knowing than by a static noun. Each person who grows up in a traditional Native American society must pass through the process of coming-to-knowing, which, in turn, gives him or her access to a certain sort of power, not necessarily power in the personal sense, but in the way a person can come into relationship with the energies and animating spirits of the universe.

Knowledge, within a traditional society, is not the stuff of books, but the stuff of life. Even in the English language that word *knowledge* has its origins in a verb or activity. In medieval times it served as a verb somewhat like our modern *to acknowledge*, and it meant to own the knowledge of something and perceive something as true. In turn, the origins of this verb lay in yet another process—the verb *to know*—which is a term of extremely ancient Aryan origins that has to do with perception, recognition, and the ability to distinguish. Thus, to the earliest peoples of Europe and Asia *knowledge* and *knowing* had more to do with a discriminating perception of the mind and the senses than with the accumulation of facts.

In time, our own indigenous view of knowledge was transformed into a a noun, something that could be categorized, conceptualized, collected, and stored within the filing cabinets of the mind. Today, Western science often seeks this more static form of knowledge, for in many cases the desire to understand has been replaced by the desire to manipulate, control, and exploit. As the French philosopher René Descartes put it, "Knowing the force and action of fire, water, air, the stars, the heavens, and all other bodies that surround it, men can be the masters and possessors of nature.'" Francis Bacon suggested that in order to gain such knowledge nature should be placed upon the rack and tortured to reveal her secrets.

In her book *Woman and Nature*, Susan Griffin juxtaposes a number of statements made by philosophers and scientists about nature and about women. Again and again a remarkable parallel in attitudes to the two can be discovered. The People of Turtle Island also speak of nature as feminine, as Mother Earth, but in the Western tradition the feminine must be possessed, controlled, conquered, compelled, owned, and exploited.

In deep and subtle ways the attitude of Indigenous science to knowledge and to the processes of coming-to-knowing is profoundly different from that of its Western counterpart. Maybe it is best illustrated by a story, for stories are one step in coming-to-knowing.

A Story About Knowledge and Knowing

In his own life, Joe Couture, a therapist and traditional healer, has explored the implications of these two ways of knowing and the clash between a Western education and his own Blackfoot background. In some ways Joe feels as at home with his laptop computer as he does in a sweat lodge, yet he has also felt that tearing dislocation that comes from living in two worlds. As for the two worlds of knowledge...? Well, one day Joe happened to be sitting with a council of Elders in a northern community when the talk turned to the role of a local school in their community. The people were predominantly hunters and trappers and the school itself took in both Native and non-Native students.

It was at that point that an old man began to tell a story about the time he was a boy and had to make a long trip along the Yukon River to Dawson City. I never did get to hear the full details of what had happened. As Joe Couture related it, the boy had "broken down"—maybe he was driving an old pickup truck. At any event he faced a journey of over a hundred miles on his own and under adverse conditions. In the end he made it through. After telling his story, the old man began to talk about his grandson who had gone to the school. His grandson could now read and write, but the old man was sure that if his grandson were to have to make the same journey alone he would never make it back.

When Joe retold this story, in a circle of Native Elders and Western scientists, it set everyone thinking, just as it must have done when the old man told it at the council meeting. The stories told by traditional people come out of their direct experiences and are ways of teaching that are very different from the simple imparting of facts.

The old man had no need to analyze the philosophy of the local school board or discuss the relative value of different worldviews. He simply told a story, and, in the context of that school board meeting, the story brought into focus some of the things that people were sensing and feeling about the school's effect on their community. Then, again, when this story was retold by Joe Couture in the context of a dialogue about Indigenous science between Western and Native experts, the same story began to operate in a new way. Up to that point some of us had been playing with ideas about worldviews and paradigms in an abstract, analytic way, but then, when we heard of someone who had survived a life-threatening experience, we began to move to a new way of thinking, one that was quieter and took us back to our own life experiences.

The story made us think about the scientific knowledge each of us had accumulated in our training and how that knowledge was supposed to give us power over nature. Yet, how useless that power would be to a young man alone in the bush in the depths of winter. Joe's story alerted us to the possibility of other forms of knowledge and a process of coming-to-knowing. It also made us aware of how people change when societies clash and the knowledge of one begins to dominate and control the ways of seeing of the other.

A Fishing Story

Rupert Ross is a crown prosecutor from Kenora in northern Ontario and has tried hard to learn about the traditional ways of Indigenous people. A sensitive man, he is very much aware that as a crown prosecutor he is the representative of a legal system that is alien to the very people it was supposed to serve. Thus, in his earlier days, he would ask advice from the Native Elders who were present in the court. Again and again he found that their answers were evasive and of little help to him. Ross wanted to do the right thing, to understand how a person in a traditional society would have acted, yet no one seemed to be telling him what to do.

It was then that he remembered an incident from the time he had worked as a fishing guide. There were a number of Native guides at the same camp, including a young man who was beginning to learn the business himself. One day Rupert was fishing with a group when he noticed the young man's boat was heading toward a region of the lake where rocks were lying just below the water. Ross was about to call out and warn the boy when, to his surprise, he realized the boy's father, an experienced guide, was also seated in the boat.

As the boat headed for the submerged rocks, the father did nothing. Indeed, it was only at the last moment that the boy saw the danger and cut the motor. Ross began to wonder; why did the father not warn his son? Why did he risk injury to the people in the boat as well as damaging expensive equipment? After all, he had simply to call out a warning and tell his boy about the rocks. But the father simply sat there, saying nothing.

This does not make much sense to anyone brought up in a Western culture. Our natural tendency is to warn, help, teach, instruct, and improve. However, the more Rupert Ross reflected on his experiences at the fishing camp the more he came to realize that, in the Native world, you cannot "give" a person knowledge in the way that a doctor gives a person a shot for measles. Rather, each person learns for himself or herself through the processes of growing up in contact with nature and society; by observing, watching, listening, and dreaming. His early experience taught Rupert Ross that there was a way to sit with an Elder and to learn what a traditional person would think and do in a particular set of circumstances.

It was another sort of learning, the one that takes usually place within the context of a school, that was preventing the young man in Joe Couture's story from coming to know the tools of his own survival. It was not so much the content the school was teaching that caused the problem, but that its approach to education was alien to a Native society. Many things can be taught out of a textbook, from quantum theory to economics, from history to poetry, but what about the art of learning itself, listening, watching, coming-to-knowing, and understanding the world?

Marie Battiste, a Mic Maq educator, spoke of the rich environment in which a Native child is immersed from birth. It is a world of songs, stories, and ceremonies; the movement of the wind in the trees and the waves on a river; the sounds of birds; the voices of dreams and animals; and the dance around the fire at night. Throughout coming-to-knowing the child is encouraged to listen and to watch, to become sensitive to the rich tapestry of the world. Then one day that child goes to school and is told by the teacher, "Listen to nothing but my voice, cut out the sights and sounds of the world outside the window, do not pay attention to your fellows; filter and focus."

It is possible that the grandson in Joe Couture's story may have learned far more about geography, astronomy, and natural history than his grandfather knew. But would he understand how to read the signs that were all about him in the bush? A map and a compass would indicate his geographical location, but would he know where he stood in relation to his own culture and traditions? Physical education and sports may have strengthened his body, but would he have had the spiritual strength to survive and make it home? School may have taught him the importance of being an individual, but alone in the night and far from any village would he have felt the presence of his own people and a direct sense of relationship to the birds, plants, animals, and rocks?

Canoe Stories

During the 1940s two Algonquin men were out trapping northwest of Ottawa, Ontario. It was spring, and while the rivers had already opened, there was still much snow on the ground. The two men had sixty miles to travel in order to return home, but, with all their furs, traps, and moose meat, their canoe was overloaded. One of the men, Kocko Carle, simply cut down a nearby birch tree and set about making a new canoe. Four days later the two men had built a second fourteen-foot canoe so that they could return to their people near Maniwaki, Quebec, with their meat and furs.

This is by no means an exceptional story, for building a canoe was once part of the knowledge of any traditional person who used rivers for transport. What is interesting about this particular story, however, is that it was told to me by a non-Native, David Gidmark, who passed through his own particular process of coming-to-knowing within a Native context.

David Gidmark's story can be found in his book *Birchbark Canoe*. As a young man he had admired the birchbark canoes that had been used for thousands of years by the peoples of North America, each group employing its own designs. He knew that, by tradition, such a canoe was built using only what is called a crooked knife. Everything else—the birchbark skin of the canoe, the cedar ribs, the spruce roots for sewing and binding, and the spruce gum to ensure that it is water-proof—is readily available in the bush.

David had seen traditional canoes in photographs and museums. He had even read scholarly articles about the way people had made such canoes in the past. If he had continued in this manner he might well have become an "expert" on birchbark canoes, a curator at a museum, perhaps. But a collection of facts is far from coming-to-knowing, and David Gidmark wanted to make a birchbark canoe of his own; to understand which was good bark and which was not; to know how to find and handle the materials; to develop the necessary skills and judgment; to learn how to use his eyes and hands and mind together. And so he traveled to Maniwaki in the province of Quebec in search of one of the last great canoe makers, William Commanda.

After many visits with William Commanda, and even after beginning to learn the Algonquins' language, David Gidmark plucked up the courage to ask William Commanda if he would teach him to build a birchbark canoe. Commanda simply laughed, "I will never teach a white man to build a birchbark canoe. If you want to learn, you'd better find some white man to teach you."

But David Gidmark persisted, staying in the area, learning the language, and talking to old people. Finally, a year later, William Commanda invited David to move in with him and his wife—and so another stage of his apprenticeship began. This time David helped around the house until one day William was ready to allow him to hang around as he went through the various processes of canoe building.

David Gidmark learned the craft and knowledge of canoe building by watching and helping someone who was an expert. His final test was critical. It was to go into the bush by himself and return when he had built his own canoe. When he finally came back, William Commanda's verdict was, "Well, at least it floats."

David Gidmark is now teaching other people how to build canoes; running summer schools where people can work and learn the many traditional skills involved. Ironically, however, the rolls of birchbark that are used to build the canoes must be shipped from Scandinavia. In the Algonquin tradition a canoe is made from a single piece of bark, and there are simply not enough birch trees in eastern America old enough to have the girth to supply the necessary size of bark.

Although the traditional knowledge and skills of the Algonquin people are still being passed on, the environment has changed so much that it would be difficult for a person marooned in the bush to build a traditional Algonquin canoe in four or five days. There is an important teaching even in this, for within the Native world there is no such thing as abstract knowledge. The knowledge of the canoe is tied to the environment, to the group, and to its long history. Now, tragically, the environment has changed. What will become of the knowledge?

William Commanda once said "I will never teach a white man to build a birchbark canoe." Today I have heard him speak openly to audiences of Natives and non-Natives about his traditional knowledge and the change that took place in his own life. William Commanda is Keeper and interpreter of ancient wampum belts that tell of the Seven Fires Prophecy. For a long period his heart was filled with anger toward white people and what they had done to his people and to the land. For this reason he would never show or speak about the wampum belts that had been entrusted to him.

A number of years ago however, he experienced a great change. He was visited by a dream, or vision, that told him the time had come to make a bridge between the two peoples. He was to show the belts and to speak about the prophecies they contain. William Commanda now speaks openly, sharing his knowledge of the wampum belts, their history, and the prophecies they contain.

The skills necessary to build an Algonquin canoe are tied

to a particular landscape, to the trees that grow there, to the game that can be trapped, to the flowing of rivers, and to the movement of winds across the lakes. The way this knowledge is learned is inseparable from the land and from the people who live on it. In this sense Indigenous knowledge is never directly transferable as knowledge is in the West. For the heart of traditional knowledge cannot be translated, written down in a book, or transposed to an individual living thousands of miles away in a totally different environment. Knowledge belongs to a people, and the people belong to the landscape.

This connection between knowledge, the land, and the People is illustrated in another story about canoe building. The Haida people live in their traditional land called Haida Gwaii (the names given to this land by Western cartographers are the Queen Charlotte and Prince of Wales islands) and their language is in danger of being lost. For a long time Woody Morrison, K'aw Daagangaas, along with some of his Elders, had been looking for a way to revive the language, culture, and traditional knowledge of his people. But it seemed almost impossible to do this exclusively within a school setting.

Woody's idea was to revive the language by building an oceangoing canoe. Once the Haida people had made great sea voyages, not only along the west coast of Canada and the United States but to Central and South America and out into the Pacific where, their stories tell, they met with the ocean-voyaging peoples of Polynesia and even with the Maoris of New Zealand. Because of the impact of white culture, these canoes had not been built for almost a century.

Several years earlier *Loo Taas* (Wave-Eater), a sixteen-meter coastal canoe had been built and with it many traditional skills revived. Later, in 1991, for example, several Haida people went to San Francisco where they carved a totem pole and built a coastal canoe. I, along with many others, was privileged to carry the canoe to the water where it was launched. No one, however, had built one of the even larger voyaging canoes in which the Haida people would undertake trips of several weeks' duration.

Building such a canoe, Woody knew, would involve the Haida people in reviving knowledge that appeared, on the surface, to have been lost, but was still contained in an implicit way within the people and the land. Not only would a canoe be built, but sails would be made using a fabric of woven bark. Cordage had to be constructed and traditional clothing woven. There was also the question of provisions for the duration of the voyage. What had people taken with them on their long ocean voyages? How much water had they needed? There were stories of the Haida people training their minds and bodies before a long voyage by drinking sea water and of their mixing salt water and fresh water on the voyage. Navigation skills would have to be learned, and stories of ancient voyages revived.

There is something half magical and yet highly scientific about Haida canoes, for they can travel at high speeds using a particular method of paddling that enables people to keep going for many hours without tiring. Through the process of recovering all this traditional knowledge, the language itself would be revived, for, as the Elders teach, knowledge and ways of thinking are contained within the language. Woody believes that as his people revive their ancient knowledge they will also come into relationship with their traditional language. Ancient words, remembered only by the Elders, would be revived and their meanings rediscovered; lost knowledge would return in dreams and visions.

This has been Woody's dream for many years, and to this end the Xaadas Voyaging Society was set up with its motto *Guutlaay Kaasgiit* (We Go, We Meet). Yet, at the time of this book's completion, the great Haida canoe has not yet been built. This has been due partly to the difficulties involved in raising funds for this great venture, but also to the fact that the Haida people can no longer walk through their traditional land to select a great cedar tree that would sacrifice itself in order to be transformed into a living canoe.

As with the birch trees of northeastern America, few of these forest giants remain today. Lands that were once the responsibility of the Haida people are now owned and managed by governments and lumber companies, and the great old trees are not an economic proposition. Companies move in and clearcut the trees, replacing them with more economical and faster-growing varieties. Most of us know about the destruction of the rain forests of Brazil, but few realize that great forests in other parts of the world are equally in danger.

Eventually Woody did locate a tree of sufficient size to build his canoe. He went through the necessary paperwork to obtain the tree for his people, but on making test drillings into its core he found that it was rotten. Other difficulties plagued the project and as I write this, Woody's dream still remains to be realized.

Knowledge as Process

Knowledge in the traditional world is not a dead collection of facts. It is alive, has spirit, and dwells in specific places. Traditional knowledge comes about through watching and listening, not in the passive way that schools demand, but through direct experience of songs and ceremonies, through the activities of hunting and daily life, from trees and animals, and in dreams and visions. Coming-to-knowing means entering into relationship with the spirits of knowledge, with plants and animals, with beings that animate dreams and visions, and with the spirit of the people.

As in all relationships, agreements must be made and obligations and responsibilities entered into with the spirits. Thus, when a person comes into relationship with certain knowledge he or she is not only transformed by it but must also assume responsibility for it.

By contrast, so much of what goes on in mainstream schools is concerned with the accumulation of facts and the practical problems of getting through a syllabus. Once during a PTA meeting I attended a parent asked a science teacher how he dealt with the ethical dimensions of his subject. The teacher admitted that ethics was indeed part of the course, but with so much to get through in a school year such luxuries as the philosophy and ethics of science simply had to be dropped.

Ultimately that teacher should not be blamed because he was merely responding to the value our society places on particular forms of knowledge. In the late 1970s I was invited to participate in a group that was raising funds to build the world's largest computer memory. Under the illusion that this would bring them considerable power the group members intended to feed a supercomputer with all the world's knowledge of science, mathematics, history, economics, medicine, literature, etc.

This image of a giant computer memory accorded very well with their attitude toward knowledge as something that could be accumulated and stored. A computer memory could be filled with the poetry of Milton, the plays of Shakespeare, the theory of relativity, the *I Ching* and the Bhagavad Gita. When the computer memory was full it could be electronically erased and we could begin again, this time feeding it with information about the world's geography, sequences of prime numbers, or the classification of plants. No one would ever think that the computer memory would be changed by that knowledge; that the computer, having been fed Darwin's theory of evolution, would begin to operate in a different way. For knowledge is passive. Within a traditional society, however, knowledge as a process transforms and brings with it obligations and responsibilities.

In one of his essays, the English writer Aldous Huxley pointed to the fragmented nature of our Western education system and the way it focuses upon the mental accumulation of facts. The cultures of the East, he observed, educate mind and body together; they are less concerned with imparting facts than with teaching how the mind actually works.

The philosopher Michael Polyani has written of what he calls "tacit knowledge"—a knowing that he says is not passed on through books or verbal instruction but is learned by direct experience through the whole of one's being. An example of such knowledge is riding a bicycle. No one can *tell* you how to ride, yet one day you find that you can. You may forget the phone number you had as a child but no matter how long you live you will never forget how to ride a bike.

Polyani's *tacit knowledge* comes close to the Native American's vision of coming-to-knowing. In both cases the knowledge is acquired through experience and relationship with the thing to be known. In both cases the knowledge is not so much stored as data in the brain but is absorbed into the whole person.

The Being of Knowing

There is one important way, however, in which the Indigenous approach to knowing differs from Polyani's. Most of us believe that knowledge has no independent existence apart from the one who knows. If everyone were to forget a particular dance, or song, or the way of doing something, and if this had not been filmed or videotaped or written down in some way, then we would say that such knowledge had been lost forever.

Knowledge, for us, is an abstraction with no independent existence. Its only manifestation is its existence as a physical record in a book, as chemical and electrical signals in a human brain, or encoded as muscular skills in the human body. Once those particular physical systems have died or been destroyed the knowledge itself ceases to exist.

When I listen to Native people I get the impression that knowledge for them is profoundly different: It is a living thing that has existence independent of human beings. A person comes to knowing by entering into a relationship with the living spirit of that knowledge.

Let us approach this thought in a slightly different way. An individual or group may "know" how to carry out a particular skill, such as beadwork, but will never actually perform the task in practice. When asked about why they don't do it they may say that it is because they have not been given authorization to do this work; they have not entered into a relationship, or agreement, with the knowledge. The authorization itself may come from an individual or from people that already has the proper relationship with the knowledge, or it may come through a special dream or vision. It will also involve an appropriate exchange.

What happens when these skills are totally lost, in the sense that no one remains alive who knows a particular way of doing certain things? Has the knowledge vanished? Traditional songs are said by anthropologists to be lost, as are certain languages. But, as far as I can understand it, these songs, languages, and traditional ways are still alive because they have existence as spirits, energies, and powers. I have been told how a song lives on after the singer has died and that it may reappear in the future as a gift in the heart and mind and throat of some other singer.

Dan Moonhawk Alford, a linguist and close friend of Sa'ke'j Henderson, loves to relate the story of the man who went to a ceremony but could not get a particular song out of his head. In the end it bothered him so much that he told one of the Elders. "Then why don't you sing it?" the old man said. The song was sung and the old man replied, "That was Joe's song. He died in 1910. I guess it got kind of lonely waiting around with no one to sing it."

I have heard stories of people who go into the sweat lodge or attend a sacred ceremony not knowing the particular songs. As soon as the drum beats they say that the song enters into them—the song sings them.

Although traditional ways may appear to be lost, some Elders are confident that when the time is right this knowledge will come back. Like the grass that grows again each spring, it will reappear in dreams or during ceremonies.

Knowing by Listening

In our schools, education tends to end in the late teens, or at the completion of college or university. But, coming-to-knowing, entering into a relationship with the spirits, powers, or energies of knowledge, is a process that must continue throughout a person's life. Pete Standing Alone is a Blackfoot from the Blood Reserve in southern Alberta and a member of the sacred Horn Society. In Fraser Taylor's biography of him (*Standing Alone: A Contemporary Blackfoot Indian*), Pete is quoted as saying about the Horn Society's knowledge: "It's something a good Indian should do, and that's give service to the people. So you should join at least once. Actually, you can't learn everything well enough in four years to teach someone else coming in for the first time. . . . maybe in twenty-five years with four times into it, to learn all the matters well enough to teach others."

There is so much to know that it takes a lifetime of relationships. But how does it all start? Danny Musqua is an Elder and traditional storyteller of the Soto people. I was

introduced to him by his adopted son, Dick Katz, who is also
the author of two illuminating books on Indigenous people,
Boiling Energy: Community Healing Among the Kalahari Kung and
The Straight Path: a Story of Healing and Transformation in Fiji. As a
boy, Danny was brought up by his grandfather, a man then in
his nineties. Danny told me how his grandfather had once set
his chair close to an ants' nest allowing the insects to crawl up
his boot and onto his pant leg. "Everything has a limit and
everything respects its limits," the grandfather told the young
boy as he set his own limit for the ants—an unseen line
partway up his leg. Sure enough, the ants advanced so far and
no farther; except for one very bold ant that began to climb
toward the old man's knee. At this, Danny's grandfather
tapped his leg gently with his fingertip to remind the ant,
which then descended. "Everything has its limits," he said
again.

Sometimes his grandfather would set Danny to watch a
particular bird and at the end of the day would ask him what
he had seen. On other occasions he would be assigned to watch
an animal that always returned to a particular spot. Day after
day, Danny sat and watched, beginning to understand what
the animals were teaching him. By watching each animal
Danny began to learn its habits, how it behaved, what its
relationship was to other animals, how it fit into the web of
nature, and how sometimes human beings did the same sorts
of things that animals did.

As Danny lovingly told me about his grandfather, he kept
moving between English and his own Soto language. It was
late and I was tired. Soon I began to hear him as one hears a
river or a distant bird, I seemed to comprehend what was being
said to me, not in any intellectual way, but directly in my heart.
There were times when I was not sure if Danny was talking
about his own particular grandfather, the historical individual
who had brought him up, or about the Grandfathers themselves, the Old Ones, the ones who had come long before, the
spirits who stretched back for hundreds and thousands of
years, the Grandfathers who can be seen moving within the
hot rocks of the sweat lodge, who appear in dreams, and whose
voices can be heard at night. In the space of just a few hours

and in what may have been a small way for traditional people—but was very important to me—I was taken into a relationship with spirits that could teach.

The Teacher

Growing up like Danny Musqua, in a traditional society young people learn that the whole of nature can teach and that they learn by being silent, by observing, and by listening. Often an older person will watch over them and introduce them to situations in which they can learn. In our society parents are usually responsible for our earliest education and discipline. But in most Native societies, although parents are the ones who feed and nourish, as part of an extended family, children spend a lot of time staying at relatives' houses and playing with their many cousins.

While the parents provide love and shelter, the responsibility for bringing up a child generally resides with a grandparent, aunt, or uncle. When Woody Morrison, K'aw Daagangaas, was seven years old, his grandfather Kun Kwiiaan, called Peacemaker, presented him to the Haida Elders and charged them to be the boy's guide and teach him of "the wind, water, trees, and fire." Normally, as Woody explained to me, the daily responsibility of educating a Haida boy resides with his father's brother.

Guided, in the case of a boy, by a grandparent or his father's brother, a child learns through the direct experience of watching and listening. Cree children play together hunting porcupine and in this way develop the skills and understanding needed for hunting larger and faster-moving animals. Later, a boy will travel with a hunter and watch how he moves through the snow looking for signs, setting traps, moving across great distances, and always knowing where he is. In this learning, no one instructs or tells the child what to do; rather, the child watches and takes things in. Then, one day, that child is allowed to go out alone and set traps, for the testing of a piece of knowledge is always done in private. And, finally, there will be some form of public acknowledgment that skills have been learned and that the young person has acquired new knowledge.

Structuring Knowledge

This may be yet another reason why Native children from traditional backgrounds often feel uncomfortable in schools where an emphasis is placed on presenting knowledge in a highly structured way through textbooks, lectures, and blackboard presentations. There is little direct experience in this. Instead teachers attempt to stimulate interest by asking questions and soliciting answers, or at least guesses, from children.

Leroy Little Bear told me of his experiences at school. One day they had had a lesson on Canadian geography. To test the children, the teacher pointed to a boy in the front row and asked: "What is the capital of Canada?" The boy began to scratch his head and think: What does this question mean? What does it *really* mean? I know things are all connected to each other, so what is really behind this question? The teacher has already told us that Ottawa is the capital of Canada, so why did she ask me this question? Why is she asking me when she already knows the answer?

Exasperated with waiting for an answer, the teacher pointed to Leroy and said, "What is the capital of Canada?" Leroy began to think: Why wouldn't the teacher let my friend answer? I know that he knows the answer. And if I answer, that's going to make him look foolish. So Leroy just sat there, scratching his head, while the teacher pointed to the next child and repeated the question. In the end she had the whole class scratching their heads and no one would volunteer an answer!

In a traditional society children learn by watching and hanging around rather than through structured teaching, questioning, or experiment. Moreover, they are not singled out and quizzed, because only after they have gained sufficient confidence would they attempt the task themselves—and this would be done in private. Having developed the necessary skills and confidence they would then return to the group and perform the new task in public.

Children in Western schools are often bored because they are passive consumers of knowledge. By contrast, the "watching" and the "listening" that takes place in a traditional society is a more active form of observation. A child is encouraged to take his or her time, for things only happen when the time is right. The attention a child gives in a school is often not very different in its quality from what we all do in front of the television set. The watching that leads to coming-to-knowing may be closer to the active watching of a kingfisher who sits poised on a branch over a fast-flowing river.

Doing and Playing

Not all schools are like this, however, some are very creative and experientially based; based on "play." Coming-to-knowing in a traditional society is based on direct experience, but there is much less emphasis upon "playing," in the sense of trying a thing out before a person really understands what he or she is doing, or has developed the necessary skills.

Knowing and Experiencing

Knowing through direct experience is also reflected in the way some Indigenous languages work. Suppose that someone wants to tell you that caribou are crossing a river. They will use different verbal forms to distinguish between their own experience of having actually seen the caribou and the experience of having been told that fact by someone else. Linguistic care is taken when, in telling a story, one must repeat what someone else has said. Native language makes it very clear that when you repeat someone else's words they are not your own.

In the West when we want to emphasize a point we may quote an important authority. In traditional societies, personal experience, what a person has actually seen or done or heard in the bush or during a dream or vision, is considered to be the most valuable form of knowledge. When Native Elders want to make a point they do not contradict or argue things out as we would; they tell a personal story and leave their audience to make the necessary connections and understand how the story illustrates and illuminates the issue in question.

Knowledge as Story

Coming-to-knowing through a combination of watchfulness and direct experience is the antithesis of programmed learning that first structures knowledge and then imparts it in "bite-sized chunks."

But there are some forms of learning that require words and these are the songs and stories that are repeated to children at night by their aunts, uncles, and grandparents. Elders also have their teaching stories, which can last many hours. One old woman told me how an Elder would begin telling a story in the evening and continue right through to the following morning. People in those days, she said, were supposed to show respect and pay attention. Of course, with a teaching that lasted that long she could not remember everything that happened; rather, she was expected to take only that part of the teaching that was appropriate to her level of understanding. As she grew up she would hear the story again and again, each time taking something more from it.

Apprentice to Knowledge

This system of learning was once common in the West. From barrel making to Renaissance painting, the apprentice system was the way most people learned their trades. Dr. Ruth Dempsey, who is an educational researcher at the University of Ottawa, has told me that if an adult wishes to learn something new the most effective way is not to ask a professional teacher, but an expert in the field. Most experts have never analyzed their skills and knowledge and may not even be able to tell a person how they do a particular task, but by hanging around them a person will pick up their skills. By contrast, a professional teacher analyzes, structures, and articulates knowledge in a series of programmed steps which, at least in Dempsey's opinion, appear to hamper the natural processes of learning.

True learning is generated by the student and not the teacher and is best when a human relationship exists between the two.

Several years ago the medical school at McMaster University in Ontario, Canada, established a radically different approach to the training of physicians. No longer would medical students be required to attend formal lectures. Instead they would attach themselves to a doctor and follow the physician around, learning his or her medical skills and knowledge through direct experience.

In the Native tradition a grandparent, uncle, or aunt does not instruct, dilute, or protect the experiences of young people, nor generally punish them when they are doing what other people may consider to be wrong. Rupert Ross's story of the young man at the fishing camp illustrates this point. It is an expression of respect for others and the way they choose to live their lives. Since no one can truly look into another person's heart, judge him, or understand his motives, it makes no sense to attempt to "help," "improve," "correct," or punish him.

Quality of Silence

Learning from nature and from an Elder involves a special quality of silence and alert watchfulness. The respect one shows to an Elder acts to create that area of quietness and receptivity into which the Elder can speak.

The Indigenous people of the Americas and their Elders have much to teach us. It is just that we have forgotten how to listen or, rather, how to create that silence within ourselves into which knowledge can speak. Therese Schroeder-Sheker, a musician and thanatologist, once told me of a medieval belief that the angels want to sing to us, it makes them happy to do so—all we have to do is listen to them.

Speaking, therefore, seems to be created out of an active silence. In quantum physics there is also a kind of vibrant silence; it is called the vacuum state, the state of total and absolute emptiness. The theories of modern physics indicate that this state of nothingness is in fact an infinite ocean of energy in potential. All the energy within our universe—the energy of suns and galaxies—is as a mere flicker on this vast ocean of nothingness. Likewise, the big bang origin of the universe—the creation of all that is—began as a tiny fluctuation within an ocean of absolute silence.

All over the world ancient peoples have said that the cosmos was created in a song, a word, or a name. Now modern physics speaks of creation out of a fluctuation or vibration. Yet not one of these primordial acts could have taken place had it not been for a preexisting attentive silence.

Coming-to-knowing arises out of silence. It is this same quality of silence that strikes so forcefully when you meet with a Native person. Native people love to gossip and will talk right through the night. Yet, at the same time, each person has a quality of silence, the silence of action suspended in potential. Their silence is like the surface of a calm pond; throw in a pebble and you can watch the ripples expand right to the pond's edge and reflect back inward again. Drop a pebble into a pond that is ruffled by the wind and its disturbances are lost in the general agitation of the water.

In the summer of 1992 the Fetzer Institute hosted the first of a series of circles in which Western scientists could meet with Native Elders and thinkers. After the meetings Carol Hegedus of the Fetzer Institute told me that what had impressed her most about the gathering was its expansiveness, the way in which each participant was able to speak and put forward his or her ideas and experiences.

Out of this power of silence great oratory is born. When Native people speak they are not talking from the head, relating some theory, mentioning what they read in a book, or what someone else has told them. Rather, they speak from the heart, from the traditions of their people, and from the knowledge of their land; they speak of what they have seen and heard and touched, and of what has been passed on to them by the traditions of their people. It is their inner silence that allows them to listen to the prompting of their hearts and to the subtle resonances that lie within each word of a language and which, when uttered, reverberate throughout the world.

What Is an Elder?

Elders are great teachers. By tradition, becoming an Elder is part of the great circle of life and renewal. It involves that period of life when a man or woman gains a particular wisdom and philosophical detachment through having seen so much of life and having traveled so far along his or her Earth Walk. Today Native society and culture has become so dislocated and perturbed that there are some who have only reached middle age but must serve as Elders, while old people who have been cut off from their traditions do not qualify for that role.

An Elder is the oral historian of the group, someone who is called upon for his or her knowledge of how to perform a ceremony or determine a protocol. An Elder thinks back to childhood when he or she was instructed by a grandfather or grandmother and told stories that had already been passed down though many generations. Among the people of the plains an Elder may tell how his or her grandparents had never seen a white person when they were growing up. Other Elders will tell stories of ancient encounters with other peoples, of old ceremonies, and of voyages that were made hundreds of years ago.

In a people whose traditions do not lie in reading and writing, memory is very highly developed and accounts of events can be passed on from generation to generation with remarkable accuracy. In addition, some peoples use mnemonic devices such as talking sticks and wampum belts to help them relate a long history.

It is not uncommon today that when an Elder is invited to speak, after saying a few words he or she will glare around the room and pick on some poor individual who is taking notes. Launching into the scribe the Elder will ask how a person can expect to hear anything when he is preoccupied in writing everything down. "You write things down," the Elder says, "so that you can forget them."

When they want to rap your knuckles, Elders can be very fierce. I remember meeting with a Blackfoot Elder who, quite naturally, viewed me with considerable suspicion. "White men come to talk to me," she said. "They write things down on pieces of paper.... And then they always get them wrong."

Luckily I did not have a notebook with me at the time. Pretty early on I had realized that if I was going to have any hope of understanding even the smallest aspect of this other world then I had to stop acting like a Western scientist. I had to trust my own observations, intuitions, and memory. Curiously enough, after I had left my notebook behind things did seem to work. Later on, when I made the decision to write this book I was astounded at how much I could remember of what people had said to me and how they had said it. I realized that by listening, and by not trying to record things or deliberately remember them, my mind had been moving in different ways. The person with the notebook and camera has chosen to maintain a critical distance, to act as an observer and resist the invitation, or the threat, of becoming too intimate with what lies outside the self.

Teachings at Night

All over the world Indigenous peoples recognize the power of the night for telling stories, giving teachings, and holding their ceremonies. Over the past few years I have been in correspondence with Dr. M. S. A. Sastroamidjojo from Yogyakarta, Indonesia, a physicist who is seeking to bridge Western science with the traditions of his own people. He has written about the famous Indonesian shadow puppet play and the levels of reality it presents. On the screen one does not see the puppet itself, but its shadow and the shadow of the one who operates it. Sastroamidjojo feels these levels resonate with those of modern physics. For him, this ancient play of the universe is similar to David Bohm's idea that the reality we normally experience is no more than the surface manifestation of a deeper implicate or enfolded order.

Dr. Sastroamidjojo cautioned me that should I visit Indonesia I would see the same play put on for tourists—a short version that only lasted several hours. The true drama, he wrote, the one that would be attended by Indonesian people themselves, begins in the evening and lasts throughout the night and into the dawn. Watching the play, a person moves through different states of perception, beginning with keen interest, then moving on to the wandering of attention, tiredness and dozing off into a sort of half-sleep half-dream, and, finally, in the morning, waking into alertness to begin again. To understand the meaning of the performance one must pass through these different stages of internal and external engagement.

Something similar happens in Native American where ceremonies begin at night and continue for several days. The act of giving attention to what is going on, of being there over such a long period, moves heart, mind, and body into states of perception in which a person reaches the deeper meanings of a teaching, or a story, directly.

A person who listens at night to the teachings of the medicine wheel begins to see the sacred hoop in the circle of light cast by the fire, in the circle of people around the fire, in the circle of the tepee, in the smoke hole above, in the way the pipe moves from person to person. They feel within their bodies the great circle of Mother Earth and the movement of the seasons. They see the four directions stretching from the center of the fire, feel the presence of the Four Winds, and see the Four Colors. They sense the movement of the hoop, the circle of a person's life from birth to old age, and the progression of the seasons. Through these movements a person moves into balance internally and in relationships with others.

Dreams and Visions

The stories told in the night reach back hundreds, thousands, and maybe tens of thousands of years. They enable a Native person to enter into a relationship with the great cycles of time, the history of the people, the land, and the cosmos.

Teachings can also come from the animals, from the movement of the seasons, from the Four Winds, and, in particular, from dreams and visions. Within this century dreams have taken on a new significance. Freud pictured the origin of dreams as lying in the repressed material of the unconscious. Jung added the collective level of the archetypes, but, above all, the origin of our dreams, we firmly believe, lies within ourselves. If a dream profoundly disturbs us we search for its meaning in the traumatic events of our childhood or as the symbolic manifestation of some universal archetype. Few of us would admit that its origin could live in the outside world. Likewise, if we hear voices in our head we assume that is we who are producing them.

Within the Torah, or Old Testament, however, there are many stories of messengers appearing from God and of great dreams that portend happenings on earth. Likewise, Indigenous science teaches that the world of the senses is only a tiny fraction of a vastly greater reality. Dreams are often the doorways into these other worlds.

When a great dream occurs it does not make much sense to look at the individual happenings of a person's life; rather, it is understood to be a message from a reality that lies outside the normal limits of our senses. It is a visit from the world of powers, energies, and spirits, from the Keepers of the Game and the spirits that give life to the rocks, trees, and winds.

To dream is to enter another world, and the information available from that world is often highly practical. Moreover, since Native Americans are not so much individuals as parts of a group, their dreams are common property, and it is not unusual for more than one person to dream part of the same dream.

In dreams people see distant relations; they spot the herds of caribou that will be crossing the river at a particular point on the following day; they see a group of strangers approaching and know that they will reach their camp in so many days time; they follow spoor on the ground and reach the place where the bear is walking. Like stock market reports and weather forecasts in our society, the information contained within dreams can be discussed and interpreted by the group.

My friend Clem Ford has told me how, when he was living with the Naskapi people in Labrador, a person would wake in the middle of the night after dreaming and begin to drum and sing—to tell the dream. I have heard how as one person relates a dream others will offer their interpretations, adding what they have seen in their own dreams.

Within Indigenous science the voices and images of dreams are not symbols of the unconscious but aspects of a reality that is far wider than anything we assume in the West. By discoursing with the beings of dreams and visiting the landscape of a dream a person can obtain useful knowledge for the whole group.

Some dreams and visions move far beyond everyday information about hunting, the movements of strangers, or the welfare of relatives. In such dreams a person may be taken up into the sky and shown the faces of the great energies of the world. One man told me how he had been given a vision of peace across the world and of sweat lodges built within the earth. He had been moved by what he had seen but did nothing about it. Some time later, however, he had another vision in which he was taken up high into the sky until his home looked very tiny below him. In the sky he was questioned as to why he had done nothing about his original vision.

One of the most famous visions to have reached the non-Native world was that of Black Elk, a medicine man of the Oglala Sioux. In his youth Black Elk had seen the Battle of the Little Big Horn and, later, the massacre of his people at Wounded Knee. But what was of greater significance in his life was the great vision he was given when he was nine years old.

For some time the young boy had been hearing voices, then, one evening, he heard a voice say, "It is time; now they are calling you." The next day the camp moved on and young Black Elk became sick. As he was lying in the tepee at night he saw two men coming down head first from the clouds like slanting arrows. They told him that the Grandfathers were calling to him. After they had left, Black Elk walked out of the tepee and a cloud gathered him up and took him to a part of the world where he saw many wonderful things and was taken to the Council of the Grandfathers. It was there that the Grandfathers taught Black Elk and showed him many things. In a teaching that took several days Black Elk was conducted through the universe by the Grandfathers, finally coming to the tall rock mountain at the center of the world.

As the vision ended, Black Elk was left alone on a great plain, guarded by an eagle. Feeling homesick, he walked back to his parents' tepee but was saddened when they did not realize how long he had been absent. As he grew up Black Elk was to treasure the teachings he had been given in the vision and became a religious leader of his people.

The vision that was given to Ganidoa'yo of the Seneca people created a great religious revival among the Iroquois people. As a young man, Ganidoa'yo, or Handsome Lake, as he was known in English, had led a dissolute life. His half brother, called the Cornplanter, had gone to Pennsylvania to learn from the Quakers and later established a school in his house.

In 1799 Handsome Lake's health broke down, and on June 15 he appeared to be dying—lying in an almost breathless coma for two hours. During this period Handsome Lake heard someone calling to him. He got up from his bed and went to the door of his house where he saw three men. At this point Handsome Lake fainted. He then heard a voice telling him that the Great Spirit was displeased with his behavior. During his coma many things were revealed to Handsome Lake and teachings were given to him. He was also told that a white dog should be killed and the White Dog Feast held.

When Handsome Lake revived, his message was relayed to the local Quakers who seemed to approve, agreeing that they too saw wonderful sights during their trances or visions and that, since people were all of one flesh, the messages that Handsome Lake had received would have universal appeal. The same day a traditional White Dog Feast was held and Handsome Lake began to recover. From that time on he began to work as a teacher and spiritual leader, directing his people away from the abuse of alcohol and urging them to return to some of their traditional ways.

Handsome Lake's teachings were never written down, but in 1840, twenty-five years after his death, his grandson Jimmy Johnson recalled and passed on the teaching. Handsome

Lake's Good Message is still spoken today in Iroquois long-houses. It is estimated that the teachings themselves take between four and five days to recount.

Traditional people open themselves to the visions, voices, and winds that surround us. Different peoples have different ways of doing this, and some of these involve ingesting plants, fungi, toad secretions, etc. I once met a non-Native who had sought out these experiences and, in the company of Native people, had ingested a variety of substances. His experiences had been profound and he had been moved to write about them in a book. Some of my Native friends said they liked the book but that the writer had sort of missed the point. The non-Native seeker had focused on plants and roots, but what he had not stressed was the ceremony itself; that was the important part, the way a person came into relationship with energies and powers of another world.

Clowns

When we think of the knowledge that comes as a person lies in a coma close to death, or watches night after night in a state of extreme thirst and exhaustion, it is good to remember that a great teaching can also come from a joke. Within the Indigenous world knowledge can come in the guise of human laughter, from seeing someone walk backward, or having a bucket of cold water thrown over your head. All this is the business of the clown.

Napi, the sacred figure of the Blackfoot people who created the land out of his body, is also the trickster who is constantly turning rules on their head and doing all sorts of foolish things. Napi's foolishness teaches us about boundaries, limits to behavior, and human nature. It is good for us to drop our Western trappings of seriousness and remember that some of the most profound teachings can come from tricksters and clowns.

The sacred figures of the People—Raven, Coyote, Napi, Nanabush, and the rest—are all tricksters, beings who turn the world on its head. Even our own Western science has its trickster: entropy, or disorder. Thermodynamics tells us that for nature to continue in her work, she must metaphorically defecate. In scientist's terms the overall entropy of a system and its environment must increase or, to put it another way, if we insist upon generating order, this can only be done at the expense of creating disorder somewhere else.

Laughter is never far away when Native people meet. I remember someone telling me about how he had been explaining the ways of the sweat lodge. He pointed out that when you take responsibility for a sweat lodge you are actually putting your life on the line. Then he pointed to one of the hot rocks, saying, "You can see the spirit moving in it?" His friend looked and nodded. "Yeah, it sure looks like Elvis."

Sometimes, in the midst of a sacred ceremony, a person will enter and make fun of what is going on. This is a clown, someone very different from our own familiar circus figure. In the West the clown has become a harmless figure of fun, but Indigenous clowns are disturbing in the way they assault, frighten, and even beat people. Clowns can also be openly sexual, waving giant phalluses and indulging in mock intercourse.

Clowns are disturbing because they turn the world upside down and openly challenge the order of nature and society. Wherever harmony and order are present, the clown intervenes. The clown makes boundaries explicit by crossing them; demonstrates the meaning of order through disorder. Most important of all, the clown reminds us that in the flux of the world nothing is certain. In Blackfoot ceremonies the circle is always open so that something new can appear.

A relative of the clown is the "contrary" who does everything in reverse. The contrary will walk backward, face the rear of a horse when riding, and wash in dirt. The contrary's behavior is also linguistic, with *No* used for assent, and *Yes* turned into a denial. Thus, through the medium of speech and action, a contrary teaches the limits and conventions of social behavior and social inhibitions.

Clowns and contraries, how much we need them in our own society today. We need the Fool in *King Lear* who constantly mocked the king, reminding him of human mortality and stupidity. The clown reminds us of the irrational within our universe, the Dionysian forces within human society that must be balanced rather than repressed or denied, and the futility of our quest for certainty, control, and absolute power.

Stories of Origin

I ndigenous science is a science of reality and place. It is never abstract because it is always firmly rooted in the concrete, in the history of a people, in the journeys they have taken, and in their daily obligation to renew the compacts they have made with the world around them. It is said that this science is enfolded within the language a people speak and, in turn, this language grows out of the spirit of a place.

When my Haida friend Woody Morrison speaks in his native tongue he tells me to listen for the sounds of the ocean, to the waves breaking on the shore, and for the cries of birds and the calls of animals. And, from the other side of the continent, the Mic Maq language is an expression of the sounds and vibrations of the Mic Maq's Atlantic coast home.

Western science—the science of analytic chemistry or elementary particle physics—can be carried out in a well-equipped laboratory anywhere in the world, because the knowledge it gives about the world is assumed to be objective, independent of the individual who discovers it and the location in which it is investigated. Indigenous science, however, refers to the particular landscape that The People occupy.

Connection to the landscape is one of the most powerful things within an Indigenous society, which explains the pain and anger The People experience when they see the land around them exploited and destroyed. The Native people I have spoken to refer to the land as their mother, and the Blackfoot say that to walk on the land is to walk on your own flesh. The memory of this landscape transcends anything we have in the West, for its trees, rocks, animals, and plants are also imbued with energies, powers, and spirits. The whole of the land is alive and each person is related to it. The land sustains and, in turn, the ceremonies and sacrifices of The People aid in its renewal.

I have heard many Native people say that they have "a map in the head." This map, I believe, is the expression of the relationship of the land to The People. Moreover, it transcends any mere geographical representation, for in it are enfolded the songs, ceremonies, and histories of a people. With a map in the head you are never lost; not only can you find your way through the bush, along a river system, or sail the ocean out of sight of land, but you know where you are in another sense. You know where your people have been for hundreds and thousands of years. You can see the marks of Coyote, Raven, Nanabush, or one of the other figures that created the land. The map in the head was something that entered your body in childhood, it was part of your coming-to-knowing and is now part of your very being.

Maybe when that old man in Joe Couture's story referred to his grandson being lost it could have been because the only maps the boy knew were the topographical maps taught in school. He may have been able to determine his position on such a map, but he did not possess within his body that map which is the relationship a people have with the spirits of the land. He did not know that maps contain cycles of time that, while stretching back into the distant past, can be renewed in the immediate present. Such a map is the songs and stories of the land, the language a people speaks, and the expression of their origin.

It is in this direct experience of a map in the head that the two sciences, Indigenous and Western, part company, for Western science has traditionally claimed to be objective and value-free, its particular truths quite independent of where or who discovers them. It is in the relationship to land and history and language, and to a wider sense of reality, that the clash of paradigms between the two cultures can be found, for, to The

People, their origin within the landscape is of great importance.

The People's Origin

All over the world peoples have their accounts of creation and origins. In some cases they take the form of stories, but others can be songs, dances, drama, rituals, music, sculpture, or architecture.

By contrast, our current Western origin stories, while they are marvelous examples of science, tend to be fragmentary. Thus we have the cosmological account of the big bang, the evolving story of the elementary particles, Darwin's *On The Origin of Species*, Freud's theories on the development of consciousness, and the many different schools of history that explain the origin of a nation or people. The problem is that, with the exception of cosmology and elementary particle theories, each of these compartments of knowledge has little or nothing to do with the others. Our scientific origin stories may be paradigms of the scientific method but they are not integrative and they provide little in the way of values and meaning that help to bind a society together. One of the last great integrative cosmologies in the West was that of Dante, who, in his *Divine Comedy*, presented the individual, society, and the divine great image; an image, moreover, that was deeply satisfying at an intellectual, aesthetic, spiritual, and emotional level.

Native America has its own stories of origin, that of the Ojibwaj peoples, for example, going back to the last ice age. I have only once heard a part of this story and only after a purification ceremony had taken place. Although what I heard represented only the tiniest fraction of a great history, nevertheless I understand that it was a matter of great controversy that even that much had been told to a stranger. Some Elders teach that the stories are sacred and must never be passed on to outsiders. Others are beginning to argue that the time has come to speak openly and share their knowledge.

The sacred stories of the Ojibwaj peoples were recorded, using a symbolic language, on birchbark scrolls. As these scrolls age and begin to disintegrate they are meticulously copied and passed on to subsequent generations. The history of these stories can also be found carved and painted on rocks. Some of these rock carvings are known to anthropologists, but I have heard stories of how the location of others remains a secret. The rocks are covered with moss and the writings are only revealed when teachings are given.

The knowledge of the Ojibwaj peoples is preserved and passed on within the initiation ceremonies of the Midewewin, or Grand Medicine Society, and, at each level of initiation, the teachers take whole nights to complete their work. Some of the stories speak of a giant of ice, the Winnebago, of the growling noises he made, and of how The People would face death if they approached too close. Today members of the society interpret this part of their history as referring to the last ice age when they were forced to move south in front of the advancing glaciers. There are also stories of a great disease and of a long migration of The People. Thus it happened that the Anishnabi, The People, came eastward and settled on the shore of a great salt water.

One story suggests that the Anishnabi lived by the shores of the salt water for so long that they began to forget their origins. Then one day a megis shell appeared above the water to remind The People of their origins. The Anishnabi followed the megis shell on a journey east that took them along what we now call the St. Lawrence River, into the Great Lakes, and on to the north shore of Lake Superior.

The birchbark scrolls are quite specific about this phase in the Anishnabi ancient migration. Symbols on the scrolls can be identified with landmarks such as waterfalls and islands in the Great Lakes region. It was from this area that the Ojibwaj spread out, taking with them their history and teachings and inscribing and painting it on rocks and scrolls. But this story represents only a tiny fraction of the long history of The People, which is quite specific about the names of locations, personages, and dates—provided in terms of the number of generations that passed after a given event.*

---

*In rereading these pages I again feel uneasy about having set down even a fragmentary account of Ojibwaj origins despite the fact that everything that

The Mohawk people also have stories and teachings that are related during special ceremonies, the telling of which can go on for many, many days—sometimes for weeks. They speak of the creation of the world, the nature of the different plants and animals, and the journeys that The People undertook. Some of these stories tell of how The People brought corn from its place of origin in Central America and traveled north, stopping along the way so that the corn could be acclimatized and introduced into a relationship with the other plants of the region.

The Mohawk people speak of the times they spent with the ancient Mound Builders of the Ohio Valley until they came farther north and settled on the south shore of the St. Lawrence River. Indeed, some of the shortest and most ancient words in their language refer to the life they led during this great migration in the long distant past.

The Soto people call themselves the People of the Middle for they occupy territory between the Ojibwaj to the east and the people they acknowledge as the Old or Ancient Ones to the west. These Ancient Ones are the Blackfoot who have always lived on the land that Napi created for them, for, as they say, the land is Napi's body. Indeed, the map of the land is the map both of the Old Man's body and the bow he carried and of his journey. Thus one can find parts of Napi's body located in Alberta and Montana; at the Belly Buttes, and on the Chin and Elbow rivers. His bow forms the Bow River.

Stan Knowlton, a Blackfoot, has been researching these stories, along with the medicine wheels and the pictograms and syllabary carved on stones in Blackfoot country. He has

---

appears here on this subject has already been written about in many other books—and probably with just as much distortion and misunderstanding. The reason is that what for us in the West is simply a story, a history, an account of the past, has a profoundly different meaning to many Native people. As I have indicated several times before in this book, such teachings are only given at special times and after special ceremonies have created a sacred space in which the energy of the story can be contained. I can only hope that what I have written is taken in the right way to show how disruptive and damaging it can be when one culture comes along and denies the validity of some of the deepest teachings of another.

even produced a map that shows Napi's body superimposed on the rivers and buttes of his land. Further east he has begun to discover the shape of the Old Man's wife.

After visiting the Blackfoot, Napi traveled north as he created the land, becoming Nanabush for the Ojibwaj, and then moving on to the Cree people. The marks of his passage can even be found in the frozen stretches of northeast Labrador.

Haida Gwaii is the home of the Haida people, on the eastern islands of northern British Columbia and Alaska. The Haida people tell how they have always lived on these islands, but they also relate some of the great voyages they undertook from their homes. The Haida stories tell of expeditions down the coast of North America and on to Columbia and the tip of the world in Tierra del Fuego. There are stories of long ocean trips across the Pacific to meet the other great voyaging peoples like the Polynesians and Maori.

The Navaho and Hopi speak of their origins as being in another world, as did the Mayan people before them. They arrived in their present world by climbing up a ladder from the world below. Today this upward movement can be seen in the ladder and circular hole in the roof of their kivas and hogans. There are also stories, told by some peoples, that their origins lie in the distant stars.

A Clash of Paradigms

Each group of people on Turtle Island has its own account of its history, origins, and relationship to the land. And, as with so many of the teachings of Native America, a story may contain many meanings and levels of interpretation. Indeed, it is only within Western society that our Aristotelian logic demands a single, unambiguous account of an origin. Some nations, such as the Haida and Blackfoot, speak of having occupied their land forever, while others, such as the Ojibwaj, tell of a great migration to their present land. In all cases, however, it is made clear that the land itself is sacred, that it was created for the People, that they have a special relationship to it, and that there are obligations that must be periodically renewed.

For hundreds and thousands of years these stories have been passed on. They are the heart of Indigenous science and metaphysics. They are what bind a people together and relate them to the powers and energies of the universe. They are what give meaning to the ceremonies of renewal. Within these stories can be found the origins of time, space, and causality. Just as the human body is kept healthy and coherent by its immune system, a field of active meaning that permeates the body, so, too, a people and the land they care for sustained by the relationships and renewals contained within these maps and stories.

Western science, however, has chosen to set these stories against its own account: the version of history and origin created by archaeologists, linguists, anthropologists, and other scientists. Most of the readers of this book, for example, will have been taught in school that the aboriginal population of North America migrated over a landbridge that connected the Bering Strait approximately ten thousand years ago. We were taught this is a matter of fact, not opinion, and thus, at one stroke the stories and ceremonies of entire peoples are wiped out and along with them the meaning of their relationship to the land.

As we shall see in this chapter, the account we were given in school is far from established fact and is, in a sense, a myth created out of the values and beliefs of our own society. Today the question of the origin of the Indigenous peoples of the Americas is a topic of hot debate in which several schools of opinion oppose each other. As we read these arguments we begin to realize how far the practicalities of academic life are from the supposedly dispassionate and objective ideals propounded by Western science. Indeed, what we are and what we do is so very much the product of our own beliefs. Western science is one of those stories that we repeat to ourselves in order to validate our society. Just as Native America renewed itself through its stories of creation, our Western society possesses its own stories of validation.

The history of contact between the so-called Old and New worlds has been one of conquest and exploitation, and this, in turn, has demanded an objectification of the conquered.

Likewise, the history of Western science has been one of exploitation and objectification of nature. Put the two together and one obtains a mythical, archetypal story of contact in which human consciousness seeks to create its symbols and stories.

Today these stories are being played out in universities and museums as academics weigh evidence, debate theories, and propose new hypotheses. This is the heady stuff of science, but, for some Native people, it has become the difference between life and death. And this, I should add, is no mere hyperbole, for when it comes to existence and stewardship of the land everything can sink or swim on an academic's theory.

Take, for example, the case of the Lubicon Cree, a people who live between the Athabasca and Peace rivers in northern Alberta. In 1899 a government commission traveled along these two rivers and signed treaties with the peoples they encountered, but since they did not venture into the bush they overlooked the Lubicon people. In 1940 the Lubicon were informed that they were not "Indians" and had no claim to their land. The following decades were spent battling with governments and oil companies to be recognized as an autonomous people.*

This story is far from unique. Many peoples across the Americas have been told: You do not exist. You have no real history. You are not a distinct people and have no special rights under law. You are to be moved from the land on which you have lived or hunted for hundreds and even thousands of years. The stories told to you by your Elders are a combination of faulty memory, myth, and fantasy.

Faced with the denial of a land claim most of us would hire a good lawyer and go to court. But at this point another problem arises: North American courts function on the basis of legal and philosophical concepts that are profoundly different from those of Indigenous people. Our courts are based upon the arguments of adversaries who are concerned with

---

*The story of Chief Ominayak and his people can be found in John Goddard's *Last Stand of the Lubicon Cree,* Vancouver, Toronto: Douglas and McIntyre, 1991.

the establishment of proof. By contrast, the legal systems of many Native groups avoid matters of proof in favor of restoring harmony and balance within the society as a whole.

Native groups who go to court will be faced with the briefs and arguments of governments, or logging, mining, or railway companies, whose claims will be supported by the evidence of expert witnesses. Anthropologists, archaeologists, and historians will offer their considered conclusions based upon an impartial, scientific examination of historical evidence. Evidence may also be presented in the form of historic treaties and land surveys.

When Native people present their own case they wish to call upon their own expert witnesses, in this case Elders and tribal historians who will present the stories they have preserved for untold generations. They may also offer physical evidence to support their claims in the form of wampum belts, birchbark scrolls, sacred bundles, and talking sticks. In many cases the courts will refuse to hear such people, ruling that they are not expert witnesses and that their evidence cannot be heard because it is based upon hearsay. Mary Ellen Turpel, a Cree lawyer, has told me about the frustration experienced by Indigenous peoples who may have lived on the land for countless generations. The problem is not the fairness of the courts, but simply the extreme difficulty that lawyers and judges have comprehending a society that operates within a radically different paradigm.

First Explanations

Two of the many puzzling questions that were faced by the Europeans who first encountered human beings in the Americas were: Who are these people? Where did they come from? The same questions were asked by the priests and scholars who followed them and, finally, are being asked by the anthropologists and linguists of our own time. In the beginning the concern was of a religious nature: Did they possess souls? Were they tainted with original sin or had the fall of man passed them by?

Later visitors began to wonder about Indigenous languages

and how they were related to the languages of the Old World. Had the Indigenous population always lived in the Americas or were they originally inhabitants of some other part of the world?

The whole issue became even more puzzling when the full extent of Indigenous civilizations was discovered. Bit by bit, amateur archaeologists began to uncover pyramids, temples, mounds, impressive architecture, and detailed artwork. In the early nineteenth century, when the Turtle Mounds in the Ohio Valley were first excavated, it was evident to the investigators of the time that such imposing structures could not possibly be the work of "Indians." These mounds were artificially made hills, some of them as high as one hundred feet and stretching over many acres. Associated with the mounds were embanked circular enclosures that encompassed up to two hundred acres of land. Some of the mounds contained human remains, pottery, copper axes, and jewelry. After all, the present aboriginal inhabitants of North America did not seem to exhibit any of the true marks of civilization. Where were their banks, universities, and libraries? Where were their kings, governments, and law courts? Where were their prisons, roads, and cities?

It seemed clear to these mainly amateur archaeologists that the Great Mounds had been built long ago by a lost civilization. Probably the people now living in the area were the descendents of slaves who had built the mounds. In short, these first attempts to explain the Indigenous peoples of North American had more to do with the projections of the world-views of European society than with the actual inhabitants of the Americas.

The New World presented a host of puzzles to the Europeans, from the monolithic stone heads left by the Olmec peoples to the pyramids of Central America and the lost cities of the Yucatan as well as the legends of the lands of gold and silver.

A variety of hypotheses grew up about the original inhabitants of the New World. People began to speculate that since pyramids appeared in both Egypt and Mexico they must have been built by the same people, and that the Mound Builders must be related to the cultures that had constructed the prehistoric barrows in Europe, and even to the ancient inhabitants of the Near East.

To add fuel to these speculations there were stories that at the time of first contact some Native American tribes had spoken a language believed to be related to Hebrew. Could it be that the Indigenous population of Turtle Island was the true "lost tribe" of Israel? Other visitors heard in these languages words that were Welsh in origin and suggested that America had been colonized by the Celts. Still other theorists spoke of visits by the ancient Egyptians, or proposed that the great statues and temples had been built by citizens who had fled from Atlantis, or from the equally hypothetical continents of Lemuria and Mu!

The Clovis Hypothesis

Stories of lost tribes or expeditions from a sinking Atlantis may seem absurd to us, but, as far as those nineteenth-century archaeologists were concerned, the New World had to have come from somewhere. Don't forget that even in the mid-nineteenth century when Charles Darwin was studying the evolution of species, many educated people seriously believed in Archbishop Usher's historical dating that placed the Creation at 4004 and the Flood at 2348 B.C. This certainly did not leave much time for human beings to have spread throughout North America. Thus, into the early decades of this century, it was supposed that the first humans had set foot in the Americas only a few thousand years ago.

Today many scientists believe that humans first evolved in Africa's great Rift Valley and from there spread across the globe. Anthropologists have compared the aboriginal inhabitants of the Americas with races from other parts of the world, taking into account hair, teeth, blood groups, and, more recently, genetic structure. Their conclusion is that they are most closely related to the inhabitants of Asia. And thus the idea began to grow that the first peoples of the Americas must have migrated from somewhere in East Asia.

The great confirmation for this theory came in the 1930s when a five-inch piece of stone was discovered in New Mexico. The stone had not been weathered or otherwise shaped by natural means, but had actually been worked into a spear point. What was particularly interesting was that the stone contained a groove—possibly for ease in attaching it to a spear shaft or, as is the case with a groove in a sword, to encourage bleeding from the wound.

Anthropologists immediately recognized that this Clovis point, as it came to be called, was quite different from spear points that had been found in the Old World. It clearly represented one of those great technological breakthroughs in human civilization; in this case, one that had led to a more efficient way of hunting. Pretty soon other Clovis points were discovered in Colorado, Wyoming, Oklahoma, and Texas, all of which suggested that there must have been a certain uniformity of culture, or at least a cultural exchange, across North America. Anthropologists called this the Clovis culture and dated it at between 10,000 and 11,500 years ago.

At the time, this date was far too early for some anthropologists—they just did not want to believe that the Americas had been peopled so far back. But, by the mid 1930s, it became generally accepted that around eleven thousand years ago a hunting society appeared and flourished across the Americas. Scientists were also quick to associate the coincidence of this date with the occurrence of the last ice age.

During an ice age much of the world's water becomes locked up as ice and, as a consequence, sea levels fall. Geologists knew that some twelve thousand years ago the level of the Pacific Ocean had dropped to such an extent that a land bridge called Beringia appeared that connected Siberia and Alaska.

These two dates—the appearance of the Clovis culture and the Beringia landbridge—coincided in a remarkable way with the supposed similarities between the aboriginal population of the Americas and the inhabitants of Asia. Twelve thousand years ago, the new story went, a landbridge appeared and linked the Old World to the New; a small hunter-gatherer group, following the animals they hunted wandered across the bridge. By one thousand years ago this small band had spread to cover the entire Americas.

The ancestors of all Native Americans, according to this theory, came from what is known as the Siberian triangle, a region formed by Beringia, northern China, and Lake Baikal. The initial group, so the scientific story went, may have been composed of some thirty people, just two or three families, who on entering the New World found abundant game and food for their gathering. Scientists calculated that only a modest increase in each generation (in this case assuming a new generation every twenty-eight years) combined with a fanning outward at a rate of four miles per year would be sufficient to populate the American continents in just five hundred years!

An even more bizarre theory emerged with this account. The combination of the Clovis point spear with a throwing stick, it argued, represented an enormous leap in hunting technology for the human race. This must have led the new inhabitants of the Americas into an orgy of overkilling of the indigenous animal population. In this way the appearance of the first humans on the continent was made to coincide with the extinction of many species. Throughout history there have indeed been major disappearances of animal species, and certainly one did occur in North America toward the end of the last ice age. By exploiting the appearance of the Clovis point, a landbridge, and a hypothetical hunter-gatherer band, scientists were able to tie all the facts together in one neat package.

Gradually, what had been only a hypothesis about Native American origins began to be taken as an accepted theory and the sort of historical fact that forms part of North American school textbooks and museum exhibits.

Not everyone felt comfortable with this hypothesis, not least the Native Americans themselves, who had never been asked about their own origin accounts. Some linguists were concerned about the large number of different language families in the Americas. This is not simply a matter of different languages in the sense of Italian, Spanish, French, and German on the European continent. Rather, it is a matter of whole families of languages, each as different as English from Chi-

nese, or Arabic from Bantu. How could it be that the descendants of a small aboriginal band came to speak not simply a
number of different dialects, or even different languages
related to the one family, but developed several totally different
language families in only ten thousand years? Some linguists
argued that there had not been sufficient time for so many
radically different languages to have developed.

Other scientists were uneasy about how, in less than a
thousand years, a single hunter-gatherer group, that arrived
some eleven thousand years ago could have spread right across
North America and down into the tip of South America,
leaving behind Clovis spear points as they went. The cat really
came out of the bag when a few anthropologists began to claim
they had evidence of human occupation, long *before* that first,
hypothetical, hunter-gatherer migration twelve thousand years
ago.

The Several Waves Theory

The B.C. Clovis migration hypothesis claimed that the aboriginal people of the Americas were all descendants of two or
three families that had left Asia some twelve thousand years
ago. But Incas, Mohawks, Cree, Hopi, and Haida do not really
look like Asians, nor do they speak an Asian language. The
supporters of the Clovis story had to present a credible account
for the way in which these differences could have developed in
twelve thousand years.

Scientists began to look at such things as the changes in
tooth structure, rates of change of genetic material in human
cells, and the way in which human languages evolve. Research
included, for example, a comparison of the frequency of
different blood groups among the Indigenous peoples of the
Americas as compared to people in Asia and the rest of the
world. Other comparisons were made between body proteins,
blood antigens, and enzymes within the red cells of the blood.

Human teeth are the favored evidence of everyone from a
police pathologist assisting in the investigation of a murder
trial to an anthropologist attempting to identify the origin of a
human settlement. The reason is that teeth are often extremely

well preserved and can give a wealth of information about diet, lifestyle, and racial origin. Scientists have established twenty-four different features that characterize human teeth, and in the case of Native Americans many of these characteristics are shared with people from Asia. For example, while the molars of Europeans and Africans have two roots, those of Asians and Native Americans have three. In a study of 200,000 prehistoric teeth from the Americas, researchers found a strong resemblance to what is called the Sinodont pattern of the Chinese. These include the molars with three roots and single-rooted lower canine teeth. Results like these seemed to confirm the hypothesis that Indigenous Americans and Asians share a common ancestry.

But as the new results started to come in it became clear that the experts could not agree on a hypothesis of a single early migration. For example, Douglas C. Wallace of Emory University, who had been carrying out a genetic analysis, postulated that the peoples of Turtle Island are descendants of four Asian women who lived some thirty thousand years ago (give or take ten thousand years). This certainly puts the date of genetic separation back way before the Clovis migration theory. Could it be that these women were part of a hunter-gatherer group that first ventured into the New World at an even earlier period?

Richard H. Ward of the University of Utah and Svante Paabo of the University of Munich hypothesized that the entire Indigenous population came from a single ancestor who lived sixty thousand years ago!

The basis for arguments like these is that genetic material changes over time. By measuring the extent to which the genes of two races differ it should be possible to determine how long ago they separated. Scientists have used similar analyses to determine the genetic distance between human beings and the apes and in this way have estimated the date at which human beings first appeared on earth. But these arguments are all based upon fairly controversial assumptions because the question of how fast DNA changes is still a matter of debate.

In addition to conflict over dates, some experts doubted that migration of a single hunter-gatherer group could explain the way in which languages and populations were spread throughout the Americas. An alternative hypothesis was that long ago a very early wave of migration entered Alaska, spreading across North America and into the South American continent. The present inhabitants of South America, as well as the majority of groups that now live in North America, are supposed to be the descendants of this first migration. Several thousands of years later a second group appeared on the continent whose descendants became the Apaches, Navahos, and the peoples of the Alaskan interior and regions of British Columbia. Finally, a third wave arrived and occupied coastal areas as well as becoming some of the earliest Inuit and Aleuts.

Support for this scenario comes in part from arguments based upon language differences and evolution. For example, certain North American languages seem to be related to those spoken in South America while others are more remote. However, Johanna B. Nichols of the University of California argues that the present richness of the different languages spoken in the Americas can be explained either by hypothesizing a single hunter-gatherer group that arrived sixty thousand years ago or by many different waves of immigration over the last thirty thousand to forty thousand years.

Even More Ancient?

Among the greatest controversies over the hypothetical arrival of the first humans to the Americas is the presence of human settlements, tools, and animal kills that appear to predate not only the Clovis-Beringia migration hypothesis but also some of the alternatives that were suggested in the section above. The result is a number of conflicting schools of thought, each one claiming that it is correct and accusing its rivals of sloppy research and unwarranted extrapolations.

This book has already questioned the dubious claim that Western science is involved in the dispassionate and objective search for "truth." A more realistic statement would be that much of what Western scientists do flows from their particular paradigms, worldviews, and belief systems. Indeed, this is clearly shown in a statement quoted by Thomas F. Lynch of

Cornell University in *Scientific American* (February 1992). Lynch accuses the proponents of a rival migration-dating of being guilty of sloppy standards and wishful thinking. "People want to believe in this, just like they want to believe in cancer cures."

As far is Lynch is concerned his opponents are being blinded by their belief systems. It is not that they are dishonest, but simply that they see what they expect to see and make the hypotheses and inferences that confirm their deeper beliefs and the way of being that gives meaning to their lives. But surely what applies to one side of an argument must also apply to the other. Is not Lynch himself also motivated by his unconsciously held values and beliefs?

Those who take sides in such a controversy are generally defending their position because it touches on something much deeper than a particular scientific point. It may have to do with their reputations and self-esteem, with their belief in the progress of science or in the power of human reason; it may have to do with who they think they are, or with their own myths of origin. For example, the early theories about who the Mound Builders could have been were all based upon a belief that there was an unbridgeable difference between Western science with its mythic cultural origins in the golden ages of Greece, Rome, and Egypt, and the Indigenous people it had discovered in the area. From within the perceptions of those nineteenth-century archaeologists Indigenous people could not have constructed such impressive monuments—the only explanation was that the Mounds were built by the same people who had created European civilization.

Today our myths are more complex, but just as compelling. They are tied to such ideas as progress, technology, and evolution; to the big bang origin of the universe and Darwin's *Ascent of Man*, to the powers of reason and the scientific method; to the objectivity of approaches such as genetic analysis, radiocarbon dating, and linguistic comparison. And so, if a person begins to question today's theories of migration and human settlement in the Americas he or she is really attacking the current underlying beliefs, worldviews, and paradigms about the meaning of Western science and culture.

What exactly are these opposing theoretical camps? The

Early Arrivals.

Monte Verde, Chile—stone fragments tentatively identified as 33,000 years old.

Meadowcroft, Philadelphia—stone tools and animal bones 15,000 and 19,000 years old.

Pedra Furada rock shelter in Brazil—stone tools that are 48,000 years old. Charcoal from the hearth at Pedra Furada in eastern Brazil has been dated at 40,000 yrs old.

Bluefish Caves, Yukon—tools 25,000 years old

Taima-taima, Venezuela—butchered animal bones 13,000 years old

The Pikimacny Cave in Peru dated between 14,000 and 25,000 years old.

In the Orogrande Cave, New Mexico, a palm print found on a clay hearth dated from 28,000 years ago, alongside tools 38,000 years old.

Santa Rosa Island, California—a hearth over 40,000 years old.

Rock shelters in northeastern Brazil appear to have been continuously occupied for thousands of years and contain rock paintings far older than any in Europe.

The Valesequillo sites in Mexico have been dated as being older than 22,000 years, but some people see them as being old as a quarter of a million years.

The Calico Hills site in the Mojave desert is seen by some experts as indicating human occupation 200,000 years ago. The famous anthropologist Louis Leakey, who had carried out some of the important excavations on the first hominids to appear in Africa, was struck by the similarities between worked stones in the Calico Hills site and those he uncovered in equally ancient settlements in Africa. If Leakey's interpretation is correct, then the tables would be turned between the Old and New worlds, for the Americas would contain some of the most ancient human habitations in the world.

Late Arrivalists stick to the original Clovis date of between 12,000 and 11,600 years ago. The Middle Arrivalists suggest a migration between 30,000 and 12,000 years ago. And, finally, the Early Arrivalists place the first human beings in the Americas at between 30,000 years to as long ago as 250,000 years ago.

Some of the evidence for Early and Middle Arrivalists comes from rock shelters, camps, and settlements that contain artifacts that can be dated as being many tens of thousands of years old. Several of these are listed in the chart below. If these dates are correct, then it means that the Americas were occupied long before that first hypothetical hunter-gatherer group could have marched across the Bering Strait. Theoretical opponents, however, systematically take exception to each of these claims. What some anthropologists consider tools, others view as naturally worn rocks. What some define as accurate radiocarbon dated artifacts are seen by their opponents as contaminated samples.

Alternative Arrivals

Up to now the assumption has been that even if migrations took place long before eleven thousand years ago, they must still have involved a landbridge that connected Siberia to Alaska during one of the ice ages. Not everyone supports this hypothesis. An alternative hypothesis suggests that people did not walk across on land, following game, but arrived in boats and worked their way down the west coast of North America. This is by no means improbable, for, after all, Australia was populated between 100,000 to 40,000 years ago and, even allowing for changes in sea level, many anthropologists believe that part of the journey to Australia must have been made in boats.

Another suggestion is that the first people came not to Alaska but to South America, traveling from Australia either via Antarctica, during one of the periods of southern warming, or using boats and a process of island hopping. Suggestions have also been made that peoples could have arrived long ago by boat from the east coast of Africa.

Most anthropologists believe that somehow, by one route or another, human beings arrived on the American continent from elsewhere. But there is one highly speculative hypothesis that human beings may have evolved in the Americas. Until recently it was believed that the Americas were like an empty continent waiting to be filled by all the higher mammals that arrived in the New World by a process of migration. However, fossil evidence now suggests that a small (primate) mammal was present long ago in the Americas. Its discovery has caused some scientists to wonder if evolutionary processes could also have occurred in the Americas, leading to more complex mammals, monkeys, apes, and even human beings.

Other Contacts

Clearly no definitive story about the inhabitation of the Americas is about to emerge. The best that can be said is that the old school history books can no longer be spoken of with confidence. In their place are a variety of conflicting stories—that groups arrived in a series of waves; that they traveled by boat from Asia, across the southern Pacific; that they came from Africa; or even that human beings have occupied the New World for as long as they have the Old.

In addition, there is mounting evidence that over an extended period cultural exchanges took place between the peoples of the Americas and those of Scandinavia, Western Europe, the African Coast, and those of the Pacific.

Some of this evidence is based upon the perceived similarity between different forms of art and architecture. Commentators have postulated connections between the myths and rituals of Egypt and Central America and have proposed that reed boats could long ago have been sailed to the Americas from Egypt by Phoenician sailors.

The great stone heads left by the Olmecs have been connected to similar statuary in both Africa and on Easter Island. Others see similarities between certain Mayan statues and the Buddhas of the East sitting in the lotus position. Pottery found in Ecuador that dates back 5,000 years seems out of context to the other pottery of that area, yet strikingly similar to the Jomon ceramics of Japan. This has led to the idea that Japanese fishing boats may have arrived on the South American coast and a small settlement established.

From ancient China come legends of a great sea voyage eastward to visit a new world. There are also noted similarities between the arts and cultures of China and Central America. Coming closer to our own times, the establishment of Viking settlements in eastern Canada and in the United States has been well documented.

Vikings had established themselves in Greenland and Baffin Island toward the end of the first millennium. By 1000 A.D. they had begun to build settlements in Newfoundland. Some of the Norse explorers even penetrated into the Great Lakes basin. Viking weapons have been discovered at Lake Nipigon in Ontario and a rune stone was found at Kensington, Minnesota. In this connection, I recall a story told to me by the Mohawk Elder Ernie Benedict. As a small boy his mother used to use a curious expostulation in Mohawk to express disaster. She explained to her son that it referred to a man covered in stone. Ernie Benedict speculated that his people may have preserved a distant memory of armed invaders from overseas.

The controversial theories of the linguist Barry Fell should also be mentioned. Fell has discovered a number of rocks in the eastern United States that bear a series of particular markings. To his critics these marks have a purely natural origin, but to Fell they are examples of ancient forms of writing, Celtic Ogam, dating from 800 to 1000 B.C. Other rocks, he argues, contain Egyptian hieroglyphics and Iberian punic.

We should always be cautious when Western scientists project their own worldview upon Indigenous peoples. Their general assumption is that cultural exchange always came in one direction, from Europe or possibly Asia into the New World. But why should journeys not have been undertaken by the coastal peoples across the Atlantic and Pacific Ocean? The Haida and other groups on the West Coast were well able to undertake long journeys in their oceangoing canoes. While on the East Coast it is possible to make journeys from the Labrador coast to Greenland, Iceland, and Scandinavia by a process of island hopping.

The academics argue their theories in conferences and scholarly journals, and as they do so The People's sense of continuity and value is denied, their stories are transformed into "legends," and their land claims said to be based upon "folk stories." The encounter between two worlds is the story of a clash between profoundly different ways of seeing and being. What is particularly tragic is that in so many cases this has resulted in the near-destruction of a culture.

For Native people the land is their body and their flesh, and its landscape can be found with the map in the head. To deny a people's origins is to cut them off not simply from the land they physically occupy but also internally—from the very sense of their own bodies.

I believe that this deep connection to landscape and origin is present within all of us. Let the reader try this simple experiment. Close your eyes and remember the bedroom you had as a small child. In your mind move around the room, go to the door and walk about the house. Now go out of the house and look around you. Think of the school you went to, or a nearby friend or relative. Leave your house and take a journey to that other location, remembering when to turn left or right, when to cross a street. As you go you will remember familiar sights, a corner store, a park, a neighbor's dog.

Practice doing this for a few hours and you will be amazed to find that the landscape of your childhood is still alive in your body and mind. As you walk in your imagination you can almost feel and taste and smell the world around you; and note how you have been looking at it from a child's height and perspective and not that of an adult.

In my case, when I do this I am saddened to realize that so much must have changed. But suppose that this land that lives in you has not changed, suppose that it is the same land occupied by your parents and grandparents and back, back for many generations. Suppose also that you have been given responsibility for the land that lives within your body and mind. Would not your actions be tempered by this knowledge? Would you not wish to renew and preserve it over the years? And further suppose that your actions and beliefs are shared and reinforced by all around you. This, I think must be what it is like for Indigenous people. Their sense of connection must be more intense, but it is, I believe, one shared by all human beings.

An Associated Press story, for example, tells how forty-two-year-old Stephen Curry of Rosemount, Minnesota, was missing for five weeks. Curry had suffered a loss of memory and personal identity, but was finally discovered outside his childhood home some one hundred miles away near Litchfield, Minnesota. Although Mr. Curry's memory had not returned at the time the story went to press he had been able to find his way back to the childhood farm guided, so the article reports, by "a map in his mind." I was struck as I read the story by the choice of phrase which, I assume was Mr. Curry's, for it sounded so close to that Native American expression *a map in the head*.

Our inner sense of our origins within the landscape has been powerfully expressed by the biologist René Dubois in his 1972 book *The God Within*. Dubois compares a landscape to a human face, something that is always changing, yet is immediately recognizable. This continuity, Dubois suggests, is the spirit of the landscape, the god within who sustains the land and resides in every rock and tree. For Dubois the spirit of a place can be so powerful that it molds, shapes, influences, and ultimately transforms the people who come to occupy it.

The Greeks had a word for it, *entheos*—the god within, the divine madness—which survives in our word *enthusiasm*, for the god can enter into us and possess us. Thus, the god of the landscape enters into and possesses the people. It is Dubois's belief that if a new people entered a particular landscape they would eventually end up being very similar to the previous occupants.

Dubois's intuitions seem very close to those of the Blackfoot teachings in which the land is said to be Napi's body. As one hears the story of Napi and his various actions, one begins to realize that Napi is also The People, and Napi's body is The People's body. The land is the body of The People, and the land is contained within the body of each Blackfoot man, woman, and child.

And thus, in a very deep sense, the origin story of the

Blackfoot and of other peoples begins with the land itself for it is from there that the spirit infuses them. The Ojibwaj speak of their great journey, and, thus, some of their origin may lie in a movement and transformation. The Haida say that were found by Raven hiding in a clam shell and have always lived in their present location.

Suppose that, several thousand years ago, a people moved into a particular landscape and came into relationship with the spirit of that place. In a sense those people would become inseparable from that land. They would, in fact, have been created by it. Thus it could be perfectly true when The People say that they have always lived there, for it was the land that created them, gave them form, language, and customs.

While some peoples see themselves as being born out of the land, others understand their origin as being created within movement, transformation, and chance. In all cases, however, The People preserve their strong identity to the land they occupy.

The Coming of Disease

The Garden of Eden

The letters and diaries of the first settlers on the eastern seaboard of North America portray it as a Garden of Eden with its Native peoples living in a state of peace and harmony, welcoming their new visitors and showing them new foods and medicines. Similar accounts of this balance, connection to the environment, and deep sense of the sacredness in all things can be found in the writings of explorers who made early contact with the Indigenous peoples in several other areas of the world.

Philosophers of the time hailed such societies as the aboriginal state of humanity. They wrote of the "noble savage" and of people who may have escaped the fall of man. Systems of government such as the Iroquoian league of independent nations and other confederations pointed the way to those Europeans who sought to free themselves from the tyranny of kings. Indeed, the political philosophy of the Iroquois people found its way into the Constitution of the United States of America, and there is evidence that Thomas More's *Utopia*, an account of the ideal state of human society, was written after the author had received descriptions of the Mayan civilization of Central America.

In *Leviathan*, the seventeenth-century English philosopher Thomas Hobbes suggested that without a common power or authority people would live in a state of war in which there would be "no arts; no letters; no society; and which is worst of all, continual fear and danger of violent death; and the life of man, solitary, poor, nasty, brutish, and short."* Hobbes, however, was wrong, for when it came to the Indigenous peoples of the Americas, and other parts of the world, his notion of "nasty, brutish, and short" couldn't be further from the truth.

Societies of hunter-gatherers, as well as those with mixed economies of farming and fishing, as well as hunting and gathering, lead lives that are far more relaxed and stress-free than our own. It takes us between thirty-five and sixty hours of work each week to provide ourselves with food, shelter, and the other things that we feel are the necessities of life. Most traditional aboriginal people work far fewer hours than this— probably two or three days out of each week is all that is required—and during the time they are not "working" they are visiting, hanging around, talking, and gossiping with one another, ensuring that the social cement that holds their society together is in good order.

The vision of a Garden of Eden has, to some extent, been confirmed by the work of scientists who have examined the skeletons of early peoples. Evidence points to the fact that, before contact with Europeans, The People were remarkably free from diseases. Indeed, epidemics only seem to have arrived when Western civilization began to encroach upon the Americas.

A Condition of Disease

Now this raises a very interesting question about Indigenous science and the condition of Indigenous people before contact with Europeans. Why were they so free from disease? Could it perhaps have been something to do with their beliefs, science, society, and way of life? How was it that, at the time of European contact, approximately one-fifth of the world's popu-

---

*Leviathan, part 2, chapter 19.

lation was living in relatively ideal conditions? Why is it that we, with all the power and knowledge of our modern civilization, are so subject to illness, cancers, heart disease, chronic autoimmune disorders, and allergies, in addition to a wide variety of mental illnesses and the slow, heartbreaking disintegrations that come about with aging? Surely if we can split the atom, travel to the moon, and communicate electronically across the globe we can ensure that our bodies and minds remain healthy. Could it be the development of the very civilization that brought about these technological advances has also been responsible for the introduction and spread of some of the world's most terrible epidemics of disease?

By the end of World War I, Europeans and Americans were stunned by the carnage that was the direct result of trench warfare. It seemed as if a whole generation of young men had been slaughtered and that every village had its war memorial commemorating the sons who had died on the battlefield. The memory of this carnage lives on today in the writings of the English war poets such as Wilfred Owen, Rupert Brooke, and Siegfried Sassoon; in Robert Graves's memoir *Goodbye To All That*; in Ernest Hemingway's novel *A Farewell to Arms*, and in the German novelist Erich Maria Remarque's *Im Westen nichts Neues* (*All Quiet on the Western Front*). But it is even more shocking to realize that within a year of the peace an influenza virus was to result in a far greater number of deaths than the totality of the war. It was as if all the wartime horrors devised by human beings—gas attacks, bombs, mines, machine guns, and bayonets—did not begin to compare with the diseases of nature.

There had been many striking outbreaks of disease in Europe's past—the Great Plague of London in 1664 caused Isaac Newton to retreat north to his family farm in Lincolnshire from which secluded environment he began to think about the nature of gravity and the laws of motion. In the fourteenth century the Black Death swept over medieval Europe wiping out one third of the population, or about twenty-five million people. Another disease, *Phytophthora infestans*, this time affecting the potato plant, caused a massive failure of that crop in 1845 and 1846. In Ireland this led to the

Great Famine with the deaths, or emigration, of millions of people.

Is this truly the fate of human societies—periodic scourges that sweep across the world? The currently fashionable science of chaos theory argues that waves and epidemics arise out of the very nature of complicated interlocking systems. Mathematical models suggest that even in an isolated environment where predator and prey, disease and host, are locked in a battle together, human populations will naturally exhibit wide cyclic fluctuations.

But I believe that the whole question of disease is far more complicated than this and that the subject is tied to the beliefs and values held by our society. This may seem strange at first, for if we have been conditioned to see disease as caused by bacteria and viruses what can be the role played by society's structure and how could an Indigenous science protect a whole continent for so long?

The Virus of Progress

My suggestion is that the West's desire for progress, growth, and increase has brought about the very diseases that have become its scourge. Take a simple example: Every farmer and market gardener knows that the more he or she attempts to increase yields per acre by farming intensively, the greater the chance is that a crop will be totally wiped out by disease or natural disaster.

In order to increase yields, monocultures are developed that can be planted ever closer together and cultivated and harvested in the most concentrated ways possible. This requires the use of fertilizers, pesticides, insecticides, and fungicides. The end result is a system in which variety and flexibility have been reduced to such an extent that when a disease strikes it can spread through the whole crop and destroy it.

The Indigenous science of the Iroquois peoples teaches that the Three Sisters, corn, beans, and squash, must be planted together and even prescribes the number of seeds to plant in each hole. Likewise, in earlier times European farmers planted many different varieties of a crop together in the same field. They also rotated their crops, leaving the land arable every four years, and farmed less intensely. Their yields may have been a lot lower, but at least when disease appeared it would only destroy a percentage of the crop.

Some Indigenous peoples periodically burned the land, which acted to fumigate and destroy insects and plant diseases. Others, like the Iroquois, periodically moved their villages to new areas to allow the land to renew itself.

When the potato was introduced into Ireland, the indigenous population adopted an efficient "lazy bed" method of cultivation that was identical to that which had been developed by the Inca. The tragedy of the Irish potato famine lay not so much in a disease of the potato plant itself, but in an indigenous population that was forced, by an occupying power, to replace its other crops and foodstuffs which this single cash crop. The ultimate cause of the Great Famine was not so much the potato blight itself but a particular social, economic, and political system.

Our thoughts, values, and worldviews cause us to see the world in a particular way and are the source of our actions. Thus, in the end, these same values come to create the world for us, a world in which diseases and disasters can flourish.

Somehow, the Indigenous science, beliefs, relationships with the land, compacts with the spirits, and energies of the world—call it what you will—enabled the peoples of Turtle Island to live in harmony for a very long time. The Native American people I have spoken to always speak of obligations rather than of rights and of the importance of their ceremonies of renewal, for, they say, nothing persists; all is flux, and unless a society is willing to renew itself through sacrifice it will pass away.

It appears that this was the worldview that enabled the peoples of the north to support themselves by hunting, fishing, and gathering; the peoples of the plains to live in harmony with the buffalo; and those farther south to practice a mixed economy that included farming. In all cases it appears that a balance was maintained between The People and the land around them. (It is true, however, that I have heard some

Native people refer to hubris and the fact that they were allowing their populations to expand too fast shortly before Europeans came to their land.)

Long ago in Europe and the Near East the same conditions must have operated, yet somehow things progressively got out of balance. The scale of farming began to increase and animals were domesticated and kept in larger and larger numbers in close contact with humans. In some cases whole forests were cleared to provide grazing land for growing herds of animals.

In neolithic times the hillsides of Wordsworth's Lake District and Charlotte Bronte's Pennines were covered by forest. Early farmers cleared out these trees to produce new grazing land for their herds. Before the advent of the Industrial Revolution the polished-stone axe was one of the most remarkable and transformative pieces of human technology.

In their original state, soils were bound to the sloping surfaces of hillsides by means of a complex root system, and vast reserves of minerals and nutrients were locked up in the ancient forests. But as the forests vanished, not only were nutrients washed away but so were the soils that had been so patiently laid down in the six thousand years since the last ice age. The final result is the present barren character of the Lakeland Fells and the Pennine hills.

Thus, even in neolithic times, an expanding human population was producing an irreversible change in the landscape. And as the scope of farming increased, so, too, the surrounding population began to grow. In turn, grain stored in ever larger quantities and people began to gather together in larger and larger cities.

It was in the wake of this change in human lifestyle that the age of disease began. Larger numbers of domestic animals were herded in closer proximity to human beings. At first diseases began to spread among the animal population and then to mutate and transfer themselves to humans. In this way humans became subject to tuberculosis, measles, and diphtheria. And, since people were no longer living in relatively isolated hunting groups but in much closer proximity to each other, these new diseases spread quite rapidly.

As cities grew, so, too, did the problems of sanitation, overcrowding, and the disposal of waste products. The historical companions of humans, rats and fleas, played their parts in the spread of disease. Sources of drinking water were contaminated by human waste, and where poverty flourished so did malnutrition and an increased susceptibility to disease brought about by a weakened immune system.

Add to this the increasing ease of travel to and from distant parts by ship and caravan, and suddenly it becomes possible to transfer new diseases from across the world into a population with absolutely no resistance. It could be argued that the history of the West is not so much that of kings, princes, and popes; of wars and treaties; of scientists, engineers, and philosophers; of arts and literature; but rather of the creation, rise, and triumph of infectious diseases like plague, typhoid, cholera, and tuberculosis.

The conditions that create epidemic disease persisted in Europe right up to the last century. In his 1990 biography of Charles Dickens, Peter Ackroyd gives a description of the conditions of working-class London at that time. Excrement lay thick in rooms, cellars, and yards; floor boards were torn up so that the hole could serve as a privy. Excrement and urine ran though the gutters of each street and privies drained into open sewers and ditches that eventually drained into the Thames so that during the hot summer of 1858 "the stench of the great river became insupportable." The same water was pumped back, untreated, into the cisterns and stand-pipes of Londoners where it emerged brown and stinking.

In a very real sense, human beings create the conditions for their own illness, out of their dreams, beliefs, values, social structures, and thought. It was not that the authorities in London were evil or stupid people, it was simply that most people could not see any way out of the conditions in which the population lived because their way of thinking, seeing, and believing was shared by the whole society.

But if we have produced the conditions of disease have we not also created triumphs of a medicine that will combat these same scourges? It turns out the true advances in medicine, when judged by the fall in mortality rate and the increase in life expectancy, have not come about from antibiotics, immunizations, or surgery but simply through improvements in sanitation and through a better understanding of diet.

The Sickness of Ideas

The First Peoples of Turtle Island appear to have avoided the problems that beset Europe in its endless quest for progress. Of course, there are always exceptions, but overall the evidence suggests that diseases were not rampant, and societies maintained a balance with the land around them and avoided these problems.

As to the absence of disease, scientists had offered their own explanation, which, as usual, invokes that Bering landbridge. They suggest the aboriginal family groups that walked across this bridge, along with all the animals that migrated before them, happened to be free from disease. Then, when sea levels rose and the landbridge disappeared, the entire American continent was sealed off like a sterile zone in a laboratory. As a result, humans and animals lived in a relative germ and virus-free area for the next thousands of years.

Well that is an explanation of sorts, but it doesn't sound too credible. To begin with, the hypothesis that the entire human population of the Americas are the descendants of an original family group has been pretty much discredited in favor of several migrations over very long periods. Neither does the argument take into account the many contacts that occurred on the east and west coasts centuries before the arrival of Columbus.

Possibly we should look for another explanation. In the previous section I suggested that sickness that sweeps through a population has its origin not so much in viruses but in ideas. A virus is information, a segment of DNA that enters into the cells of a healthy body and instructs them to operate in a different way, manufacturing more viruses and, in the process, causing the host to sicken. Healthy bodies, however, have their own system of defense, the immune system, that recognizes the pattern of an intruder and manufactures antibodies that act to destroy viruses and bacteria. When the body has been weakened by poor nutrition and lifestyle the immune system does not work so effectively to combat an invader.

Thus, at the level of an individual, disease could be thought of as a battle between systems of information. This image also applies at the social level because the conditions under which viruses mutate and are passed on, as well as the conditions under which human immune systems become debilitated, are the direct result of social conditions. Disease is a manifestation of human thought because it is ideas, worldviews, and beliefs that create the conditions in which a society can be riddled with disease, strife, and poverty, or can continue in health and harmony.

The Alliances of Harmony

If, in effect, diseases grow out of the human thought process, then maybe the ability to maintain health has a similar origin. I have been told that in ancient times The People negotiated alliances, compacts, and relationships with the powers of the world such as the Keepers of the animals, and with sacred plants and medicines. Among the Iroquois peoples, for example, the Three Sisters (corn, beans, and squash) are specifically acknowledged in the Thanksgiving Address. The actual method of planting of the Sisters takes place according to the outcome of the sacred Peach Stone Game—how the three plants must always be planted together and how many seeds of each must be placed in a hole.

The Iroquois people's relationship to the food they eat is really their direct spiritual connection to the powers, spirits, or energies that guard and generate the crops. This statement can be put in another way: The Iroquois peoples, through their ceremonies, renew the direct relationship that was once established with active genetic and biological information that informs the processes of nature. This alliance between the molecular level and the world of powers and energies is the practical side of Indigenous science. The idea of direct access to the molecular basis of life may be a big jump for many readers but it is something I am going to expand on and attempt to justify throughout this book.

The customs and ceremonies of the Iroquois that lead them to interact with the Three Sisters in their characteristic way are also what we would today call a form of ecological wisdom and are yet another example of the profoundly different visions of nature between the two worlds. As an example, in high school you may have been asked to pick out the major themes of a novel or short story. One of these themes would no doubt have been "man against nature" and would have dealt with the human struggle against a hostile environment. For example, *Apocalypse Now* is a reworking of Joseph Conrad's *Heart of Darkness*. In both portrayals the farther one travels upriver the more one leaves behind civilization and enters into a disturbing, hostile, and terrifying environment. Nature is "red in tooth and claw," and human beings can only survive through struggle with its dark forces.

But this is the vision of Europeans who, for centuries, have sought to dominate and control the natural environment around them. It is profoundly different from the view held by the Indigenous societies of the Americas. To them, nature is not competitive or adversarial. Rather, all things live in cooperation; the Three Sisters sustain and protect each other, a stem of corn gives physical support for the bean, which in turn fixes fertilizing nitrogen within its nodules.

It is difficult to imagine an Indigenous scientist having written Darwin's *On the Origin of Species*. Its hypotheses about the survival of the fittest and progress through competition are essentially the values of Victorian politics, society, economics, industrial progress, checks, and balances projected onto the natural world. By contrast, an Indigenous scientist would view nature as cooperative and operating through relationship and alliance. In a universe in which time turns in a circle, and in which the ceremonies of renewal are the continued obligations of The People, the emphasis is always upon balance and harmony as opposed to progress, advancement, and accumulation. Within such a world the whole idea of sickness and health must have a profoundly different meaning. I think that is the real reason for the aboriginal Garden of Eden the first settlers encountered, rather than talk about a sterile, isolated continent.

Alliance With Health

Elders tell stories of a time when humans and animals could freely talk together. This era has long passed, but the two-leggeds are still able to communicate with animals in their dreams and many Native American people talk to rocks and trees. Before the coming of the Europeans who knows how extensive that communication between all aspects of nature may have been?

A friend of mine, the psychiatrist Paul Grof, has given me examples of how perfectly ordinary people can look into themselves and "see" their own organs, often picturing them in striking detail and producing drawings or paintings that show unexpected anatomical knowledge, even down to the correct color for each organ. In some cases this ability seems to involve a sort of "zooming-in" on the microscopic detail of a cell or organ. Other people can enter into the bodies of those around them and actually "see" the exact nature of disease.

From the Native American community I have heard accounts of medicine people who have made accurate diagnoses of the state of internal organs. In many cultures the rituals and ceremonies surrounding healing involve the medicine person entering into a heightened state of "seeing" in which the illness can be concretized, as it were, and removed by sucking, blowing, or pulling.

Naturally, modern doctors and psychiatrists have, within their own paradigms, explanations of what is happening during such cures. But we should remain open to other possibilities, that some genuine understanding exists of the inner nature of sickness and disease through the ability to communicate directly with the body and spirit of a particular sickness.

When Western doctors speak of a "medicine man" or "medicine woman" they generally have in mind someone who has accumulated lore about certain roots, herbs, and fungi, a combination of "old wives' tales," "herbal medicine," and the sort of folk wisdom that has been painstakingly accumulated by trial and error. Today, thanks to the spectroscope and other tools of the analytical laboratory, they can analyze these medicinal herbs and isolate their active medical ingredient. In so doing, scientists believe that they have accounted, in a scientific way, for folk remedies—they are biologically active chemicals adulterated by a variety of other substances. How much better, therefore, to administer a 100 percent pure drug that has been synthesized in the laboratory than an unpleasant concoction of herbs and roots. Scientific knowledge has advanced beyond the superstition of folk medicine.

Again, what is really happening is not the perfection of knowledge or the replacement of myths by objective knowledge, but really an encounter of two worldviews. Traditional stories speak of the People having been given healing plants as gifts from Mother Earth. Some tell of how the Bear brought medicine and taught the people how to use it. Above all, plants contain spirit, and in using them one is essentially entering into relationships with the powers and energies of another world.

Could it be that there is another science of healing, one that is profoundly different from our own? In times gone by, did The People possess a direct perception of the inner nature of the plants around them and enter into a dialogue with the spirits of the plants? Did the animals, birds, and insects exchange their knowledge with the People and teach them how to come into relationship with healing medicines? Just as the gift of corn came about through a direct process of relationship, acknowledgment, and obligation for renewal, so, too, exchanges may have been made and obligations entered into for the use of medicine plants in healing ceremonies.

Harmony and Health

If human thought creates the conditions of disease, then human thought can also prevent them. With some exceptions the Indigenous peoples of the Americas lived in relatively small groups and were not the victims of rats and lice as were the town dwellers of Europe. There is evidence that they practiced a form of birth control to maintain their populations at an appropriate level.

Such a lifestyle would prevent the conditions under which disease and epidemics flourish and when sickness did visit there were medicines to be used and ceremonies of healing. Above all, the society relied upon its ceremonies in order to renew, on a daily and a seasonal basis, the relationships it had entered into with the spirits of sky, earth, animals, trees, rocks, and healing plants. As to the healing ceremonies themselves, while individuals may have been cured of body sicknesses, their deeper meaning may have been to bind the people together and renew their sense of lived meaning. A Native American may say, "That was a powerful healing" even when the physical body still suffers from the same disease; what is being healed is something far deeper and perhaps more important.

The Great Disease

Before contact there were two worlds, two visions of reality, two views of time, balance and harmony. Inevitably, as the first settlers, explorers, and traders began to move across the continent a confrontation of worldviews took place. I have suggested that Indigenous America was pervaded by a field of active meaning, a relationship that had been created in a world beyond the immediate senses, and which involved the whole of nature in a web of exchange, relationship, obligation, and renewal. What happened next was a perturbation of balance, a virus in a field of meaning, the epidemic spread of a alien set of values.

Within a relatively short period of time after the arrival of the first Europeans, between 90 and 95 percent of the population of the New World was wiped out. It was a disaster unparalleled in the recorded history of the human race. Whole societies, peoples, languages, and civilizations were brought almost to the point of extinction. The great shock wave of disease that spread across the Americas far exceeds in its impact the Black Death that swept Europe in the Middle Ages, the Great Plague that gripped England in the time of Newton and Samuel Pepys, or the carnage of two world wars.

The nature of the disease that swept across the Americas can be read in different ways. For instance, through thousands of years of isolation, inhabitants of the New World lacked resistance to the diseases of the Old. Clearly this makes objective, scientific sense. But the story can be read in another way, for not only did bacteria and viruses invade a new territory, but ideas, values, and ways of thinking also spread out and expanded without first seeking to establish a relationship and a harmony with the Keepers of the land.

No relationship existed between the Keepers of the Animals, the powers and energies of nature, and these new ideas, diseases, and viruses that arrived from another continent. For tens of thousands of years the peoples of Turtle Island had maintained a balance. Now they were faced by values of progress and growth, expansion and change, by a society that had externalized reality and sought the control of nature. The invasion of sickness was at the level of concept, idea, and way of seeing. It was the clash between an open system, a society that sought balance and harmony, that maintained a cyclic time of renewal, as well as an alliance of dreams and spirits and one that sought security through control—a society that had accepted the sacrifice of disease in return for mastery over matter and time and the accumulation of wealth. Like a cancer, new perceptions, worldviews, political, and economic ways of thinking spread throughout Turtle Island.

The Sickness Spreads

As to the sequence of events that followed the large-scale movement of Europeans across the Americas, that order depends upon which historians you choose to read. (In the sections below I have relied on Calvin Martin's *Keepers of the Game*, Andrew Nikiforuk's *The Fourth Horseman*, and "Bugged by Progress," a review by Roy Porter, lecturer in history of medicine at Wellcome Institute.)

Contacts occurred between the Old World and the New for hundreds, and possibly thousands, of years before Columbus.

Several decades before the arrival of Christopher Columbus, fishing was already taking place on the great cod banks off Canada's eastern coast. As the fishing banks around Europe began to deplete, boats from Bristol, Normandy, Brittany, and the Basque areas ventured further west in search of better fishing. The location of a vast wealth of fish off Newfoundland was at first kept secret to avoid competition.

Probably these early fishing crews landed and traded with the Mic Maq, Beothuk, Montagnais, and Naskapi for furs. In exchange, the Native American population was given glass beads, pieces of metal, and something of much greater implication—colds, influenza, smallpox, typhoid, diphtheria, measles, chicken pox, whooping cough, tuberculosis, yellow fever, scarlet fever, streptococcal infections, gonorrhea, and syphilis.

It is generally assumed that the first diseases to enter the New World were brought by human contact, but Calvin Martin suggests the additional possibility of cross-species contamination. Rats leaving the European fishing ships, as well as chickens and other animals carried on the ships for food, moved among the indigenous animal population and, in so doing, passed on a variety of diseases. Among some Native American groups there are legends of a time when the caribou vomited blood and the beaver were dying of a great sickness.

A great epidemic of many diseases may have begun in the animal population and spread westward from the coast. In turn, these diseases mutated and passed into a human population that had no natural resistance to them.

For tens of thousands of years the two-legged and the four-legged had maintained a harmonious relationship, now they were becoming locked together in a terrible symbiosis of diseases. Martin reports stories of wolves and dogs eating the victims of smallpox and themselves falling ill.

A wave of sickness, affecting humans and animals alike, radiated in advance of the first missionaries and explorers. Maybe a decade before Europeans arrived at a given village the population would have already suffered the ravages of a variety of diseases.

Estimates put the depopulation of Central and South America at between 90 and 95 percent within two hundred years of contact. The population of Central Mexico has been calculated as 25 to 29 million in 1519, but by 1605 it had dropped to just over one million. Some scholars have put the population of the precontact New World as high as 100 million, with 10 million people living in the Northern Hemisphere. By the time contact had been well established there were fewer than one million Indigenous people in North America.

Imagine what effect such a widespread toll of death would have on a people who, for tens of thousands of years, lived in harmony and balance with nature. Martin imagines a world in which everything was dying, the two-legged and the four, yet none of the traditional healing ceremonies would work and no answers came from dreams and visions. Did this mean that their compacts and relationships had somehow failed? Did the first settlers encounter a people in the interior who were not only dying of disease but whose very social fabric had lost its meaning?

If we accept Calvin Martin's hypothesis, and it is after all a speculation based upon contemporary reports, then we begin to see the colonization of the Americas in a very different light. We see a dying people trying to find meaning in the terrible punishment that had been imposed upon them. We see them struggling in the face of explorers and settlers who bring with them alien worldviews and values. Thus, a people who had obligations to renew the land met people who believed in land ownership. A people who believed in balance and the renewal of time met those who believed in progress, control, accumulation, and linear time. Those who had based their lives on consensus met treaties and hierarchical government. Those to whom justice was the return of harmony of the whole group met adversarial trial and punishment.

The initial spread of disease was followed by a variety of official policies that included extermination and assimilation. Buffalo were massacred from slow-moving trains by so-called sportsmen. The original inhabitants of Newfoundland, the Beothuk, were hunted to extinction; internment camps were established in which the Cherokee people were placed, and many deaths were suffered during their forced march to their new reservation. In residential schools children were beaten for speaking their own languages, and bottles of whiskey were given to those who had come to negotiate a price for their furs. See, for example, *Bury My Heart at Wounded Knee,* by Dee Brown.

Yet, in spite of all this, The People did survive. Although some languages are now endangered and others have vanished, many are still spoken; ceremonies are still performed, teachings are repeated; and a philosophy of balance and harmony has been preserved. In spite of alcohol and violence, sickness and disease, extermination and assimilation, the spirits live on. Today many Elders speak of the need for a great healing and call for red and white brothers and sisters to sit in the circle together and listen to each other.

6

The Medicine Ways

The circle goes round; sickness and disease give way to healing, decay is balanced by renewal. The previous chapter spoke of the near devastation that resulted when worlds and worldviews met. This chapter must therefore deal with the processes of healing.

Healing, Wholeness, and Meaning

Modern medical science, with its biochemistry, X-rays, and biopsies, is a marvelous triumph of our technological prowess, yet it is representative of a worldview that has fragmented mind and body, the individual and society, spirit and landscape. From this perspective, dominated by the linear relationship between cause and effect, it is difficult to understand the nature of healing within Indigenous science.

Yet, increasingly, there are indications that we are becoming of one mind. If I have stressed the gulf between the two worlds, it has been in part to illustrate and make points. A chasm exists because my Native American friends hear and see a profoundly different world from mine. At the same time, however, we must not forget that we share a common humanity. Ernie Benedict, a Mohawk Elder, once reminded me that Natives and non-Natives have married, they have loved each other and raised children together. At a certain level we all experience the same loves and pain, the same hopes and anger. It is for these reasons, I believe, that we can come to understand the meaning of healing arts within Turtle Island.

Recently the West has been calling for a different quality of healing. While we acknowledge the wealth of knowledge inherent in modern medicine it does not present us with a truly convincing account for the ways in which we get sick, how we are healed, and the ways in which we are able to remain healthy. It is true that many infectious diseases have been eliminated and miracle cures developed, but in other ways people feel that medicine does not reach them at the personal and experiential level.

My friend Paul Grof, a psychologist who is interested in why some people get sick and other remain healthy, asks how it is that when one hundred people drink water infected with the hepatitis A virus only a certain percentage develop the symptoms of the disease, others experience flulike symptoms for a few days, while the rest remain perfectly healthy. Hepatitis A perfectly fits our Western scientific model of cause and effect. The cause is a virus ingested from fecally contaminated food or water. The effect, following an incubation period of two to six weeks, is fever, nausea, enlargement of the liver, and the symptoms of jaundice.

But why, if it is a matter of cause and effect, do only some people get sick while others remain perfectly healthy? And why, in an emergency ward or after major surgery, do nurses "know" that, irrespective of the official prognosis, some patients are going to die while others will recover? It is possible that the answer to these questions cannot exclusively be found at the level of matter, cause and effect.

The same questions intrigued the psychiatrist Viktor E. Frankl who, as an inmate of the Auschwitz, Dachau, and Theresienstadt concentration camps, asked why some people continued to survive, irrespective of their general physique or state of health.

Frankl's answer became the basis of a new treatment he called logotherapy; it is a psychiatry concerned not simply with being, *ontos,* but also with meaning, *logos.* For Frankl, we are "oriented towards meaning" and the essence of our lives is "the tension between being and meaning." Indigenous scientists would perhaps rather speak of the human as inhabiting a world of both matter and spirit, and of the process of renewal and relationship that grows out of the entire society. Thus, if we are to understand the nature of health and healing we must learn to enter a reality that contains additional dimensions to the purely material.

The Medicine Way

The stereotype of Indigenous healing is that of a beaded and befeathered medicine man or medicine woman carrying a medicine bag. But just what is "medicine" in Native context? Certainly it is not synonymous with the capsules and tablets of a Western pharmacy. A medicine person may refer to the herbs and plants in her bag as being medicine, but Native Americans will also say that a ceremony they attended, an experience they had, or the food they are eating is "good medicine."

So what is "medicine"? The problem is that this is an English word, an attempt at translation, and not a word in a Native language. So much Indigenous science and worldview is enfolded within the languages spoken by the people. *Medicine* is an attempt to convey within a single word a whole spectrum of concepts that belong to a profoundly different vision of reality and the human body.

English, and for that matter French, German, Italian, and the other European languages are noun-oriented. They are employed to divide the world into physical objects (nouns), and thinking into separate concepts (again, nouns). Many Native American languages do not work this way. They are verb-based. Thus, when in English we speak of "medicine" we automatically seek a referent, a substance, an object, something tangible, something that can be conceptualized. But suppose we begin with something verbal, with activity, process, a movement of harmony and balance. Medicine could then be felt in the beating of the heart, sensed as a movement around the sacred circle, the wind blowing through the leaves of the trees, the growing of green plants, and the astronomical alignments of the medicine wheel.

Even food can be good medicine. This reminds me of what I was once told by a medical officer who worked in Labrador. He said the incidence of cancer and heart disease was very low among those Native people who still hunted and trapped their food, but once they began to purchase meat and other foods from stores the rate of these illnesses rose to that of the general population. Scientists have discovered that the fat content of wild animals differs from that of their domesticated counterparts. While the latter appears to contribute to heart disease the former contains substances that appear to protect against the same disease.

Medicine could be approached as energy, power, spirit, relationship; as movement, balance, a way of life; and as walking the Good Red Road.* Yet, at the same time, a medicine bag may contain plants, roots, herbs, fungi, pieces of bone, fur, feathers, and other things used in doctoring that are also referred to as medicine. We are not really going to be successful in capturing the essence of Indigenous science within our comfortable logic of "either/or."

Indigenous Pharmacopoeias

At one level the contents of a medicine bag relate to what we in the West know as drugs or medicines. As an example, one of the first explorers within North America, Jacques Cartier, traveled along the St. Lawrence River in winter until his men contracted what we would now diagnose as scurvy. Fortunately, the local Indigenous population taught Cartier how to make tea from the bark of the birch tree. Today we know that birchbark tea is a good source of vitamin C.

Sa'ke'j Henderson smokes a mixture containing red willow bark for muscular pains in his back. Willow bark contains, among other things, the molecules directly related to aspirin, or acetylsalicylic acid. Thus, the smoking mixture quickly provides the level of pain relief required for muscular tensions.

Inca runners were required to travel with messages for long distances and chewed the leaves of the coca plant, which

---

Life's journey. Also known as taking the Earth walk.

contain cocaine, to suppress appetite and increase endurance. Hunters dip the points of their spears or arrows into plant or animal preparations (the secretions from toads, for example). Derivatives of one of these, curare, are used in modern anesthesia to block the breathing reflex of the patient and permit "breathing" to be performed by a machine that controls the flow of oxygen, carbon dioxide, and anesthetic.

Substances used by Indigenous peoples all over the world have subsequently been found by Western scientists to contain valuable pharmaceuticals. An appeal that is sometimes made to save the rain forests and other threatened areas is that valuable cures, at present known only to isolated Indigenous tribes, may be destroyed in the process. People speculate in a romantic way about miracle cures for cancer or for AIDS being discovered in a remote forest, or within the bag of a Native healer.

This raises an interesting question that touches yet again on the differences between Western and Indigenous science. If certain traditional medicinal herbs contain biologically active substances related to drugs used in modern hospitals, does this mean that Native medicine is a more primitive form of what Western technology has developed?

To answer this question we first have to enquire as to what philosophers would term the ontological status of Native medicines. What, in other words, is the nature of their existence? Sa'ke'j Henderson once asked me what I thought a molecule was. I offered him an explanation from modern science, that a molecule is a geometrical arrangement of atoms. Of course, he knew this sort of answer, but replied that a molecule was an alliance of spirits, and that when taken into the body this alliance dissolves and takes up new configurations.

At the time I was inclined to bridge the gap between our two ways of thinking by calling on concepts from modern quantum physics. A molecule is an arrangement of atoms but it can also be represented by a wave function, which is, in a way, a sort of vibration of matter and energy. Maybe it is possible to think of the molecules that make up medicines as patterns of vibrations or more subtle forms of matter-energy.

But, in that case, the same description would apply to a

chair or a table as to a medicine. The more I thought about it the more I realized that "spirit" cannot really be reduced to our words *energy* or *matter* as they are currently understood in Western science. The idea of using plants and herbs to cure sickness may at first sight appear close to our scientific idea of "medicines," suggesting that the powers of animal and vegetable substances lie in their biologically active molecules. But this cannot be the whole of the story. For example, the way in which these plants are collected is important, and before the medicine bag is used, the bag must be smudged with the purifying smoke of sage, sweet grass, tobacco, or cedar. Medicine itself has a life of its own. It is the tangible manifestation of alignments with the world of powers, energies, and spirits. Trying to understand how and why a particular plant is "medicine" stretches our Western paradigm to its limit.

Let us push this question of the ontological status of "medicine" a little further. I buy brand-name nondrowsy hay fever tablets at my local drugstore. They tend to be fairly expensive, but next to them is a "no-name" package whose active ingredient is chemically identical. According to our current view of science, a molecule that has been synthesized in one laboratory is identical in its effects to the "same" molecule made in another laboratory, even when the two manufacturers have synthesized their products in totally different chemical reactions. And most westerners find both will work equally well to relieve their hay fever.

A Native medicine may contain the same biologically active molecule and yet, as far as I understand it, Native healers would not consider these two medicines to be identical. One way in which they differ is that, in addition to the significant biologically active molecule, the plant medicine contains a wide variety of other chemicals. It is possible that, in their natural form, some of these act in complex ways to enhance each other's effects. Physicists and chemists are now coming to realize the very complicated nonlinear effects that can occur when substances interact together. This could, in part, account for the reason that certain naturally occurring substances are so effective.

But this avoids the full issue of ontological status—the way in which a Native medicine exists. Traditional people speak of a plant as "having spirit" and in a landscape in which large-scale logging, mining, or road building has taken place, may claim that the plant has lost this spirit. Analytic chemists may dispute this as superstition, but healers will argue that the medicine has lost its effectiveness.

Spirit is part of the ontological existence of medicine. When medicine is passed around the circle there is an exchange of this spirit, with some people giving spirit to it and others taking spirit. As the medicine circulates a balance must be maintained; thus everyone may give their energy to the medicine so that it is available for the sick person. A woman who is "on her moon" (menstruating) will step back and not touch the medicine. The reason is, I have been told, that a woman has such power during that time of the month that she would disturb the balance of energy and spirits within the medicine.

To approach medicine herbs only in terms of biologically active molecules is to see them in only one dimension. Within the dimensions of chemical analysis this may be correct, but it leaves out the other dimensions of spirit, energy, and relationship.

A Natural Ecology

Clues as to the ontological nature of a plant can be found in the way it is gathered. At certain times of the year people collect sweetgrass, sage, and many other medicine plants. Suppose a non-Native person spends several hours searching for a particular rare plant and finally spots one. His or her natural inclination would be to pick it at once, but the Native person will pass it by. It is only when they discover the third such plant that they will feel able to take it.

This third plant is a gift from Mother Earth and, as with all gifts, if a person is to take it, it can only be as part of an exchange. The spirit of the plant must be acknowledged, for the medicine person seeks to come into relationship with its power. No one would wire up a house without having the correct knowledge of electrical polarity and circuitry. In a similar way, a Native person makes contact with the powers of nature in the proper manner; to act in an unthinking way would indicate a lack of respect and could also disturb a person's equilibrium and energy.

When a person reaches the third plant he or she will speak to it, offer a prayer, and request the aid of that plant. Then, after taking the plant from Mother Earth an offering will be made into the hole that has been left—a bead, perhaps, or some tobacco.

Back at home the plant is handled in an equally respectful way. When a powerful object is passed round the circle, for example, there may be someone present who desires to use that energy for his or her own personal power, or who may be corrupt in some way. Such a person may take part of the spirit from the Medicine and, in exchange, impart something of him or herself. Thus others are cautious in touching the object when it is handed back to them and may first purify it with the smoke from sage, cedar, or sweetgrass.

The gap between the two worlds, of molecules and of spirits, is illustrated in this story of a traditional healer who acts as trickster. A Native person asked that a medicine man should be allowed to visit him in the hospital. The doctor agreed but the Native healer was uneasy about working in a non-Native environment. Nevertheless, the healer visited the man and spent some time with him. When he left, and being careful to do this within the doctor's hearing, he handed the patient a bottle and told him to take the medicine it contained, but to be very careful that no one else should touch it.

The next day when the Native healer arrived he encountered a very angry doctor. "What's going on here?" he asked. "We analyzed the bottle and it contains nothing but tap water. You're a fake!"

The medicine man smiled back. "You see," he said, "when I left that bottle I knew all along what you would do with it."

The nature of Native medicine lies both in the plant and the ceremony, in the way that plant was picked, the exchanges and relationships that were entered into that would lead to its use, and in the relationship between that plant and other people in the circle and the relationship to the sick person.

Energy and the Subtle

Sometimes this word *spirit* is used interchangeably with words like *power* and *energy*. As we seek to understand the nature of Medicine it is natural to ask if *energy*, when it is used by Native people, has a connection with *energy* as it is used in Western science. It is interesting to note that ancient healing traditions from many parts of the world also make use of what is translated into English as *energy*. In India there is *kundalini*, or serpent fire, an energy that circulates through the body, ascending from the bottom of the spine up to the top of the head and then descending again. Activating and maintaining the proper circulation of the kundalini ensures continued health and is also said to open up extraordinary powers within the individual. Japan has its *ki* or *qi* energy which somewhat corresponds to the Chinese *chi*. These energy flows are activated through body movements and can be balanced with traditional medicines such as acupuncture. The !Kung of the Kalahari make use of the boiling *Num* that is activated during their healing ceremonies.

The fact that concepts from the traditional medicine of several different cultures have been translated by this word *energy* does not necessarily mean that they are all equivalent, or identical to the *spirit* of Native American medicine and the *energy* of Western physics. Sometimes the distinction is deliberately made by speaking of "subtle energy."

Energy is experienced as a feeling of internal power and an underlying movement and transformation. It may also be connected with a meaning and integration within the body. Recently, Western medicine has begun to take the idea of subtle energy seriously; indeed an International Society for the Study of Subtle Energies and Energy Medicine has been established and boasts fifteen hundred subscribers. Although not part of the mainstream, some scientists have begun to study claims made by traditional medicines of the East as well as those made by Western healers who claim to be able to "balance energies" in the bodies. Most of their investigations involve attempts to measure energy flow or to correlate traditional practices with changes in neurotransmitters, metabolic function, and the immune system. Thus Western medicine is using the natural processes of the body as indicators of the functioning of something more subtle.

I have tried to gain some understanding of this field myself by attempting to discover correlations between ideas in Western physics and traditional medicine.* The human body is a complex interrelationship of biochemical processes, it contains flows of matter and energy, the passage of information along nerves and through the immune system. Health could be thought of as the coherent working of these complex properties; it is a constant dialogue within the body, a flow of meaning, and an interchange of information.

Many of the biochemical processes within the body involve exchanges of physical energy, but these grosser forms of energy are not what I take the terms *healing energy* or *subtle energy* to mean. Rather, the latter are like the activity of a conductor of an orchestra or the choreographer of a ballet, that integrates and coordinates into one cohesive movement all the biochemical and energy processes of the body. Seen in this way, death is not the cessation of biological function, for many of the cells in the body continue to function after death. It is, rather, the breakdown of this symphony of coherent meaning that differentiates a living individual from a mass of functioning cells.

Let me suggest a metaphor. In a candle flame individual atoms are heated and gain energy to the point where each can emit a photon of light. Throughout the flame individual atoms are emitting photons. The result is candlelight, but in itself it is a random, uncoordinated process and the illumination fades as it reaches the edges of the room.

Now take a laser, whose light is intense and penetrating. What happens in the laser is that energetic atoms, rather than emitting photons of light at random, all fire at the same moment. The result is a coherent burst of light with great penetrating power. The overall energy expenditure may be no

*See F. David Peat, "Towards a process theory of healing: energy, activity and global form," *Subtle Energies*, vol. 3 (1992): 1–40.

more than that in a candle, but by acting cooperatively within the laser the effect is enormous. What happens is that a wave of stimulation, or coordination, moves back and forth within the laser until all its atoms are coupled together. It is at this point of total coherence that the atoms simultaneously emit their photons of light.

Laser light is the manifestation of what could be thought of as a circulation of coordinating relationships, or of an activity of information that relates each atom to the whole. Something similar may operate within the healthy body, involving a circulation of meaning, an activity of information, and the movement of a global form that brings together all the cells, organs, and biological processes within a coherent whole. Thus, subtle energy is itself not so much the physical energy within the body, but rather it is the *form*, or pattern or activating potential that has been superimposed upon that energy.

Think of watching a film on your television set. The actual processes within the set itself are purely physical, energized by electricity that flows out of a plug on the wall. But the content of the program arrives as a very subtle electrical signal that, while its energy may be negligible, is filled with information. It is this information that acts within the television set to produce particular sound and pictures by modulating the "gross" energy supplied through the power plug.

Likewise, the subtle energy of the body may be important not so much as a material manifestation but in the way its information or "field of meaning" acts to orchestrate the body's functioning.

When you are faced with a daunting physical task you pull from somewhere within yourself the intention to act. You know an instant before you begin if you will be successful or not, for the result does not so much depend on your own physical strength as on the power of that inner will, that "energy" you feel within you. Just as within a laser a small energy can have a tremendous effect, so, too, by coordinating the body's forces one can, in an emergency, lift incredible weights or walk great distances. Likewise, when a people are filled with "spirit" they are able to do great tasks and overcome great obstacles.

Healing is the activation and renewal of spirit in the individual and the group. The operation of spirit may, in some way, be connected with that experience of power we all feel within ourselves, with recovery to health that sometimes comes about when we discover a new meaning to our lives, and with the way in which a small group of individuals can perform great tasks.

Subtle Matter

If energy can be expanded into the subtle domains of meaning and an activity of information, what then of matter? Is there, as Tibetan medicine suggests, a subtle body that corresponds to our own everyday physical body? And can cures of the physical body be affected by addressing its subtle counterpart?

Again, there are difficulties in moving between paradigms, worldviews, and languages. Our Western minds attempt to categorize and compartmentalize so that the subtle is distinguished from the manifest. It is interesting that the scientific revolutions of this century have all demonstrated the errors of such compartmentalization; thus, matter has been conjoined with energy, and space with time. My experience of Indigenous science has been that Native people do not differentiate and categorize in this way. It is not so much that there is a world of stones and trees and another one of spirits, powers, and energies, but rather that they are all one, and it is our particular human way of seeing, or the limitations to our seeing, that causes us to relevate* one particular aspect over the other.

To the Native healer, matter and energy, gross and subtle, spirit and manifest, may be the only verbal appearances that conceal the flux of the world.

---

*The word *relevate* (re-levate) was coined by the physicist David Bohm to sugest the act of bringing something into explicit manifestation or into conscious awareness from a deeper underlying flux. It seems descriptive of the way our minds and perceptions work.

With these reservations in mind, let us look at the concept of subtle matter from our Western perspective of homeopathy. While homeopathy is not part of conventional Western medicine it does have a tradition and a serious following in some European countries. Its philosophy goes back to Paracelsus' maxim of the early sixteenth century that "what makes a man ill also cures him."

Homeopathic procedures of diagnosis differ from those of more conventional Western medicine. The physician is not so much concerned with labels like *goiter, hypertension,* or *schizophrenia* as with the individual pattern of a person's life, his or her diet, personality, likes and dislikes, and pevious illnesses. Once this overall life story has been revealed, then, on the principle that "like treats like," preparations are administered that, when taken in higher concentrations by a healthy person, would produce all the symptoms associated with a particular sickness.

If the treatment is successful, the symptoms the patient originally complained of will begin to disappear. But since those symptoms are only part of a larger overall pattern, the physician may now expect to see others surface and increase in intensity. Using a sequence of homeopathic preparations the overall "cure" could take months or years to affect and is supposed to result in a person who is healthy in mind and body and filled with energy.

One difficulty Western medicine has with homeopathy is that, as the treatment progresses, the preparations become more effective when their dilutions are most extreme. Indeed, the practice of dilution with distilled water is continued to the point where there should theoretically be no active molecules present in the medicine that is being taken by the patient! The end result is a little like the bottle of tap water left by the Native medicine man. How could pure water possibly cure the illnesses of body and mind?

If homeopathy works in the way it claims, then nothing material brings about the cure. Could a form of subtle matter exist in the preparation? Some homeopaths have offed explanations. They suggest that the processes of progressive dilution and sercussion (repeatedly tapping the vial that holds the water onto a table top) introduce subtle information from the active molecules of the "medicine" into the water, information that is then conveyed into the patient's body.

Scientifically speaking, this is not altogether too farfetched. It may come as something of a surprise to most readers to learn that the most common of substances on our planet remains a considerable mystery. We know that water is made out of hydrogen and oxygen and that its building blocks are the molecules H_2O. But how are these molecules arranged together? It turns out that physical chemists cannot agree. They know that a weak force—called the hydrogen bond—attracts the oxygen atom on one water molecule to the hydrogen atom of another. This tends to make the molecules in water orient themselves. Some chemists theorize that this weak attractive force causes water molecules to congregate and form islands of order within liquid water—the overall effect is something like a collection of loosely bound crystals. Others suggest that water is not unlike a polymer, or even that the astronomical number of H_2O molecules in a glass of water order themselves in such a way as to create a single giant macromolecule.

If water does consist of a subtle but complex arrangement of a vast number of molecules, this means that information could indeed be "written into" water by very slightly changing the nature of this arrangement. Just as a Beethoven symphony can be "written onto" an audiocassette by changing the orientations of metal oxide molecules on the tape's surface, so, too, information could be "written into" water through subtle changes of global molecular arrangement. The processes of sercussion and successive dilution that go into the creation of a homeopathic remedy could transfer information from the active molecules in the preparation to the water in the form of, for example, subtle reorientations of its overall geometrical structure. Within the body this information might be "read" by the cells and used to bring about active changes in the whole body.

The more we think of the human body not as a machine, or a set of biological reactions but as the physical manifestation of fields of meaning and processes of information, the more we can be open to the presence of subtle levels of energy, matter, and spirit within healing.

The Implicate Order

Sa'ke'j Henderson opened up yet another aspect of the meaning of medicine when he told me that the plants, herbs, pieces of bone, feathers, and fur found in a medicine bag allow people to come into contact with a much wider reality that includes the various animating spirits within the world. He gave the example of a piece of bone from a particular animal that allowed a person to enter into relationship with the Keeper of that animal. On another occasion he explained how a certain gourd contained the whole world.

Here it is possible to make connections between Indigenous science and some recent ideas in Western science. In the 1960s the physicist David Bohm began to develop what he called the implicate (or enfolded) order. Bohm has argued that while the classical physics of Newton described what could be called the surface of reality, by contrast, quantum mechanics has forced us to move to deeper levels of perception of the world.

Bohm suggested that, in its deepest essence, reality, or "that which is," is not a collection of material objects in interaction but a process or a movement, which he calls the *holomovement*—the movement of the whole. This flowing movement throws out explicit forms that we recognize through our senses of sight, smell, hearing, taste, and touch. These explicate forms abide for a time and we take them as the direct evidence of a hard and fast reality. However, Bohm argues, this explicate order accounts for only a very small portion of reality; underlying it is a more extensive implicate, or enfolded, order. The stable forms we see around us are not primary in themselves but only the temporary unfolding of the underlying implicate order. To take rocks, trees, planets, or stars as the primary reality would be like assuming that the vortices in a river exist in their own right and are totally independent of the flowing river itself.

For Bohm, the gourd that Sa'ke'j Henderson carries is the explicate or surface manifestation of an underlying implicate order. Within that implicate order the gourd enfolds, and is enfolded by, the entire universe. Thus, within each object can be found the whole and, in turn, this whole exists within each of its parts.*

Song

It is not that difficult to become lost and confused when we venture into worlds of spirit, energy, subtle matter, dreams, and visions and leave behind our familiar territory and what can be held in the hand or grasped conceptually within the mind. But some things stretch across the gaps of culture and one of these is song.

A few years ago I was in San Francisco on the occasion of the launching of a Haida canoe. It was also an opportunity for Pam Colorado to gather several of her Native and non-Native friends together. Pam envisions a science that connects Indigenous peoples all over the world. In San Francisco we were to explore the nature of these connections and two Miwok spiritual leaders, Lannie and Ester, had been asked to conduct a healing ceremony for the circle. Lannie spoke of the Ones who had lived in the old times, of what they had experienced and of the wisdom that could be seen in their eyes. Then, as the Miwok healing song was sung, Lannie approached each person in the circle in a ceremony of healing.

Later that evening we heard one of the stories surrounding the song and its power to heal. As settlers spread out across the continent, traditional lands were claimed for farming, ranching, and mining, as well as for roads, railways, towns, and cities. As a result, many Indigenous peoples were brought to the point of extinction. In the case of the Miwoks things were made even worse by the fact that they were being hunted with guns.

So it was that the last group of survivors was tracked down and surrounded. As the Miwok people faced their executioners

---

*Some months before David Bohm died it was possible for him to meet with me and my Native friends Leroy Little Bear and Sa'ke'j Henderson. All of us were struck by the deep underlying similarities in their visions of the nature of reality.

they made a last request: Before they died they wished to sing their sacred healing song. As Lannie and Ester told us that while the song was being sung the guns were lowered and the posse turned away and rode off, leaving the Miwoks to survive and carry their songs into the future.

A year or two later I passed this story on to Therese Schroeder-Sheker, a harpist and singer who is using medieval music within a hospital setting for the dying. It evoked for Therese similar stories of the power of song, stories that come from all over the world. She told me how, during the Second World War, a group of rabbis had sung the Kaddish before their execution. She spoke of the shaming songs of Africa—when a man has raped or violated a woman, the women from the surrounding area, carrying their children, gather around this man's hut to sing their shaming song. There is no need to punish the offender, to have him arrested or put on trial; the women simply sing throughout the day and into the night until the man leaves the village and is never heard of again.

The more I have tried to learn about Indigenous science, the more I have heard of the power of songs. Songs come to us from another world, they have their own existence and power. Songs create and renew, they heal and make whole. I have heard people say how, when they arrive at a ceremony or enter a sweat lodge, they may not know the right songs, but as soon as the drumming begins the words enter into their minds without conscious effort.

There are other stories of how a song can be given in a dream or vision. In one case a man dreamed he was seated around a drum with some of the great singers of the past. In his dream one of the singers nodded to him, indicating that it was now time for him to sing. When he awoke the song remained with him and could be passed on to be used in a ceremony.

We would probably say that the song had been composed unconsciously and was the essential product of that individual, albeit from deeper areas within his mind. But this explanation is a projection of our own particular beliefs about the nature of reality and of our separateness and individuality. To others, a song has its own autonomous being apart from human minds and voices and, in exchange for something undefined, it can be given to the singer.

The song sings the singer. A famous Zen koan asks what is the sound of the tree that falls in the forest when no one is present to hear it. One could also ask what is the sound of a song when no one sings it.

Song is spirit. Song is being. Yet song is also a set of physical vibrations moving outward. Many traditional societies speak of the power of such vibrations to operate within the worlds of matter and spirit. Leroy Little Bear related to me how an Elder had told him about the four races—the blue, yellow, red, and white people—and how each one had a special task. It turned out that the blue people—what we call the black races—had been given the song, which he interpreted as being the song of creation.

In many cultures the primal act of creation begins with the word or the song whose vibrations animate the void. In the Sufi tradition, it is said that Allah brought all things into existence by calling out their names, thus, when the sacred names are pronounced one partakes in that primordial act. Mantras from India involve both the repetition of sacred names and the creation of highly specific vibrations that act within the mind-body to bring about transformation.

Sound, vibration, and song are believed by many to be the creative, generative forces within the cosmos. In those societies that understand time as a cycle, acts of creation must be renewed and the songs repeated again and again. Colin M. Turnbull, in his book, *The Forest People*, speaks of the African people sometimes referred to as pygmies and the significance of their music. In their ceremonies a sacred instrument is taken through the forest to make music. Blowing the instrument produces a variety of sounds that are similar to those heard in the forest itself—sounds of birds and animals. When Turnbull asked why the people did this they explained that it was to make the forest happy; for the forest looked after everything, the insects, the birds, and the people. If the forest slept, maybe it would forget about them, but if they sang to it and made music, then the forest would be happy, and the people would also be happy and not get sick.

When I mentioned this story to Leroy Little Bear, he pointed out that everything has its role to play, everything does what it must. The ants do their thing, the birds do theirs, and so, too, must the people—which is to sing to the forest. When all things act as they should, nature remains in balance.

Songs connect us to the world of dreams and to the visions in which healing can take place. As I understand it, for the Naskapi and the Montagnais of Labrador and northern Quebec, song is the central focus of healing. Again, the nature of this healing is very different from anything we understand in the West.

My friend Clem (Alan) Ford studies the Indigenous languages of northern Quebec and Labrador. One afternoon as I was visiting him I noticed the *Apparat Français et Montagnais,* a dictionary compiled in 1729 by a Jesuit priest, Le Père Lavre, lying on his desk. It is a very large book and by a curious synchronicity when I opened it the pages fell open to the phrase

HIPISKAPIGOKA IAGUSIT

which the priest had translated as *le jongleur chant un malade,* "the magician/sorcerer sings a sick man." I passed the book over to Clem, who explained that the translation was not really correct. To begin with, the missionaries of the early eighteenth century believed that all the ceremonies and traditional ways of The People were the work of the Devil. Hence the healer is described as *le jongleur,* the magician, for it was believed that his powers were a mixture of cheap conjuring tricks and deviltry. But really the mistranslation goes deeper, for it destorts the very thought processes of the Montagnais people.

The importance of the Montagnais phrase is that it is about a process; it is a verbal form that the translator had attempted to transform into our European noun-based, concept-dominated language system.

What is really happening is "singing"—the action, the process. The healer cannot really say that it is "he" who is singing, rather the process of singing is going on.

Within our Western worldview agents carry out actions, nouns/objects interact and bring about changes in each other.

The author of a process is a noun; an object and the verb is its action. But for the Montagnais reality is profoundly different; it is flux, process and change within which individual human beings are transitory forms; and manifest expression of temporary alliances of powers, spirits, and energies. Thus, no human can bring the song into existence. Rather, the singing itself is the primary reality, the vibrational process that floods across the world.

The image that began to emerge from that phrase was of a sick person and a healer, and a process of singing taking place. The singing is the primary reality, for it did not originate with either person, nor was the healing something that passed in a transitive way from one to the other. The singing sings itself. The healing heals.

In our Western hospitals healing is something that is done by the doctor and nurse to the patient. If Western doctors were to employ singing as a treatment, the doctor would sing to, or at, the sick person. But within Montagnais reality, healing is the animating principle within the spirit of the song.

This is reflected in another phrase from the same page of the *Apparat*:

MATUTICHIU-NIKAMU

which, while it is translated as "he sings in the sweat tent," is really again an expression of a pure process of singing. It is as if many nouns emerge out of the verbs, the object out of the process.

In a similar way, the Montagnais reality does not need nouns to describe snow, rain, heat, or cold, morning, afternoon, or night. Rather, there are verbs that express the processes of nature, a world of transformation and animation.

This idea of the song that sings opens up the ethical dimension of Native medicine. Within our society it is a high ideal to perform "good works," which can range from healing the sick to seeking ways to save the planet Earth. The ethical dimension of healing within an Indigenous society appears to be quite different. If a person is suffering or in pain one does not immediately enter his or her home to perform an act of healing, no more than one would without invitation seek to help or improve a person in some way.

Rather, a person only acts in response to being invited and, as with all such actions, a relationship must first be established through an exchange of some sort—tobacco or gifts. The result may be a healing that could, for example, involve sucking or blowing the sickness away. But, as far as I understand it, it is not so much the medicine person who does the healing in an active way; rather, it is the song, or the spirit within the medicine, or the relationship that moves in a circle of balance within the sick person, the medicine person, the plants and herbs, and all the powers of sky and earth.

In his book *Boiling Energy: Community Healing Among the Kalahari Kung* Dick Katz discusses the healing, through singing and dancing, of the !Kung of the Kalahari. During a long night of singing, dancing, and rapid shallow breathing a special energy called *num* is generated within the body that enables the dancers to enter the state of *kia*. It is while they are in this state that healing takes place. The business of healing is no easy matter, for the *num* can burn and harm the one who is healing. Thus it is important not only to heat up the *num* but, in certain cases, to cool it down and maintain it at the correct temperature. This means that the process of healing cannot be done by a lone individual, for rather all the dancers in the group must support the healer and help control the temperature of his or her *num*. Healing involves sacrifice and personal danger and can only be achieved through the sanction of the whole group.

When the *num* is boiling, the healer is given special powers to see into the nature of disease and to cure. In this state, called *kia*, he or she may also see over great distances and exercise other special powers. Entering *kia* brings with it pain and fear. Indeed, the state is described as death—and Dick Katz is quick to point out that by death the !Kung do not mean what in our terms would correspond to an ego-death or psychological death but an actual process of death, and later rebirth, with all the fear, pain, and disorientation that this implies. While in a state of *kia* the healer himself is sick and in great danger, so that the healing process itself must involve the whole group. Indeed, the healing ceremony itself is called *num chxi*, that word *chxi* implying a gathering together to sing and to dance.

Healing for the !Kung is a community matter, something that arises out of the group as a whole, and, while the *num* may be focused into the body of certain individuals, responsibility still lies with the people as a whole. It is important to emphasize this point because many non-Native people are drawn to exotic powers and abilities evoked through altered states of consciousness. But, as Dick explained to me, it is no very special thing to change your consciousness; peoples all over the world have developed well-defined techniques for doing this. What really matters is not the altered state itself, or the special powers, but the ethical dimension—what you do with it and how you act. In an Indigenous context this always means responsibility to the group and relationship to all of nature.

Dick Katz has also told me about the feeling of "a good healing" which is shared by the !Kung and by Indigenous peoples the world over. After a night of singing and dancing people will know that something very powerful has happened, that a good healing has taken place. It may turn out that a person who has experienced this healing power is still left with an illness or body defect, but the illness of the body is not as significant as the sense of wholeness and relationship that the healing produces.

Cluniac Alchemy

Song provides a way of linking the Western healing tradition to that of Native America. In the tenth century the monks of Cluny, France, began to develop Europe's first infirmary practice. Their healing was based upon two sources, plants and song, and it is this latter practice that has been revived by the harpist Therese Schroeder-Sheker and her Chalice of Repose Project at St. Patrick Hospital in Missoula, Montana.

The Cluniac philosophy is in many ways similar to that of traditional healing. Therese is very careful, for example, to dissociate herself from such titles as "healer" or "music therapist," nor does she speak of having a special ability to heal. Rather, as with Native medicine people, she will only attend when specifically invited into the room and once there will allow the music to do its work.

When a Cluniac monk felt that the hour of his death was approaching he would inform the abbot and meet with his brothers for leave-taking. The monks, in turn, aided his process of dying by chanting a prescribed series of musical modes. Using voice and harp, Therese has continued this practice with many thousands of dying patients. The process is described as "anointing with sound." Two harpists weave a web of sound substance across the body of the patient, actively responding to changes in skin pallor and other vital signs. Sometimes, when a dying person is in a deep coma, the output from the electronic monitors of her respiration, heartbeat, and blood pressure shows that she is responding to the music. Other patients in severe pain may be removed from a morphine intravenous to die painlessly and in clarity of mind. For Therese, the skin of the entire body is an ear through which musical vibrations enter and do their work.

To the monks, death was such a natural, though marvelous process, that they used the metaphor of birth to describe it, and the musical practice as "sacred midwifery." The monks also employed the imagery and language of alchemy to describe the way in which music acts to loosen the series of attachments within a person and so allow him to move though the processes of death. Just as in alchemy the repeated processes of sublimation, distillation and condensation, dissolution and recrystalization bring about purification and the separation of the subtle from the gross, so, too, tonal substance works its alchemy within the body to free the spirit from matter and allow its rebirth in a more subtle realm.

Indigenous people consider songs to be living beings, as does Therese, for whom each musical mode is a being in its own right. When she first learned about the tenth-century tradition Therese felt that she was being introduced to each of the particular musical modes and in the process, being given an authorization to use them. In certain cases this sense of relationship, or authorization, did not come and for this reason she will not play those particular modes.*

What is particularly exciting about Therese's work is the way in which an ancient tradition that makes use of alchemical imagery works hand in hand with modern medicine and how the subtle changes brought about by music can be recorded by modern technology. For Therese, there is nothing incompatible in the old and new working together, provided that this is done with respect and sensitivity. This suggests that worldviews and paradigms can indeed be transcended and Western and Indigenous medicine can support and learn from each other.

Anger and Transformation

When Native and non-Native people sit together for the first time anger and pain are not far away. As a Native person relates the story of his life or his people there is often an anger in the heart toward a society that could have done such things. The presence of white people in the room evokes oppressive memories and, in turn, it is extremely difficult for non-Native listeners to maintain their own equilibrium while listening to such a story. Anger, guilt, resentment, rejection, and aggression begin to surface. Yet so often it is out of this emotional chaos that a healing begins, for as people begin to relate at the level of the heart they discover their common humanity. All of us have families; we have watched a child in pain or sickness, have known the stomach-tightening fear when the future of a loved one is threatened. Each of us has the potential for friendship and forgiveness, not only of the other but also of ourselves.

---

*For the past few hundred years (until the advent of Schoenberg and atonality) Western music was composed of key signatures, related to scales. Such music has a tonal center and makes use of the tension and resolution that is created in moving away from and toward this tonal center. Earlier music, from the time of the Greeks until the Middle Ages, employed modes that, while they are also sequences of notes arranged in ascending or descending order, do not hve this same sense of a tonal center. Such music often has a timeless, eternal quality.

In so many instances the spiritual and political leaders of The People have passed through a dark night of drug abuse, alcohol, and prison. The wheel balances and the darkest shadows are created by the brightest light. Healing wells up out of the pain and fragmentation of our lives.

The previous chapter dealt with the waves of disease that destroyed between 90 to 95 percent of the original population of the Americas. In its wake came further assaults. People were moved from their traditional territories and their land was converted to other uses. In many cases this was accompanied by warfare, in others the weapons were alcohol and appropriation. Behind it all was a deliberate policy designed to break down resistance through the systematic destruction of a culture.

One of the most effective ways to dismantle the order of a society is to cut off its children from their roots. I have often heard Native people speak of their experiences in the residential school system, a particularly effective system of social genocide. In most cases this extinction began with children being removed from their families, sometimes by the use of force. The children's first experience of school consisted of being stripped, having their clothing burned, their hair doused in kerosene, and, in the case of boys, their heads shaved. The schools forbade children to practice their traditional ways, which included prayer, and they were beaten for speaking their own language. In so many cases excessive physical abuse on the part of the staff was coupled with the sexual abuse of both boys and girls. Today, many of these abused children have grown up to become community leaders, Elders, and faith carriers; others are alcoholics or abusers of their own spouses and children. But, in one way or another, all of them bear the scars of that terrible treatment.

Residential schools may now be closed but discrimination continues. At a conference of the Administration of Justice for Native Canadians, held in Banff, Alberta, in 1991, I heard that within that province, 75 percent of adult Native people have been arrested at some time or another; when brought to court, 86 percent of them will plead guilty, and 98 percent of them will be found guilty, figures excessively higher than for any other group. The extremely high rate of convictions and guilty pleas indicate that these are a people who are being exploited by all aspects of the justice system, including those lawyers who, working on legal aid, maximize their profits with a quick turnover of clients.* Alberta Natives joke that they are the best employers in the province, for without them, most police, lawyers, courts, parole officers, and social workers would be out of work.

The Renewal of Spirit

Indigenous societies cohere and have their being through the power of spirit. It is the source of their existence, the meaning that lives within them, and the balance they must maintain throughout the circles of time. In turn, this spirit is a part of the land the people occupy and care for. The traumas of forcible displacement and the requisitioning of lands, the disruption of traditional ways and forms of governance, the importation of alcohol and drugs, the loss of language, and the education of children in an alien world have all contributed to a breaking apart of society and a fragmentation of its meaning. Spirit departs and the relationships with the powers, energies, and Keepers of the land are weakened. Without them the people will die.

It is here that healing must begin, a healing that brings back the spirit and renews the people. Miraculously this

---

*As I understand it, these lawyers are paid by the state or province at a fixed daily or hourly rate that would be less than they could obtain from private clients. Thus, while they cannot make too much out of a prolonged case, they will do better by having a very fast turnover of clients and cases. Simply spending a few minutes with each client and then entering a plea of guilty to a lesser charge, the lawyer will take his fee, discharge the case, and not even have to bother to study the papers involved. Lawyers I have spoken to point out the very high rate of guilty pleas among Native people and have suggested to me that in many cases if they had chosen to fight the case they would probably have been found not guilty or would have received a noncustodial sentence. In most cases, Native people are cynical about the justice system, for they become pawns in an alien legal process and may not even be fluent in the English used in the courts.

healing still works, despite all that has occurred over the last five hundred years. It takes us beyond specific sicknesses in the body and into the healing of spirit, society, and the planet itself. Healing also comes when Natives and non-Natives sit in a circle to listen to each other. Healing begins when we reach down into ourselves and understand the narrowness of our own perspectives and lives, show respect for another way of life, and are willing to learn from it.

Sacred Mathematics

Introduction

Sacred mathematics—the very term seems magical, with its evocation of hidden knowledge and the secrets of long-lost civilizations. Sacred mathematics and sacred geometry speak to us of a wisdom veiled from our own age, of practices that, to use the original meanings of these words, are hermetic, esoteric, and occult.

We picture the Pythagorean brotherhood of ancient Greece; the numerology of the cabala; the twelfth-century Masons who concealed within the construction of the great cathedral of Notre Dame at Chartres a wealth of numerical and geometric symbolism; the preoccupation of the artists of the Renaissance with the connections between nature, mathematics, geometry, and perspective; and Kepler's discovery that the numerical relationships between musical intervals are mirrored within the order of the solar system as the harmonies of the celestial spheres. Today the same sacred mathematics is alive in the Americas where it occupies a key place in the lives and ceremonies of many of the First Peoples of Turtle Island.

Number and Control

Sacred mathematics is a living form, a manifestation of energy, spirit, and mystery. This may at first sight seem strange to us, for within our society numbers have come, in the popular mind, to be associated with static and abstract things. To mathematicians, however, number is a door that opens into the farthest reaches of the human imagination.

For most people the dehumanizing role of number has become overemphasized. We have a Social Security number, a telephone number, a driver's license number, numbers for our bank accounts and credit cards, and other number codes we use to gain electronic access to our accounts. The stories of our lives can be found on educational, tax, banking, employment, and medical records, all identified as a series of numbers on a computer network. Some may feel that we are close to that nightmare world predicted by the science fiction writers. In Eugene Zamiatin's novel *We*, the citizens of the future have all been reduced to ciphers. In the 1960s cult television series *The Prisoner*, each episode began with the hero (played by Patrick McGoohan), being addressed as Number 6, and protesting "I am not a number, I am a free man." This same policy of stripping away the personality by the use of a number is one of the first disorienting shocks a person experiences when being confined to a prison or inducted into the armed forces.

The scientist or mathematician is sometimes portrayed as a wounded schizoid character who flees the world of emotion and insecurity into an abstract universe of number and certainty. Bertrand Russell said in his autobiography that he turned to mathematics as a young man because: "I wanted certainty in the kind of way in which people want religious faith. I thought that certainty is more likely to be found in mathematics than elsewhere." In the end Russell was to discover that deep within the foundations of mathematics there can be no certainty, "I set out with a more or less religious belief in a Platonic eternal world, in which mathematics alone shone with a beauty like that of the last cantos of the *Paradiso*. I came to the conclusion that the eternal world is trivial, and that mathematics is only the art of saying the same thing in different words."

Sacred Number

Within Native America, number is seen in a profoundly different way; not as dry, abstract, and dehumanizing, but as alive, real, and immediate. mathematics is a sacred practice related to the dynamics of the whole cosmos. Through the meaning and manipulation of number many Indigenous people maintain balance and harmony within the ever-changing world of flux, energies, and transformation.

For aboriginal peoples all over the world, as well as for many ancient civilizations, number and mathematics have always played a special role. Sometimes its importance is so high that number may not be used for secular or commercial purposes since its symbolic representations are reserved for sacred ceremonies and the great cycles of time and the gods. Numbers are symbols and manifestations of the transformations, dynamics, and cycles within the world of nature and spirit. Numbers are the manifestations of beings.

Indigenous Number

All over Turtle Island numbers and other symbols can be found inscribed on sacred rocks. Some of these have been photographed and studied by archaeologists, but many others are known only to Native people. Rocks may be deliberately left covered with moss and vegetation and only exposed during special ceremonies or teachings when the rocks are to be read. Tom Porter, a traditional Mohawk, said that he would approach such rocks in a special way by praying and offering sacred tobacco. If the spirit of that rock wished to speak to him and shake hands with him, then that would be good. Thus the voice of the rock heard by a traditional person will be very different from what is read by a non-Native.

Western scientists who study petroglyphs (writings and markings on rocks) have observed, in addition to hieroglyphs and picture writing, series of lines, or holes, sometimes inscribed in rows, that are referred to as "tally marks." The sequence of marks, they say, is evidence of a numerical representation that may have been used, for example, to count game. Other rocks display what they believe are the records of astronomical observations, such as the number of nights between each new moon.

At one level rock markings refer to number and computation, but their significance may go far beyond records of days and months or the numbers of game that have been killed.

Since they were a sacred subject Tom Porter did not say much about the markings, but when I spoke to him he did convey the sense that these markings can be read as a map, or as a journey though life. As an analogy, he pictured someone driving from New York to Los Angeles. Such a person does not need to know the detailed geography of the United States, simply the particular highways that must be taken for that journey and the changes that must be made at intersections. The tally marks made on stone can also be read in this way; they refer to a journey, but a journey that goes beyond that of a single individual and one that is connected in some way with the land, The People, and the cosmos.

Numbers, tally marks, and writing are also inscribed upon the sticks used by many different peoples, such as the Condolence Cane of the Iroquois or the Walking Stick of the Mic Maq. The Iroquois speak of a stick that is associated with each person at birth. This stick contains the map of a person's life and the number of its days and can only be seen by the creator.

Number and Chance

The world is flux. Nothing lasts forever. Whenever we have made our plans and laid down the path of our future the trickster will come along and play a trick on us. The celebration of chance, through gambling, becomes important to Native people. But gambling is not simply a "game"—in our sense of the word as entertainment or diversion—but a sacred ceremony that acknowledges the basic metaphysics of the cosmos, including the power of the trickster and other spirits. The Mohawks have the Peach Stone Game that must be played before corn is planted, the Mic Maqs have the game Waltestaqaney. These are played on behalf of the whole society and may, for example, act to renew the compacts and alliances made with the spirits of the universe.

Playing gambling games and creating their rules implies that such people have a knowledge of the laws of probability and are able to compute the odds of various outcomes. A role taken during such games is that of the tally keeper, who must not only carry out rapid mental arithmetic but must have devised a method of recording the tally of points. Tally keepers were also required on the Northwest coast where, during the Potlatch, records of the exchanges of copper and other very valuable gifts were kept.

Sacred Architecture

The sciences of geometry, surveying, computation, and number representation were all involved in the architecture of traditional buildings and in the construction of temples and earth works. The Hopewell people, whose culture flourished from around 1000 B.C. to A.D 500, and who may be the distant ancestors of the present-day Iroquois, must have practiced sophisticated surveying skills to have been able to build their elaborate mounds and earthworks.

The buildings and temples of the lost Anasazi people of the Chaco Canyon were aligned astronomically with the position of the rising sun on certain days of the year. What is particularly striking is that in some locations the horizon cannot be seen because of an intervening hill or building—nevertheless the walls of the building are aligned, not with where the sun happens to be first seen at that location, but with *where it would be seen if there was nothing obscuring the view*!

In many other cases architecture is tied to cosmology and special directions. The traditional longhouse of the Haudenosaunee is made in the likeness of the cosmos, its curved roof representing the sky and its floor Mother Earth. Likewise, the orientation of the building ensures that its two openings meet the rising and the setting sun at a certain time of the year. The buildings of many other peoples also have doors or windows that open out onto some astronomical event, or that channel light onto a wall or marking. The ability to place an opening so that it will be aligned with the rising sun at the solstice or equinox, or with some other event, clearly implies the ability to predict and calculate the location of these events in the sky. Indeed, the design of a building represents a perfect integration of mathematics, astronomy, surveying, and architecture.

In celebrating these triumphs of Indigenous mathematics one should not forget that the astronomers and mathematicians involved may not necessarily have been men. It is so easy to be blinded by our own history of Western science and technology to assume that the leaders of scientific evolution must always be male. A story told to me by the University of Ottawa ethnomathematician Michael Closs illustrates how easily we can jump to assumptions.

Some time ago balls of string were discovered by anthropologists on the Northwest Coast. When they were unraveled they were found to contain long knotted strands to which pieces of cloth had been tied at periodic intervals. The anthropologists quickly figured out that the knots represented days and that the regularities of the pieces of cloth at every twenty-eight days represented the appearance of a new moon. Clearly these strings were astronomical records, the "lab books" left by the Indigenous astronomer-mathematicians of the West Coast.

This account was generally accepted until someone noted that these balls of string were usually kept by women. Suddenly the penny dropped—the regular markings were not recording the phases of the moon, but a woman's menstrual cycle. And so one interpretation was replaced by another.

In an Indigenous community a woman's period is described as her "moon." It is a time of great power, when a woman will be very careful of the medicine and the sacred objects that she touches, for during her moon her own spirit can overwhelm everything with which she comes in contact. In a culture in which everything connects and is related, it is no coincidence that the knots in a string refer both to the cycles of power and fertility within a woman's body and to the waxing and waning of the moon. Indeed, each is a reflection of the other, and it could well be that women first began to study and represent the harmonies and regularities of cosmic and human cycles. For the interrelationships of the cosmos are expressed through the periodicity of heavens, earth, and the human body.

Number Systems

Algonquian, Siouan, and Iroquoian people use a base-ten system as we do, while the ancient Mayan practice of counting by twenties is still preserved in Central America, in parts of California, and by the Inuit people.

The basis of these number systems is reflected within language. In English our use of the base-ten system of counting is shown by the way we reuse the numbers one, two, three, etc., as we reach thirty, forty, fifty, sixty and so on. Thus, after twenty-nine we go to thirty and begin counting again with thirty-one, thirty two and so on. On the other hand, counting by twenties was practiced by the Celtic people of Europe, just as it was by the Mayans and Olmecs. Its remnants still survive in the Biblical-sounding phrase "three score years and ten" for seventy, or in French *quatre-vingt* (four twenties) for eighty.

Words for numbers indicate the way a people counts. In many cases they show that counting began with the hand. How natural it is to represent numbers as the fingers of one hand as do the Zuni:

1. *topinte* "taken to start with"
2. *kwilli* "that (finger) put down with its like"
3. "adding one more finger"
4. *awite* "all (of the fingers) all but done with"
5. *opte* "the cut off"

Following the five one moves to the other hand with:

6. *topalikya* "another brought to add with"

and so on to

10. *astemthal* "all of the fingers."

If you begin counting on the fingers of the left hand and continue onto the right, it is natural to refer to the number seven as being the index finger of the right hand. Thus, the Yurok refer to seven as *tserucek* or "pointer," while eight, identified with the middle finger, is *knewetek* or "long one."

At the number ten, one has completed counting on the fingers, and thus the southern Wintun refer to ten as *pampa-sempta* or "two hands" and the Maidu refer to it as as *ma-tsoko*, or "hand doubled."

Following ten one can begin all over again, or continue, using the toes. Thus, the Unalit people of the Arctic refer to eleven as *atkahakhtok,* "it goes down," and sixteen, which they begin to count on the other foot, as *qukhtok.* Finally, when counting is completed with all the toes and the fingers, some peoples refer to this number twenty as "one person."

In some languages a particular number does not have a word of its own, but is formed by addition or multiplication. Thus in Crow the number ten is expressed as two (*upa*) and eight (*pirake*), i.e., as *nupa-pik;* while in Kutchin the number six is expressed as *neckh-kiethei* (which is two (nakhai) multiplied by three (kietheir). Likewise, the number eight is expressed as two times four.

The fact that number words occur in a language means that counting and other mathematical operations must have been used in the culture over a very long period—often these words are quite short, indicating that they have a very ancient use. (In most languages the shortest words generally tend to be the oldest, longer words having been created at a later date in a compound way.)

So far we have only seen the smaller numbers that can be arrived at by counting on fingers and toes. Counting can go on indefinitely and some languages are able to accommodate extremely large numbers. The Ojibwaj people, for example, represent one million as *me-das-wac da-sing me-das-wac me datching me-das-wac me-das-wac.* It is also referred to as *ke-che me-das-wac* or the "great thousand." Indeed, just as we in English can speak of ten million, one hundred million, and one billion (or one thousand million in the British Isles), so, too, the Ojibwaj language is able to vocalize numbers.

What is particularly impressive about having words for such things as one billion is that the human mind, and human language, are referring to what lies outside the realm of direct sensual experience. While it is abstractly possible for the mind to generate the number one billion through mathematical operations it is not possible to appreciate the nature of this number directly. Yet, because so many things within Indigenous science are based upon experience one wonders what use these numbers could have been put to. If they were not experienced through references to things within the physical domain of nature possibly they may have had some cosmological correspondence, or connection to the world of processes, spirits and energy.

The Four Directions and the Teachings of the Hoop

Numbers are contained within the languages of Turtle Island as well as being represented as marks, notches, and symbols on rocks, canes, knots on a string, or fragments of shell on a wampum belt. But there is far more to number than its representation. While to us number can be thought of as quantity without quality, to The People each number possesses a quality and a spirit of its own. In this case Indigenous mathematics goes further than the mathematics of the West, for its number celebrates, acknowledges, and mirrors the animating and transformative processes that go on in the world of spirit and nature.

Let us begin this exploration of the deeper nature of number in sacred mathematics with the number four. As far as I know, all over Turtle Island this number expresses, on the one hand, a state of balance and harmony, and, on the other, a dynamic movement of spiritual forces within the cyclical nature of time.

For most Western mathematicians, the heart of their topic lies in abstraction. But in seeking to understand sacred mathematics we should never forget the great principle of Indigenous science, that it is based on both traditional knowledge and direct experience, which includes the whole world of dreams, visions, spirits, and powers. Within sacred mathematics, a number is never abstracted from the animating spirit that gives it life, nor from the concrete situations in which it is used.

The number four is not an abstraction that stands on its own without reference to any process or object in the world of spirit and nature. The number four is the Four Directions and the Four Winds. It is embodied within powerful concrete devices, images, or algorithms—call them what you will—such as the medicine wheel and the sacred hoop. The number four is a spirit and its various representations are manifestations of the dynamics of the cosmos that are animated by that spirit.

The great teachings of the People from all over Turtle Island can be found within the sacred hoop of the number four. In their Thanksgiving Address the Mohawk people acknowledge the Four Winds that come from the Four Directions and bring strength to the people and rain to the earth. Through the activity of the Four Winds the cycles of the seasons are manifest upon the earth. And so the Four Winds are the animating powers or spirits or energies that bring about maturity, continuation, renewal, and refreshment.

The Four Directions are pictured as spokes on the medicine wheel and refer not only to the transformation of the seasons but also to the movement from birth to death; to health and of healing; to the dynamics of the individual psyche; to the concept of justice; to the meaning of the sacred colors; to the history of a group; to the tasks that must be carried out by the different peoples of the earth, and to a host of other teachings. Again and again one sees that, from the perspective of Indigenous science, sacred number is not abstract but concrete and experiential: The spirit of each number unfolds into an interlocking multiplicity of different meanings and teachings.

But what are the Four Directions? At one level they could be compared with the four points of the compass, east, south, west and north, but they are also the directions of the Four Winds, and they are associated with the spirits or energies that can be found in each of these directions. They are also the sacred colors.

Sacred mathematics is not a branch of knowledge or a particular discipline that can be taught separately from other subjects and disciplines. The famous mathematician John von Neumann said that mathematics is the relation of relationships. The whole notion of relationship is central to Indigenous science. While we in the West place emphasis upon objects and categories, the Native mind deals with process and relations of relationship. The Mohawk language, for example, is rich in the various terms it employs for human relationship.

My Mohawk friends tell me that their language contains over 120 terms to express family relationships. To speak

Mohawk is to enter into a web of interconnections to family, relatives, and clan that are the Mohawk people. Their language itself stresses the complexity of relationship and this also is the basis of mathematics.

Number and Spirit

Although we in the West use numbers every day we may never have actually sat down to think what number really means to a mathematician. Writing in James R. Newman's famous four volume collection, *The World of Mathematics*, the philosopher Bertrand Russell offered the following definition for number: "A number is anything which is the number of some class."

This may not be of too much help to the philosophically uninitiated, indeed it may sound a bit like a circular definition. Russell offers a further definition: "The number of a class is the class of all those classes that are similar to it."

Let us not bother too much about the details of this definition; the thing to be taken from it is that numbers are seen as concepts within a worldview whose language is based in nouns; a worldview that deals in the concepts of classes, or collections, of objects. While numbers cannot be held in the hand, they are abstractions that can be grasped in the mind; they are the objects of thought that can be manipulated and moved around in a mental universe.

To the mathematician and scientist these mental objects exist through their interrelationships of addition, subtraction, multiplication, and division. Otherwise they are without quality, and when we speak of them as "having value" we mean this only in the quantitative sense and not as referring to any intrinsic spiritual or moral value.

Within Indigenous science, number is a being—a living entity immersed in flux. To enter the world of numbers and sacred mathematics is not an act of abstraction but a sacred process. To understand the transformations of number, for example, is to seek a relationship with the dynamic processes of energies and spirits. This was once true within our own Western culture as well. Number was sacred to the Pythagorean brotherhood of ancient Greece, it lies close to art and poetry and to the world of enfolded metaphors and numinous symbols, and, for some mathematicians, its sacred qualities remain.

Number and Balance

An insight into the sacred nature of number and its transformations can be gained by further considering the number four and its representation as the spokes of a medicine wheel, or in the sacred hoop. In many of the world's cultures four is both the symbol of balance and harmony, and of process and movement. Early medicine in the West spoke of the four temperaments and four humors, and science pictured matter as an equilibrium of four elements.

The psychologist Carl Jung made a study of symbols whose power transcended the particularities of individual cultures. Again and again he returned to the number four as the intersection of vertical and horizontal, the four-fold division of the sacred hoop.

Jung believed that the human psyche was a dynamic process involving four forces, or psychological functions. One of these was called the thinking function and Jung pictured this as occupying one side of a duality in opposition to the feeling function. Likewise the sensate function of the psyche was seen as being at the opposite end of the spectrum from that of intuition.

Jung imagined the psyche as being structured in a way that is similar to that of the sacred hoop, with the four psychological functions lying along the sacred directions. Ideally, the human psyche should occupy a point of balance within the center of the hoop, but most of us live out of balance. A person who approaches different events, including human relationships, only in a rational, logical way can be seen as living from the thinking function, having consigned the feeling function to the shadow world. Eventually this undeveloped and undifferentiated feeling function will begin to exert its subversive power on the personality.

We generally first approach life's decisions through the thinking function, by considering the pros and cons and analyzing the situation, but the final decision is usually based upon the feeling function, that is, upon a general sense, or gut feeling, of what would be the right thing to do. But a person with an inferior feeling function may arrive at a purely logical decision without having an underlying sense of conviction of the essential rightness of his or course of action.

Conversely, a person with an inferior thinking function may, with great conviction, take an important step in life without having a proper understanding of the implications involved. Such a person invests this new phase of life with great energy, only to encounter unforeseen difficulties and practical obstacles.

A person with an overdeveloped psychological function is not centered within the circle of his or her personality and is in danger of being flooded and overwhelmed with the undifferentiated energies of the inferior functions. Clearly the health of the personality depends upon reaching a balance with all four functions. It involves moving to the center of the circle and being at that point of balance within the four functions through what Carl Jung called the process of individuation.

For Jung, the number four was the essence of balance and harmony. In this respect his observations are not far from the traditional Native American teachings of the medicine wheel in which a person or a society seeks to respond to the dynamic movements of the wheel in order to maintain a state of harmony within the flux of the world.

The connection of the four directions to the sacred hoop and to the central point of harmony and balance can be approached through a variety of images. It is the human being standing in the center of the bowl of heaven. It is the central point of the observer within the circle of the horizon. It is the fire in the center of the tepee. It is the center within the council circle.

The four points of the hoop can be thought of as the

different poles of two sets of dualities while, at the center, is the resolution of all conflict and duality. Thus the number four is created out of the opposition of dualities and resolved within unity. The dualities themselves can be pictured as the vertical movement of gravity set against the horizon of the world, or as the vertical movement of energy along the spine of the human body and its extension outward into the fingertips. It is the tree of the world that rises vertically out of the earth; it is the cottonwood tree of the Sun Dance; it is the human being who stands at the central point of connection between the Sky World and the world of Mother Earth; and it is the domain of physical experience that extends horizontally outward from this point.

The connection between balance, harmony, and equilibrium contained within the number four is also found within the world of Western physics. This can be illustrated by the example of a stool whose legs serve as an example of the movement toward harmony. It is not difficult for an amateur carpenter to make a serviceable three-legged stool, for as soon as you set it on the floor it will be in balance. Even when its three legs are not exactly the same length the stool will not rock and, even if the floor is uneven, it will be balanced.

To the mathematician this is no surprise, for: Three points define a plane. Mark two points anywhere on a piece of paper and it is always possible to draw a single, unique line through them. As the mathematician would say, "Two points define a line."

Put down three points in space, and (with the exception of the special case in which they are in line) the third point will *not* lie on a line. What these three points do is define a plane. One could take a card and maneuver it until it would just touch each of these three points. In this way a flat surface, a two-dimensional plane can be uniquely defined by only three points. No other flat surface, angled to the first, will exactly touch these three points.

Back to the stool. The tips of its legs can be thought of as three points; these three tips define a unique plane or flat surface—it is this same flat surface upon which the stool sits! It is a fundamental fact in mathematics that it is always possible to put down a three-legged stool so that the tip of each leg just touches the floor. Moreover, this is a unique result, for no other plane will touch the three tips of the legs. This means that there is only one single orientation of balance, no other orientation is possible. If there were, for example, two different planes, or flat surfaces, then the stool could wobble between them. No matter if the lengths of the legs differ, the stool will always rest on the floor without rocking.

Now add a fourth leg and the whole picture changes; for equilibrium is lost. If you put four points in space it is not generally possible to have a of card touch all of them; one will always be outside the plane. We can arrange the flat paper so that it touches any three of the four points, but not all four at the same time. So it is with our four-legged chair. Any three of the legs will define a perfectly flat plane where the chair is in balance; the fourth leg will either be too long or too short. And this means that there will be different orientations for the chair in which three of the tips touch the floor while the fourth remains in the air. When you sit on the chair you wobble between these different balance points.

This example demonstrates that the very sensitive and difficult process of achieving balance is a fundamental property of space, the universe, and the number four. Since four legs will not, in general, balance, the act of coming to balance means that we must carefully adjust the length of the legs until a unique plane is defined. In the old cartoon, the carpenter shaves a little wood off one of the legs, only to find that another leg has now become too long and so on. Achieving a final balance involves a dynamic process of constant adjustment.

The four-legged stool serves as a simple metaphor for the way in which a series of adjustments must be made in order to achieve balance through the number four. For, while in the case of a three-legged stool whatever wood we shave off from one leg is done quite independently of the other two, when it comes to the four-legged stool any adjustment to the length of one leg must always be made with reference to the lengths of the others.

For a stool, coming to balance is a holistic, integrating process, for any change in the length of one leg must involve all four legs. Likewise, for a person, or a group, or an environment, to come into harmony involves a cooperative working in all the four directions. Coming to balance is a process of renewal in which movement in one direction immediately connects all others. There is no individual who is apart from the group, no group that is independent of nature, for as we attempt to change ourselves in one direction we affect an overall change in the whole.

All this is contained in the number four.

And more.

Number and Change

Number, as defined by Bertrand Russell, is static, an object within the mind. But as we have seen from the teachings of the sacred hoop, the number four involves the movement of "coming to balance." Four is a dynamic process in which equilibrium must be constantly renewed.

Within Indigenous science the number four is not a thing, it is not a mental abstraction, but a living spirit; likewise the sacred hoop is not a static diagram on a piece of paper, but an unfolding process. The hoop is a movement in which each of the sacred directions gives way to the other, for it is always in rotation. And so within the number four stands each of the sacred directions, each one being also a point of arrival and of departure. Each number, therefore, also contains its neighbor—for it gives birth to it and dies away from it.

Numbers are in a constant state of transformation and becoming. They are the symbolic manifestation of the alliances that exist between the different powerful spirits and energies of nature.

The center is the point of balance within the medicine wheel; it is the person on the mountaintop who stands at the center of the bowl of the earth; it is the fire at the center of the tepee; it is that point that both participates in the rotation of the cosmos, and yet, being above it, also stands still. In the language of Carl Jung and his friend the physicist Wolfgang Pauli, the center is the *speculum*, the mystical mirror that stands between two worlds and reflects each into the other, yet belongs to neither.

What is this center? It is the process of completion that

leads beyond the fourth. It is the fifth direction—the number five. Yet the center is also the first number, the self, the I, the number one. At the center of the medicine wheel a person will find him or herself, for it is here that they come into balance at the one. Within a traditional ceremony a person acknowledges the four directions and this acknowledgment becomes the fifth direction.

The essential processes of sacred mathematics lie beyond our Western operations of addition and subtraction. Number is dynamic, it is a process in which the number five is born out of the acknowledgment of the number four, and is at the same time the origin of that four. Five is contained within four, it is born out of four, yet five is greater than four since it contains the four. And so the four directions are five.

This aspect of sacred mathematics can be seen within the sacred pipe ceremony, in which, as the pipe is passed from person to person, its bowl is held at the stationary fifth point while its stem is rotated to acknowledge the four directions. Yet that same static point itself participates in a greater movement as the pipe is passed from person to person around the circle of smokers whose center is the sacred fire—and so the fifth point is in a rotation that returns to its starting point.

In that same ceremony the pipe carrier acknowledges Mother Earth and the sky. The ceremony begins at the center, in the heart, the number one that is also the number five. Out of this five are acknowledged the four directions and through them Mother Earth and the sky. So out of the one and the five, the four directions become six (north, south, east, west, up, and down). Returning to the center this six becomes seven. The dynamics of the sacred numbers are constantly rotating, unfolding one out of the other, folding back into each other. Each number is a starting point and an ending point. Number is no longer an abstract object, it is a process, a dynamic, a moving alliance of spirit and energy. In mathematical terms Indigenous numbers act as an algebra.

Number and the Implicate Order

In the previous chapter David Bohm's idea of the implicate order was introduced as a metaphor for understanding reality within Indigenous science. Bohm argued that discoveries at the subatomic level suggest that the quantum world is much closer to the implicate order than it is to the explicate. The mathematical formalism used in quantum theory, however, is still locked within the order of explicate forms.

Up to his death Bohm and his colleague Basil Hiley were searching for a mathematics better adapted to this notion of an implicate order and the holomovement. One of the mathematical forms they were exploring is called Grassmann algebra. It was developed by Hermann Grassmann, the famous German mathematician and expert on Sanskrit, in the nineteenth century as an attempt to express the nature of thought. Thoughts, Grassmann argued, do not belong to our explicate world of causality and linear sequences in time; rather, they unfold out of each other and fold back again. One thought follows on the other, they are not distinct objects with clear boundaries; rather, one thought anticipates the next and thereby contains it. The thought that comes afterward contains the memory or trace of the former. Thus, the movement of thought within the mind requires a mathematics of implicate forms.

I believe that this mathematics of enfoldment and unfoldment is close to the spirit of the sacred mathematics of Indigenous science. In order to acknowledge, celebrate, and come into relationships with the flux and movements of the world, and the spirits and energies that lie behind the appearances of things, Indigenous science developed a mathematics in which the numbers are not static objects of thought but dynamic processes and actual living beings.

Number and the *I Ching*

Something very similar happened four thousand years ago in ancient China. It began during the Shang dynasty and resulted in the *I Ching*. It is commonly said that the "broken" and "unbroken" lines of the *I Ching* are a form of binary arithmetic, corresponding to our more familiar 0, 1 notation. But this is an oversimplification that misses the *I Ching*'s deeper nature, for each line within the system can be either static or transforming. While the static lines remain the same, the moving line transforms into its dual opposite—a broken line transforms into an unbroken line. Likewise, the moving lines within a pattern of the static lines cause the nature of each of the *I Ching* characters to change. Each character is created out of a pattern of six lines. Yet, by virtue of its moving lines, as a particular character emerges out of the chance manipulations of the dried stalks of the yarrow plant, it is in the process of transformation and movement within the circle of the *I Ching*.

Like the thoughts presented by a Grassmann algebra or the implicate order of Bohm and Hiley, the character that emerges out of the permutation of the yarrow stalks contains the other characters, and meanings, within its process of transformation.

The sixty-four characters of the *I Ching* are arranged in a circle and become part of an underlying movement that transforms the characters and takes them to various points within the circumference of the circle. In this way I believe that there are deep connections between the meaning of the *I Ching* with its transforming relationship to the flux of the universe and the sacred mathematics and gambling games of Indigenous science.

Flux and the Trickster

The meaning of number four was discussed through the medicine wheel and the sacred hoop. We must not forget that, for the Blackfoot, this circle is always left open so that the new may enter. Nothing is permanent, no situation is ever fixed, and no category is ever closed. The trickster is ever present in all aspects of Indigenous science. The trickster may appear as coyote, as raven, or as Napi—the Old Man. The trickster was even metamorphosed into the rabbit, manifested as Br'er Rabbit, when his stories were passed on to black slaves.

The significance of flux and the power of the trickster is present in what anthropologists refer to as gambling games, ways in which The People come into relationship with the deepest processes of the universe. Sa'ke'j Henderson describes the meaning of the Mic Maqs' Waltestaqaney (or Waltes Game) as connecting The People with their ancestors who first made alliances with the spirits and energies of the universe. Waltestaqaney was created by the hero Glooscap and by playing the game one is taken back into that world through the great circle of time.

I have never seen the Waltes Game played but Sa'ke'j Henderson and Marie Battiste gave me photographs and explanations about it that had been written by their people. To begin with I was struck by the implements used to play the game. In a world of categories and abstractions a game is just a game, and it does not much matter from what materials a pack of cards, or a chess board is made. By contrast, Indigenous science deals in direct experience and these things do matter.

As we have already seen, a person who holds a piece of bone senses it as the bone of a particular animal and, moreover, as a particular part of that animal. Since all things are connected, and all things are contained within each part, to hold that bone in the hand is to be connected with the spirit of that animal, and through that to the Keeper of the animals and to all the other animals of that species. Bones and feathers, leather, and fur are direct connections—the apparatus of Indigenous science.

Each piece of the Waltes Game is not a symbol of something but a thing in itself, a direct connection to a world of spirits. The *waltestaqan'ogan*, or bowl used in the game, is made from the burl of a hardwood tree that has been boiled in salted water for many hours before carving. The six dice (*waltestaqank*) are made from the bone of caribou or deer. They are flat on one side and curved and marked on the other. In addition there are fifty-one sticks (*kitmaqank*) that are counted in groups of three; plus three *kisikui'skwaq*, who are wives of the Old Man and notched on one side; and one *kisikuo'p*, or Old Man, that is notched on both sides.*

Playing the game is complicated and takes all night to complete. As befits Indigenous science, the mathematics used

---

*As recently as the mid-1950s, police raids were made on Mic Maq homes and Waltes Games confiscated.

to keep tally changes during the game's three phases. From the point of view of mathematics, the Waltes Game deals with the laws of probability, of computation, and of tally keeping; in the game transforms itself, for the system of counting used from the perspective of metaphysics it deals in exchanges that must be made within a world of flux. One element of the Waltes Game has entered Western culture, for in their early contacts with white settlers the Mic Maq people adopted an aspect of their game into the game of poker by making certain cards wild—"Indian poker."

What is striking about the Waltes Game is that a person who has been losing to such an extent that he or she has almost no sticks left can stake everything on a final throw of the dice. By "dancing with the devil" in this way, the losing player stands a chance of winning the game outright. One wins by sacrificing everything and, in a world of flux, reversal of fortune may always be around the corner.

The origin of this game of chance is told in one of the many stories about Waltestaqaney: An old man and an old woman longed for a child and finally a son was given to them. The man loved his son dearly and taught him all that he knew. One day the boy died. The old man grieved and, finally, accompanied by a few brave men, went to the Land of the Souls to ask that his son should be returned to him. At first the Keeper of the Land of Souls was very angry and refused to allow the old man to see his son. But finally he was so impressed by the great love shown by the old man that he agreed to play Waltestaqaney with him. If the man should win, then his son would be returned, but if he lost he must return empty handed.

The game began, and continued day after day. Gradually the old man's strength began to fade, but he prayed that he could continue. The game went on until the old man had lost almost all his sticks. His only chance was to "dance with the devil" and stake everything on one last chance. In his final tossing of the dice the old man won the game and the Keeper had enjoyed the game so much that he allowed the spirit of the son to return to the land of the Mic Maq people; in addition he gave The People the gift of fruit trees and bushes.

The Haudenosaunee also have ceremonies that are related to the drawing up of contracts, and each year the Mohawk people gather in the longhouse to play the Peach Stone Game and determine who will carry out certain of the year's tasks. The Peach Stone Game is played to decide, for example, if men or the women will plant corn for the coming year—the women say that if the men win then they know it is going to be a bad year for corn!

Contracts, Chaos, and Harmony

Giving such importance to chance is one of the ways in which the metaphysics of Indigenous science differs from traditional Western science. Within Indigenous science all is process, and the various aspects of nature that we see around us—the sun and moon, winds, rocks, trees, and animals—are manifestations of this underlying flux. But there is an order within this flux, for there are alliances, compacts, and relationships between the energies and spirits of the world. Sacred mathematics, as reflected in number, architecture, symbolic representation, and in the ceremonies of gambling, places The People in touch with this order. It is an order that itself is always in a state of transformation; the world is movement, and movement of that movement, and movement of the movements of movement. Its mathematics consists of relationships, relationships of relationships, and relationships of relationships of relationships.

In the distant past the Elders made contracts with the powers and spirits and energies of the world to enter into relationship with the plants, the animals, the winds, the sun, and the movement of the heavens. In the world that lies between the Sky Kingdom and Mother Earth, The People renew these relationships through their ceremonies that help maintain harmony and balance in the world.

The basic element of this worldview is that balance lies in flux, transformation, and chance. Harmony always requires the presence of the trickster, the one who overturns laws, transcends boundaries, and can win everything when down to the last counter.

By contrast, the Newtonian worldview pictured the cosmos as material bodies moving under fixed laws against the backdrop of space. Newton's universe was perfect order and predictable mechanical motion and held no room for the trickster. As the quantum physicist Wolfgang Pauli put it: There is no place for the irrational within the world of classical physics.

Within such a classical worldview there is no room for the lone Blackfoot who, early each morning, stands on the hilltop and prays for the renewal of the sun. Within a Newtonian cosmology, the sun will rise tomorrow no matter what we do; nature is dead and our contracts with its supposed spirits are illusions. The deterministic universe of Newton and Laplace is impervious to all that we want or desire and has no need for our ceremonies of renewal.

In fact it is only recently that Western science has begun to entertain a picture that, on the face of it at least, appears closer to that of Indigenous science. Chaos theory (or, more generally, the science of nonlinear systems) explores the different consequences that randomness, chance, and probability can play in our world. It demonstrates that our universe is far from being simplistic clockwork because chance plays a guiding role in a vast number of processes, including weather, fast-flowing rivers, the shock waves from supersonic aircraft, the growth of materials, and the fluctuations of insect populations.

One tool in the description of chaotic systems are fractals, which are capable of modeling the details of extremely complex objects. Fractals are geometrical patterns of infinite complexity. Magnify a tiny portion of one of these fractals and a new world of detail will be revealed. They have been used to portray fractures in metals, the shapes of trees, river deltas, lungs, the circulatory system, clouds, coastlines, mountainsides, the electrical activity of the brain, and the beating of a healthy heart. Fractals are related to both order and chaos. Thus, the heart of nature, it appears, is more concerned with this chance than with simple order.

At one time order was considered to be the norm, with chaos pictured as the breakdown or disintegration of this order—thus chaos was equated with lawlessness. Now scientists are discovering, as Indigenous science has long taught, that stability and harmony can also result from chance. The chemist Ilya Prigogine has studied a host of what he calls "dissipative systems," which range from living cells and periodic chemical reactions, to the growth of cities and the flow of traffic. In each case regularity and order emerges out of a world of chance fluctuations.

In so many ways scientists are beginning to perceive the underlying duality of chaos and order, the one emerging out of the other. Order and chaos are like the two brothers in the stories told by the Iroquois people. When one of the brothers produce something, the other creates its opposite; when one of the brothers produces order, the other will turn this order upside down. Non-Natives interpret these brothers as "good" and "evil" and see an image of the Western picture of the battle between God and the Devil in their eternal confrontations. Yet to Native people this loses the deeper meaning of the stories, for both brothers are necessary, and each must be acknowledged. To have one brother without the other would be to create disharmony in the world, for order cannot exist without chaos, nor chaos without order.

The Nature of Laws, and the Laws of Nature

Acknowledging the power of chaos and chance is one way in which Western and Indigenous sciences are bridging their worldviews. But a distance remains between them in the way they interpret physical law. Western science seeks ever more fundamental laws, expressed in mathematically elegant ways and applying to a wider and wider range of phenomena.

In a sense, these laws lie beyond the realm of matter. As an example, one of the most fundamental laws about elementary particles, the grand unified theory, applies to processes occurring at incredibly high energies comparable to those that occurred during the big bang creation of the universe. Indeed, physicists believe that once this ultimate law is discovered it will describe the big bang origin itself. In other words, such a law describes the coming into existence of matter and energy, space and time. The law has an existence and a rule before the appearance of time and the universe itself; it existed prior to all existence!

Western physics attempts to discover the most basic laws that lie beyond all contexts, and all exceptions. These laws somehow exist outside matter and are imposed upon it. By contrast, the laws, or the alliances, relationships, and compacts of Indigenous science can never be abstracted from the spirits, energies, and forms to which they refer. These laws are like the relationships between members of a family. And if that family were to cease to exist then the law would have no meaning. Rather than law being an abstraction, it is an expression of the rich activity of the world.

But, in other ways, maybe an Indigenous perception of "laws of nature" would not be that far from the ideas that are now emerging within Western science. In my book *The Philosopher's Stone* I explored the idea that nature in its deepest essence is an inexhaustible and indescribable *inscape*. The laws of science are expressions of the regularity of nature, but are always limited and prescribed according to some particular context. Since no context is ever closed and complete, but always open to something that lies beyond it, so too, no law of nature can ever be exhaustive. What we see as the laws of nature are not impositions from some abstract domain that lies above matter and energy, space and time; rather they are expressions of the regularities within the world; they are the forms and patterns of process created out of the inner relationships of matter and energy.

Indigenous science expresses the harmony and balance of nature by sacred numbers. These numbers are never static, they cannot be exhausted through abstraction and logical analysis. Each sacred number is an *inscape*, an animating spirit and a moving process. Within the heart of Indigenous harmony there is always room for the trickster. The circle contains a gap to allow the unexpected to enter.

Time, Number, and the Mayans

One thing that strikes non-Natives as they first try to learn about Indigenous America is the different ways in which its various societies have chosen to live. Some, like the Naskapi of Labrador, are predominantly hunters who travel long distances in small family groups. The Haida, by contrast, have lived for countless generations in their villages by the sea, making periodic raiding trips down the west coast of British Columbia and Oregon, or taking long voyages into the Pacific Ocean. The Iroquois people practice farming, hunting, fishing and gathering, live in villages, and, in traditional times, moved periodically to allow the Eastern woodlands to regenerate and renew themselves. The people of the plains made their compact with the buffalo and, while they spent each winter in permanent housing in fertile river valleys, they spent the rest of the year moving camp and traveling with the buffalo, and coming together for their Sun Dance.

To our eyes, the world of the Haida looks structured and bureaucratic. Under the leadership of The Peacemaker, the Iroquois peoples developed a new system of government, a league of independent nations bound together under the umbrella of the Great Law of Peace. The peoples of the Americas, each speaking its own language, chose to live their lives in different ways: some in longhouses, some in hogans or kivas, some in tepees, some in cliff dwellings, and others in wigwams. Each group was in a unique relationship to the land it occupied, having entered into compacts with the spirits of the rocks, trees, and animals.

Yet despite their apparent differences the Native people I have talked to acknowledge a universality within the culture of the Americas. They tell me that despite variations in language and society The People all share something in common.

Once I was discussing about these things with Leroy Little Bear and he told me a story about the Blackfoot people. In their tradition small groups occasionally take long journeys, lasting for months or even years. Long, long ago one group voyaged south and, on their return, told their friends how they had visited people who lived in houses in the desert and after living with them for a time went farther south to visit the people who lived in cities.

Leroy believed that this latter group they spoke of were the Mayans. Although they lived in a very different way, the Blackfoot visitors acknowledged the city dwellers as relations, as a people who could be referred to as brothers and sisters. While to me, an outsider with a European background, the city dwellers of Central America with their panoply of gods and elaborate calendar system seem profoundly different from the Blackfoot of the plains, to Leroy's ancestors they were people with whom they shared an inner relatedness. "The Mayans were not different from us," Leroy said. "When it came to real strangers, it was those first Europeans who made contact with the Blackfoot who were alien; here was a group of human beings who did not share in the values we held dear." Let us keep this in mind as we explore the Mayans' mathematics and their vision of time, for within them may well be a universe that is common to all The People.

The Circle of Time

According to Ingidenous science, everything that exists is bound within the great cycle of time. There is a time to be born and a time to die. Each of us moves from the baby to the child, from the child to the young adult, from young adult to maturity, and finally into that special interval of wisdom and serenity of the Elder before the final turn of the cycle when the old person becomes the infant again and moves toward death. A society is like a human being; it too has a time of birth and development, a time in which it flourishes, and a time in which it moves toward death. Life and society are bound within the circle of time and, thus, there exist ceremonies that acknowledge and assist in its renewal.

Mayan society was very much concerned with these cycles of renewal and with their inner numerical significance that reverberates throughout the cosmos with the movement of the stars and planets, the waxing and waning of the moon, the planting and harvesting of corn, the processes of birth and death, and the flowerings of society. In acknowledging these cycles the Mayans expressed their basic connection with Indigenous societies across the Americas. As we look at the Mayans in more detail and attempt to understand their relationship to number, time, and the spirit of corn, we are touching upon something universal within Indigenous science.

The Gift of Corn

The story of the Mayans begins with the gift of corn. For many thousands of years small groups of Indigenous people lived in Central America until an event occurred that was to transform the entire continent. Long before the human race put in its appearance on the face of the globe, grasses covered the earth. For millions of years these grasses took their place in relationship to the other plants until, around the time human populations began to grow in size, they mutated and the first cereals appeared.

In different ways this miracle occurred right across the globe. In the "fertile crescent" of the Middle East, a particular sort of grass, evolved into wheat. In order to undergo this transformation grass had to adapt to the needs of human farmers. For example, its seeds no longer were dispersed by blowing but fell to the ground for easy collection or winnowing. In addition, the size of each grain, rich in protein, increased. In this way it became possible for the land to support a much larger number of people than ever before. In the Far East a different grass developed, this was the rice that today feeds other great areas of the world. The third of these transformations occurred when yet another grass, this time in Central America, mutated into corn.

Was this purely a series of fortuitous accidents? Modern science teaches that genetic mutations take place by chance—all that happened was that corn, wheat, and rice grasses happened to undergo a particularly striking, though random, genetic transformation. Observant human farmers, the Western scientific account goes, amplified this chance effect by collecting and replanting seeds from the best plants, practicing a method of selection and even crossbreeding.

Is there another explanation as to why new sources of food should have appeared across the earth? Does Indigenous science offer a different kind of answer? The traditional ways of the People place them in a relationship with all living things; they give offerings and make exchanges and compacts with the spirits of animals, plants, rocks, rivers, and trees, and renew these relationships through a variety of ceremonies.

I believe the ancient peoples of Central America entered into a deep relationship with the plants around them, including the grasses. The grass that gave birth to corn was not simply a plant but a manifestation of a spirit or energy that moved within the complex pattern of relationships of the natural world. When a people entered into direct relationship with the spirit of the corn, there was an exchange of obligations, a contract between the god of the corn and the needs of the human race. Within this exchange a new alliance was struck that resulted in actual physical transformations.

Within Western science it turns out that there is another way of looking at corn or any other plant or animal. The physical form of corn is the manifestation of genetic information, for within every cell of that plant are an unfolding set of directions that chart the course of its biochemical processes.

Corn is the material manifestation of the activity of this unfolding information. And when this sequence of information changes, then, too, the physical corn itself is changed.

Indigenous science also teaches that corn is the manifestation of something deeper, of something that transcends the particular individual plant and links all corn together—in this case spirit. Moreover, it is possible for human beings to enter into relationship with this spirit, this active power, that brings about the form of the corn plant.

Could it be that the spirits of corn and The People entered into a new form of mutually supportive relationship? From that point on corn would grow in a new way, not by chance or hazardous mutation, but in response to a request that it should feed The People. In return, The People acknowledge the power of the plant and care for it in special ways, conducting the necessary ceremonies of renewal and acknowledgment of that initial compact.

The gift of corn, and the obligations it entailed, could then be passed on to other peoples. The Iroquois have many stories of their origin. In some of these they hint at a time when they came north from the land of the Mound Builders, which anthropologists have come to call the Hopewell culture. Some of these stories speak of an even longer journey, from Central America, the land where corn first grew.

According to these latter stories the Iroquois people traveled north very slowly. At each stopping point they planted the corn and introduced it to the other plants of the area. Thus The People and the sacred corn established new alliances, new relationships, and new obligations with the spirits, powers, and energies of the regions they were entering. Western science would say that they were allowing the corn to become acclimatized, an account that fails to include the new sense of obligation and ceremony that the Iroquois people were acknowledging and undertaking.

Not only did the Iroquois bring corn, as a material plant, but they also brought the stories and ceremonies to accompany it. Today they continue to carry out the seasonal round of ceremonies, beginning with the Peach Stone Game, connected to corn and its relationship to its sisters, squash and beans.

It is remarkable that the majority of plants and vegetables found on tables all over the world had their birth in Central and South America. Were they the results of random mutations or were they given as gifts by the spirits of the plants to their two-legged relations? Today Western science can repeat such processes in the laboratory, adapting, for example, tomatoes for ease of harvesting and packing. Genetic engineering enables us to create designer plants and animals, even to modify our own bodies. The technology is impressive and its implications awesome. The problem, however, is that scientists don't really understand the implications of what they are doing. The relationship of a plant or animal to the general ecology of its region is incredibly complicated. It may be possible to make a computer model of, say, the introduction of a new bean hybrid upon a particular environment. But, as mathematicians would say, models are highly nonlinear, containing many feedback loops. Predictable behavior can suddenly change in abrupt ways, from gradual trends to wild oscillations or even chaos.

It is beyond Western science to fully understand the impact that various aspects of genetic engineering could have upon the environment and our future. Indigenous science, if we are to believe its metaphysics and its claims, moves in a slower way. It is based upon generations of painstaking observations and upon a perception that looks into the heart of things, upon knowledge that is given by the plants and animals to the two-legged. Thus, when changes take place they do so from within an acknowledged web of relationship. Moreover, the power of the trickster is always acknowledged, for the People know that all human plans are subject to the forces of chance and transformation.

The Olmec Compact

The compact between The People and the spirits of the grasses must have taken place around six thousand years ago, for Western scientists say that corn began to appear in Central America around 4000 B.C. The People of that period were hunters who supplemented their diet through the cultivation of beans, squash, chili peppers, peanuts, avocados, and tomatoes. The first ears of corn that appeared were probably no bigger than a fingernail, but as people began to care for and cultivate this grain a variety of hybrids were produced until, by 2000 B.C., the ear was some two inches long and a field planted with corn had become a rich source of protein. By this time farmers were also practicing irrigation and drainage.

Archaeologists suggest that the size of farming communities began to increase over the next two thousand years and soon villages and trade routes grew up. Around 1400 to 1200 B.C. The People entered into a new relationship together that resulted in a flowering of the Olmec society with its elaborate buildings, ceremonial sites, pyramids, sculpture, art, and new technologies. At the explicit, surface level the Olmecs displayed all those attributes that we in the West tend to associate with "civilization." From the perspective of our Western paradigm, the society of Central America had made a great leap forward, but from another perspective, The People had simply chosen to explore another form of alliance together. From within this Indigenous perspective the change may not have been so marked, for life was still based upon the gifts of the corn god, ceremonies of renewal, and a sense of wholeness with all creation.

In this same period mathematics and writing developed, and highly sophisticated astronomical observations were carried out. And, thus, the Olmec peoples, sustained by the corn god and by other fruits, vegetables, and game, developed a variety of skills that they were to pass on to their descendants, the Mayans.

Seeing Olmec society from the distance of time we are struck by its monumental sculpture. The great helmeted stone heads, some nine feet high and weighing as much as twenty tons, evoke the same sense of remoteness and awe as do the heads of Easter Island. We know that in 1250 B.C. a town containing a 150-foot clay platform, or courtyard, was located near what is today the town of San Lorenzo in Mexico. Rocks were quarried in the Tuxtal mountains some fifty miles to the north, dragged over land, and then floated down to the city where they were sculpted into colossal heads.

As cities grew up in different locations, many feats of engineering were attempted. In one case an architectural complex was dominated by a 103-foot cone built to look like a volcano. In another, a great courtyard for the sacred ball game was constructed. The Olmecs were not only skilled in working with stone, but also with iron ores and in creating curved metal mirrors. There is evidence that the Olmecs used lodestone, a naturally magnetic mineral, as a compass for navigation. As with many other peoples of the Americas, the jaguar was held in great respect, and there was a story that the Olmecs were descended from the child produced by the copulation of a human being and a jaguar.

The Olmec people continued to flourish until, between 900 and 300 B.C., the compact, or spirits or energies, that had brought them together ceased to be renewed. The Olmec cities ceased to function and their statues were deconsecrated.

From our Western point of view we speak of a people as vanishing, or a civilization as breaking apart, being overwhelmed by barbarians, or replaced by some other culture. Such descriptions do not seem to work when it comes to the Americas. Archaeological evidence suggests that the Olmecs were not attacked or destroyed from within, neither did the population die out. Rather, The People seem to have made the deliberate choice to lead their lives in a new way. To this end their great statues were first mutilated, then laid in long lines and buried; in addition, fires were lit and pottery broken.

Again and again a similar pattern can be seen within the Americas, as The People apparently decide that the end to a particular cycle had come and they must voluntarily withdraw from the cities and from the alliance that was their former society in order to partake in a new cycle of being. And so the mystery of the waxing and waning of societies and civilizations in the Americas is tied to the mystery of spirit and time.

The Mayan Compact

While The People remained, that compact for living that we call the Olmecs had disappeared. Some time later a new contract was drawn up with the spirits of the land and the Mayans appeared. Within the Mayan society, which flourished for some one thousand years, can be detected much of the spirit and knowledge of the Olmecs. In its power and scope it has sometimes been compared to the civilization of ancient Egypt. One Mayan city had forty thousand inhabitants, which made it only slightly smaller than London under Henry Tudor. Indeed, the population of the Mayan territories was probably some three million, comparable with that of all of England during the time of Chaucer.

The society itself kept elaborate records, and their books and pottery show pictures of scribes who were skilled in writing and in mathematics. There are even depictions of what appear to be schools or universities of scholars. One of the Mayan achievements that strikes our modern age so forcefully is their highly developed system for representing number and time.

At its height, the Mayan compact extended for some 125,000 square miles and lasted until the end of its cycle loomed, at which time the temples were closed and the great buildings deserted. As with the Olmecs, The People decided not to renew their alliance with the spirit of a particular society and withdrew. And, thus, the first visitors to the New World met an apparently simple agricultural society living in small villages. As far as the Europeans were concerned, the Mayans themselves had vanished and all that was left were legends of lost cities deep in the jungle.

In their books the Mayans recorded the story of their own origin and spoke of the great cycles of time in which different worlds, or suns, appeared. With the appearance of each sun there was a new race of people and as one transformed into another the human race underwent a change and a new emergence. The Mayan society flowered within the world of the fifth sun, and today the Mayan people look ahead to the coming of the sixth sun, the transformation of human consciousness, and the dawn of a new world.

And what do anthropologists say of the origin of the Mayans and the societies of Central America? Using an approach known as lexicostatistics, linguists have attempted to develop a quantitative measure of how closely one particular language is related to others. Assuming a certain rate of change when a language separates from its origins it becomes possible, in theory at least, to determine how long ago a particular people split off from their parent language. Similar studies have attempted to relate the languages of Turtle Island to those of Asia and to determine the dates of the hypothetical great migrations.

In the case of the Mayans, these studies suggest that they originally inhabited North America and were distantly related to groups in Oregon and Northern California, among others. Migrating south the small tribe eventually settled in the highlands of Guatemala during the third millennium B.C. It was from this beginning that the Mayans began to grow, and, carrying on the knowledge that had been developed by the Olmecs, they brought mathematics, astronomy, and a philosophy of time and the calendar to a level of great sophistication.

Certain elements of the Mayan religion may also have come from the Olmecs, such as the belief in the power of the jaguar. Their great ancestor was spoken of as the Plumed Serpent, also called Quetzalcoatl. It was he who taught the people how to carve stone and make pottery and who was tricked by his brother Smoking Mirror (Texatlipoca). It is so easy for us in the West to see Quetzalcoatl and Texatlipoca as the embodiments of good and evil. But this is to miss the essence of a worldview that extends across Turtle Island—the idea of harmony and balance. For in a world of process, activity, and relationship, both brothers are necessary. We have already met a similar story of two brothers as told by the Iroquois people. Each is the complement of the other, and if one brother were to create an eagle the other would create a bat—and within the web of the world both forms of life are necessary. It is only if one brother were to gain too much power over the other, or if the People were to acknowledge only one of these powers, that imbalance and disharmony would come to the land.

The Burning of Books

The Mayan peoples, with their schools, scribes, and universities, kept full records of their society and wrote books about religion, mathematics, and daily life. Tragically, today we in the West know even less about them than we do about the ancient Egyptians. The reason is that a great burning was ordered in 1562 by Spanish priests, on the grounds that the Mayan writings were pagan. As a result the libraries of the Mayans, with the descriptions of their history, literature, ceremonies, science, astronomy, cosmology, and philosophy, were destroyed. All that survive today are fragments. It was as if all the works of the Greek culture had been burned—the ideas of Socrates, Plato, and Aristotle; the plays of Sophocles, Euripides; and Aristophanes; the mathematics of Pythagoras; the geometry of Euclid; the foundations of law and democracy had all vanished and all that survived were the ruins of temples and dim legends of a lost people.

At the hands of the Spanish colonizers, a whole history of knowledge was wiped out, and all that survives are a few codexes in museum cases, inscriptions on pottery, carvings on monuments, and the ruins of abandoned temples and cities. Some of the Mayan inscriptions have been deciphered and their mathematics figured out, but to us in the West much remains a mystery.

To other people, however, this knowledge may not be totally lost. Knowledge and stories may have been passed on orally from generation to generation of the Mayans and to other Indigenous people who live in Central America today. It need not be a knowledge known explicitly, but rather one that has been passed on in an implicit way, enfolded within certain ancient words, symbols, songs, ceremonies, stories, and dreams. One day, at the appropriate time, this knowledge may be revived. Indeed, there are Mayan people who look forward to the start of the next great circle of time, early in the next century, and to the creation of new compacts that will lead to the renewal and revival of their culture and traditional ways.

The Abstraction of Mathematics

What anthropologists know of the Mayans' culture, their writing and mathematics, has been pieced together from a variety of sources such as inscriptions on pottery and monuments and from the few books that survived. From this information, Western scientists have attempted to reproduce the past glory of the mathematics of the Mayans. How successful they have been depends on exactly what you feel this mathematics to be.

Mathematicians assert that their topic is the art of abstraction and relationship. It is concerned with moving beyond the particular and the uniqueness of things into the general. Hence, mathematics is able to add two sets of very different objects together—two sets of trees, of knives, of eagles, of rocks, of apples and oranges, and obtain a new number. The power of abstraction lies in ignoring what gives each thing its individuality and apartness and instead seeing them only as representatives of categories and sets. When Cezanne painted a bowl of oranges he saw each one as being set in its own space, separate and unique. A mathematician, however, would simply see a certain number of similar objects, all members of the same set—oranges.

This may be a rather crude example, but it is the beginning of how mathematics is able to move progressively through a series of higher and higher levels of abstractions. While a farmer may be concerned with the characteristics of a particular piece of land, a surveyor sees it only as a length, width, and area. Euclidian geometry is even more abstract, for it the study of the properties of shapes alone and deals in the properties of squares, triangles and circles irrespective of their size. Topology is based on yet another level of abstraction; it ignores the differences between particular shapes, such as circles, triangles, and squares, and classifies them all merely as closed figures. Thus, topology would treat a ball and a cube as having the same abstract properties, while being different from a tea cup and a donut, each of which possess a hole. (The hole in the tea cup is formed by the handle.) Finally, the study of algebraic cohomology in effect abstracts geometry even further by dispensing with the necessity to talk about an underlying space at all! All that remains are abstract algebraic relationships.

Mathematics, in the minds of many philosophers of the subject, strives to be free of particular objects and, indeed, of particular cultures. The highest mathematics is identical for Europeans, Mayans, Arabs, Chinese, and Indians. Mathematics should translate across cultures, for it is the study of the basic logical relationships of the world, and if it is tied to anything, then it is to the deepest levels of symbolic processing within the human brain. From this point of view there is no reason why Western scientists should not be able to reproduce and perfectly understand the totality of Mayan mathematics.

But there is another possible approach to all of this, and that is to see mathematics as inseparable from language and culture. After all, those who talk of the universality of mathematics, and the common ground shared by Europeans, Arabs, and ancient Indians alike, tend to be professors who speak and think within a common Indo-European family of languages.

Some linguists have argued that mathematics is a particular, formal expression and extension of the various relationships, transformations, and interconnections that exist within language. And language, in turn, is to a greater or lesser extent connected to culture and the particular way people live. Thus, what we take as our universal and value-free mathematics may be connected in certain very subtle ways to the set of common paradigms and ways of thinking that are embedded in all Indo-European languages. These include, for example, the strong role of nouns (objects) in the languages, the importance of categories, as well as certain notions of time and causality.

There is another aspect to treating mathematics as abstract and value-free. In doing so one tends to lose sight of an idea that is common to so many of the world's Indigenous peoples— something that was known to the ancient Greeks as well—and that is the idea that mathematics is sacred and deeply connected with the whole nature of time and ceremony, with the proportions of architecture and the human body, and with the structure of the cosmos and of sacred sites.

Number and Mystery

Numbers resonated though all aspects of Mayan life and ceremony. Number was the synchronicity that connected the inner world to the outer. Whereas to us in the West number is an abstract object to be manipulated within the mind, to the

Mayans each number was the representation of a particular deity.

Numbers are the wheel that is constantly rotating—the wheel that connects to the cyclic movements of time, birth, death, and renewal. In this sense Mayan number is closer to what mathematicians call algebra than to arithmetic because algebras are about the way things transform into each other, and Indigenous number is about the transformation of forms within the manifest world and about the flux of alliances and relationships between that underlying world of spirits and energies. Right across Turtle Island we see how the forms of the world are in the process of flux and transformation for they, like numbers, are manifestations of the spirits, gods, and energies of the universe.

The Mayan Number System

Leaving aside for a moment its sacred aspect, the Mayan number system is vastly superior to the system devised by the Romans. When it comes to the ability to represent large numbers, the Mayans appear to have been centuries in advance of others. This is because the Mayans invented the number zero, or, to put it more accurately: They had developed a metaphysics and a way of living within the world that was of such subtlety that it enabled them to incorporate that most mystical of processes—the emptiness that is total plenitude, the perfect movement that is stillness, the nothingness out of which everything unfolds, the identity of birth and death, the motivating essence of all transformation—the void, the zero.

Writing Numbers

The Mayans had many sacred teachings about the number zero; but let us first approach zero from the point of view of a practical number system so we can discover just how freeing that number can be. Let us therefore revisit a world without zero, the world of Roman numerals.

The first number in the Roman system is one, unity,

represented by the symbol *I*. To represent the next number, two, you put two of these unities together—*II*. In a similar way the number three is represented by the symbol *III*.

It would be too cumbersome to continue indefinitely in this way, so the Romans used a symbol for five which is obviously a symbol for one hand of five fingers, *V*. In this way six becomes one more than five, *VI*, while four is one less than five, *IV*. The next symbol is introduced at ten and consists of two hands of five fingers, represented by *X*. Thus the number nine is written as *IX*, while sixteen is *XVI* and thirty-seven becomes *XXXVII*.

The system continues in this way with additional symbols for fifty, *L*; one hundred, *C*; and one thousand, *M*. But clearly the system is a messy one when it comes to large numbers. For example, 3973 is written as MMMCMLXXIII. And how on earth do we multiply XXXVII by LXXII?

The key to a more sophisticated number system lies in what is called a place-value system in which the value that the particular numerical symbol represents depends upon its position in relationship to other numbers. In this way, for example, the symbol *1* can be equally employed to symbolize unity, ten, one hundred, one thousand, one million, or whatever.

In our present Arabic numerical system we arrange numbers horizontally, by reference to columns of ones, tens, hundreds, and so on. In this way three thousand, four hundred and twenty one is written:

thousands	hundreds	tens	ones
3	4	2	1

But how do we represent three thousand and one?

3			1

If we are using only the symbols *1, 2, 3, 4, 5, 6, 7, 8, 9* we are forced to write it as *31*. But then how is one to distinguish this from thirty one, or three hundred and one, or thirty thousand and one? The place-number system fails unless we can come up with a systematic way of indicating gaps. This is exactly what the symbol *0* can do, for 31, 301, and 3001 are all clearly different numbers.

Of course one can invent any symbol one likes to represent gaps between the 3 and the 1 in three thousand and one. Zero is special as well as serving as a marker of gaps in columns because it is also a number in its own right. It is a number, moreover, that has no quantitative value! For when zero is added to another number the value of that other number does not change. Thus $1 + 0$ is the same as 1. In order to achieve what the Arabs discovered only several centuries after the Mayans, it is necessary to introduce the whole concept of a zero, a void, or the absence of value, within the processes of a mathematical system.*

Mayan Numbers

It should come as no surprise to learn that the Native American culture, which has always placed such a high value on the notion of relationship, should have developed a system for representing the values of large numbers based upon the relationship of symbols. Add to this the fact that zero is also a number, and one realizes the enormous advance that could be made by the Mayan people.

Let us focus upon that great mystery, this plenitude of nothingness, which of itself can give birth to the infinitely great. Zero is symbolized by the figure

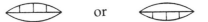

which seems to evoke in us the image of a shell, or even of a galaxy.

Some years ago I met Hunbatz Men, who founded the Mayan Indigenous Community near Merida, Mexico, and who

---

*It has been generally assumed by writers on the history of mathematics that the Mayans were the first people in the world to specifically develop and use the number zero. However, some researchers have suggested that zero, or at least the use of certain of its mathematical properties, may have been known by the peoples of the Near East in ancient times.

has studied the meaning and symbolism of Mayan mathematics from within the traditions of his people. For Hunbatz the symbol for zero is identified with the Mayan letter G or "ge" which is symbolic of the beginning, the moment of creation, the essence of existence, the Egg-Creator out of which all is born. In his book *Secrets of Mayan Science/Religion*, Men indicates the association of the letter G with the Milky Way. And, recalling that numbers are spirits, the number zero is that spirit which is the creation of all number and which itself mirrors the creation of the cosmos.

This notion of the void out of which the totality of the cosmos was created has astounding resonances with the physics of our own time. A development of quantum theory, called quantum field theory, deals not only with material particles like electrons, protons, and atoms, but also with energy fields like light (electromagnetism) and the forces that hold the nucleus of the atom together.

Within quantum field theory, both particles of matter, like the electron and proton, and the quanta of energy such as a photon of light, appear as vibrations of quantum fields. But what is particularly interesting about the field is that its lowest energy state, called the ground state or vacuum state, is the state of total emptiness, the quantum void, for within this state no excitations exist. One would expect the vacuum state to be empty of all vibrations and all energy. But paradoxically this absolute zero of the quantum world is totally full of energy. It is packed with an infinity of energy, so that there is more energy within this tiny dot " . " of the vacuum state than in the whole observable universe!

The entire visible universe, with its planets, stars, and galaxies, is no more than a tiny fluctuation upon an immense sea of nothingness, that boundless zero-point energy. The stars and planets are like clouds in the air; clouds that from a distance appear as solid patterns in the sky, but, when we fly into them, dissolve into an insubstantial mist. Within the "zero" of the quantum field is the totality of creative energy in the cosmos.

Out of this same void many physicists believe that the universe was born. The universe, we believe, was created within the big bang. But from what did this big bang originate? Physicists believe that it was literally generated out of nothing—out of the vacuum state, out of the infinite void—for this aboriginal state of nothingness was subject to quantum fluctuations. Out of these fluctuations of the void an actuality was manifested—the zero manifested itself into unity. And from the infinite potential of the vacuum, from the infinitely empty and the infinitely full, was born all that exists.

Many of the world's spiritual and meditative traditions share the same notion of the infinite potential of the void. It is sometimes said that the goal of meditation and of spiritual transcendence is to reach a state of emptiness in which all thought and attachment ends. When this is achieved the seeker is open to the infinite flux of the void and the ultimate state of no-mind.

For the Mayans, zero is the Egg-Creator of the universe and, mathematically speaking, the womb out of which the numbers are born. Out if its nothingness we arrive at unity, the first number, the *one*, that is complete in itself yet seeks its dual image to make two. For *one* is the fundamental distinction between something and nothing. And so unity becomes the fundamental duality, for of the one is born two.

The great circle rotates, and out of zero the numbers are born and will finally return to their place of birth at the end of the cycle.

To unfold the numbers of the Mayans is a sacred act that brings us close to the mysteries of creation. A similar sense of mystery may also have existed in the civilizations of the West. The Jews had their cabala in which the sacred mysteries of creation and the transformation of the human soul were displayed as a tree of numbers. And the highly symbolic language of alchemy also expressed the movement of the Creator within the world of matter and spirit.

As we follow the movement of the Mayan numbers we are participating in mysteries that extend across Turtle Island, mysteries that express creation and renewal, the processes that bridge the world of everyday consciousness to that other world of spirts and visions, a world of energies as great as those which created the universe in the primordial big bang.

The Writing of Numbers

To write down such numbers, to build pyramids and temples in the image of the inner relationships and movements of number, spirit, and energy, or to compute the movement of the heavens, is to touch the animating processes of the cosmos.

The mysterious number zero is written as

One is written as ●

Two as ● ●

and so on.

The number five is written as a bar. ▬▬▬

And six becomes

It is probable that the dot and bar system of representing numbers was created even earlier, by the Olmecs. But the discovery of zero, or, rather, of a way of making the Egg-Creator the essence of their sacred number system, belongs to the Mayans, who used it a thousand years before its appearance in India.

Ten is represented as two bars

and so on up to nineteen.

We in the West use a base-ten system with columns for tens, hundreds, thousands, etc. The Mayans, however, employed a base-twenty system. Curiously enough, a base-twenty system was also used in Celtic Europe. In the case of the Mayans the number twenty is also connected to their concept of cyclic time and their method of counting days.

Rather than writing down their numbers in a horizontal row, the Mayans arranged things vertically.

Thus the number twenty-one becomes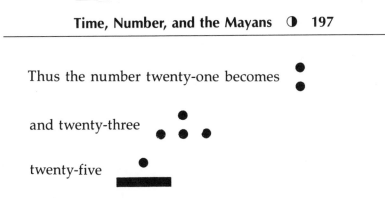

and twenty-three

twenty-five

For forty we have two units in the twenties row, thus

and to represent one hundred we have five entries in the twenties column

In this way the Mayans had the capacity to represent ever larger numbers, by moving from the units row, to the twenties and so on.

Value of row		
160,000		12 x 160,000
8000s		0 x 8,000
400s		8 x 400
20s		2 x 20
units		0

1,923,240

Value of
row

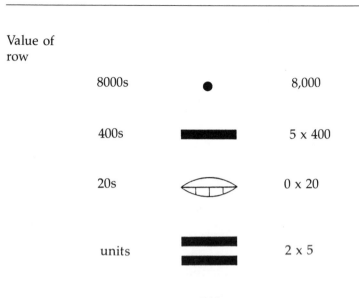

8000s		8,000
400s		5 x 400
20s		0 x 20
units		2 x 5

1010

Rather than arranging their numbers in groups of ones, tens, hundreds, thousands, etc., the Mayans employed the twenty, using a column for twentys; then, in the place of our familiar hundreds, there was a column of four-hundreds (20 x 20); and instead of our thousands column there was one for eight-thousands, etc.

Each of these had its own name:

1 hun	1
1 kal	20
1 bak	400
1 pic	8,000
1 kabal	160,000

Using this system it is possible to represent astronomically large numbers.

But why should a civilization need to develop a system capable of dealing with such large numbers? The reason is not hard to see, for these large numbers are connected to the Mayan measurement of time and the great cycles of the solar system.

Time and Cycle

For the Mayans, number and time were inseparable aspects of the same dynamic reality. Therefore, if we are to go any deeper into the nature of Mayan number we must first investigate the nature of time. Indigenous science is nonlinear and cannot always be approached in a structured, didactic way. We must now, therefore, set aside our journey through the world of number and begin to explore the resonances of time.

Time is one of those deep metaphysical ways in which Indigenous science differs from its Western counterpart. To enter more fully into the whole notion of Mayan culture and sacred mathematics it is necessary to have a new experience of the nature of time. Let's leave aside the representation of number for the moment and begin to focus upon time.

Time, as conceived by Isaac Newton, was an ever-flowing stream that moved, without resistance or change of pace, from the past into the future. Time was conceived of as external to the movements and dynamics of the physical world. And so, to our scientific way of thinking, things take place "in" time, as if time were some gigantic body of water in which we are all suspended. Bodies are immersed in the constantly flowing river of time and nothing that we do can alter the speed or direction of this flow. Time is linear and totally independent of us and of all the workings of the cosmos. Like space, time is the backdrop to motion, it is given *a priori* and exists independent of all physical laws and processes.

The concepts of time that are shared by the people of Turtle Island are far more dynamic. For them, time is animate, it is the activity of spirit. Time is alive, it is not independent of us nor of the rest of nature. Time is addressed in ceremonies and a people's relationship with its movement must be renewed. And in this way all of time can be accessed from within the present moment; or perhaps it is better to say that within the sacred space of the ceremony one can enter the flux of time and move within its vastness.

To the Australian Aborigine the Dream Time or the Dreaming, when the ancestors walked the land and created the landscape, is not a historical "time past" but a living time that has not passed away, one in which a person can still participate through dreams, visions, and ceremonies.

At the central point of the Catholic mass, during the consecration of the host, the door of time opens, for within that act of consecration are unified and revealed all other acts of consecration, past and future, down to the first consecration by Christ Himself.

Within the Sufi tradition, I have been told, Allah created each thing by calling its name. During the *ziggurs*, or sacred acts of meditation, the holy names are repeated, and through the sacred vibrations of these names the Sufi is able to participate in that primordial act. Likewise, the song reunites the Blackfoot singer with singers who passed away centuries earlier.

Both the song and the sacred name are living beings that exist outside the confines of the linear Newtonian time of Western physics. To the Native mind time is alive, and, if it must be pictured as a flowing river, then it is a river in which the mind is free to swim and move. Time does not exist apart from, and independent of, the spirits of nature and the lives of the people; its processes must be constantly acknowledged and renewed.

All beings move from birth, through growth and maturity toward death. In a similar way, societies move through the cycle of time, and if they, too, are not to decay they must be periodically renewed by contracts made with time.

Each group of Native people on Turtle Island recognizes the movements and cycles of time—the cycle of a life, the cycle of the day, the cycles of plants and animals, the cycle of the moon and the seasons, the cycle of civilizations, and the great cycles of the cosmos. And, in each case, the Native mind seeks a relationship with the spirits of these cycles, and, thus, each hour, each day, each season, each year, and each era, they participate in its renewal.

"Indian Time"

One of the most difficult things for a non-Native to comprehend is what is often called Indian Time. In fact, the jokes about Indian Time made by Natives and non-Natives alike point to the tension that exists when two very different paradigms collide.

A notice may say that the powwow will commence with a grand entry at noon. A non-Native visitor turns up in good time only to find what appears to be a total absence of any organization—the grand entry is not taking place until later in the afternoon. Indian Time becomes equated with things being late, and with people who are never "on time."

An even deeper puzzle occurs when an outsider learns that a group has decided to go hunting the following day. When the next day dawns nothing seems to happen and people say, "Oh, we'll go tomorrow." The following day people are occupied with other tasks in the camp. Nevertheless, one morning, very early, the group is assembled in the bush, well-prepared to go hunting.

The outsider wonders how such a spontaneous decision could ever have been made, for no one seemed to have decided on a precise time or location, and certainly no notice was posted. Nevertheless, when the time was right, everyone came together, as if by magic, at exactly the right spot. In the end, Indian time simply remains a mystery for most people!

Time, for us, is something registered by watches and clocks. We are driven by time's whip, by a mechanical process that takes no account of who we are and what we think, or feel or desire. Leroy Little Bear has a good story about our obsession with time. When he was a young man he was listening to an Elder but kept glancing at his watch. In the end the Elder said, "Do you have somewhere else to go?"

"No," said Leroy.

"They why do you keep looking at your watch?"

"Oh! Well, to see what time it is."

"No, you don't. You look to see what time it isn't!"

We have to go to a meeting at 2:15, and so we keep glancing at our watch to make sure that it isn't close to 2:15. It's not as if we want to know the time *now* but that we are always looking to see what time it *isn't*.

A Native husband and wife are driving their pickup truck along the highway on their way to a ceremony. The wife is getting very agitated, saying "Hey, you're late. We've got another eighty miles to go." Her husband looks at his watch and says. "Don't worry. We're not late, it's only quarter of twelve."

He drives along for a bit and looks at his watch again and says. "Now it's twelve, the ceremony's started. *Now* we're late. *Now* you can worry."

The Time Is Right

Those of us who live by the clock have our lives ruled by abstract points of time that do not yet exist, for they live in the future. That 2:15 meeting may be set a week in the future and thus we know, come what may, a certain event has been fixed and in the future we will all sit down at a certain 2:15 and talk about a particular topic.

Native people tend to meet and act only "when the time is right." They may sit together in a circle and continue to meet over many days with no urgency to arrive at a conclusion or general plan of action. They do not plan for the future; rather, when the group as a whole feels that the right moment of time has arrived, they will act in a consensual way. For us every moment of time is equivalent. Within Indigenous science, however, particular moments of time may have special powers or qualities.

An Iroquois therapist, Wendy Thomas, once told me that if, when the day arrived, the time did not feel right for her to carry out an interview or meet with a client then she would postpone the appointment.

Another aspect of Indian time is preparation. For us an important event may begin on June 12. For a Native person it begins now, for the next months will be spent in a long preparation out of which will unfold that special moment in time. For ceremonies this preparation may involve an aware-ness of subtle movements within the cosmos because cere-monies themselves celebrate time through the cycles of nature such as the rotation of the seasons, the movements of the heavens, the appearance of Thunder Birds, the appearance of strawberries or new corn, the renewals of contracts with the spirits, and the launching of new enterprises. Each ceremony takes place within a precise cycle of time, but one that cannot necessarily be measured on a clock.

What Is Time?

This question of the particular moment in time at which people come together to hunt or to celebrate is one of the most puzzling aspects of Indigenous science for the non-Native. In the first chapter I explained my confusion as I tried to find out the exact day on which a Sun Dance would occur. It led me to speculate that the very nature of time, within Indigenous science, is different from what we in the West normally experience. Or to put it more precisely, that Indigenous people have access to dimensions within the spirit of time that we have forgotten.

Could it be, for example, that the Sun Dance that lay many days in the future already existed and was calling people toward it? That the power, energy, or spirit of the ceremony unfolds and manifests within a particular region of space and time that we call the future and then acts as a magnet to attract the people, winds, and spirits toward it?

Western physics has recently developed the notion of a "strange attractor," a region that attracts the behavior of the system toward it. The strange attractor does not pull and trap things in a mechanical way; rather, it exerts a more subtle influence so that the system weaves and dances around it, always relatively free, yet never escaping from its influence. Could it be that the time of the ceremony acts in this way, so that for days or weeks earlier people feel within themselves the need for preparation and sense a subtle attraction? While they are perfectly free to go about their business, nevertheless something is drawing them forward into a particular region in time and space?

Within Western physics the strange attractor is an expression of all the interactions and relationships within a complex system and its environment. In a sense, therefore, the system itself generates its own complicated behavior. This leads me to speculate whether a strange attractor of time could be generated out of the rhythms and relationships within the world of nature and spirit. This strange attractor in time does not exist within our Western "now." Its existence lies in the future. A ceremony begins; *that* is the time of the ceremony. People come together, through the action of a general consensus, or a group mind, or in response to the movements of the winds and heavens—and the ceremony commences. *It is at that moment that a time is created for the ceremony.* From that numinous instant time is broadcast backward into the past and forward into the future.

The moment of time of the ceremony is like a stone thrown into a still pond that creates a ripple that will spread out ever wider. And so the ripples of the ceremony reach into the distant future and call back into the past. They reach us in our "now" and call us to prepare and move forward to meet the ceremony. In the paradox of cyclic time this moment did not exist until the ceremony began, but once it had been created it made its influence felt within the cycles of time that stretch back to the days, weeks, and years that precede the ceremony.

Time and the Calendar

For the Mayans, time was a living force that could be celebrated in many ways. Moreover, the movement of time and the unfolding of number formed a perfect synchronicity that could be celebrated through their system of calendars. Just as numbers unfold out of each other and return to their origin, so, too time becomes a cycle of movement.

For the Mayans, time and the calendar formed one whole, complex movement. Western anthropologists who have tried to analyze this subtle movement suggest that time, for the Mayans, existed as a series of interlocking calendars. The simplest of these is called the *uninal*. Used to count the daily intervals, or *kin*, the *uninal* covers a cyclic period of twenty days. Each day of the *uninal* has its special name and association, starting with the Crocodile and ending on the twentieth day with a Flower. The basic rhythm for computing days is the same as the base system of twenty used in Mayan counting.

Just as time cycles from the past into the future and back to the original point of renewal, so too the numbers move, by a process of counting, through their cycle from their origin around the cycle to return back again. Within the movement of time and number each of the spirits of the different days gives way to the next through a process of eternal change and renewal. The starting day of the calendar is also its point of return and renewal, a point that is the same and yet different, for time returns within an ever new context.

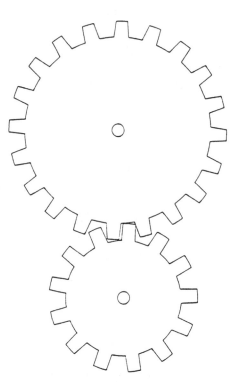

In addition to the twenty-day *uninal,* the Mayans used another cycle of thirteen intervals that intermeshed with it. Each time the *uninal* completes its twenty-day cycle of renewal the second wheel of time advances by one cog. The Mayans named the first day of the *uninal* the Crocodile and the last one the Flower. But after one complete cycle of renewal, when the second cycle advances by one cog, the first day must now change its name from the Crocodile to the Jaguar. After a further period of renewal the spirit of the Jaguar itself gives way and 2 × 20, or 40, days have elapsed. The renewal cycles of the *uninal* continue and the spirit of the Crocodile does not return until the *uninal* has made its way through thirteen such rotations—corresponding to the thirteen cogs on the second calendar. This happens after 13 x 20 = 260 days—a period when the cycle of cycles is itself renewed.

This 260-day cycle is the basic unit of time within the sacred calendar, also called the *tzolkin,* or Count of Days, or the Book of Good and Bad Days, or the Book of Fate. This sacred calendar indicates one of the great teachings of Indigenous science—that there is always a motion within the motion and, indeed, that there is a motion within the motion within the motion.

It is possible to picture these two rotating cycles as cogged wheels as we did above, but we must be careful not to make the association with something in our own culture—the cosmic clockwork of the mechanistic Newtonian universe. For the Mayan calendar-wheel is also the sacred circle, the sacred hoop, and the medicine wheel. It is the wheel of transformation, of birth and death, the unfolding of number that must ultimately return to itself. When we picture the Mayan calendar as a series of cogged wheels we must not be trapped within mechanistic paradigms but must keep in mind something closer to process and transformation.

The Mayan Calendar and the *I Ching*

The 260-day cycle is the province of gods and spirits and a celebration of the processes and transformations of nature and the cosmos. It reminds me of another cycle of process and change, the *I Ching, Book of Changes,* or *Book of Transformations,* which evolved out of the bone oracle of the Shang in ancient China (around 1700 B.C.). Popular accounts of the *I Ching* speak of it as being a book of divination, and certainly it has been used in this way by Chinese people for the last hundreds of years, but in its deeper nature it is a book of wisdom and knowledge about the nature of transformation within the cosmos.

Could it be that there are analogies between the *I Ching* and the Mayan calendar? Both are concerned with number and process, with the transformation of energies, with the rotation of a cycle, and with the harmonies and power of nature. The *I Ching* provides an algebra of transformations not unlike the mathematical metaphysics of Native America. My friend Quang Nguyen, who is an ardent scholar of the *I Ching* and the ancient knowledge of China and Vietnam, points out to me that the *I Ching* is also song—and how important are songs to the peoples of Turtle Island, for a song is a vibration of energy and a living spirit that requires expression from time to time. The original language of ancient China was richer in tones than is modern Chinese and I have had the pleasure of listening to Quang as he sang part of the *I Ching* to me.

For Quang, the *I Ching* contains the Indigenous science of ancient China. It is a book of meteorology, astronomy, earth sciences, and statecraft. As with all Indigenous science, it makes no separation between spiritual and practical knowledge, for the heavens, the earth, and everything in them are sacred.

Why 260 Days?

The sacred calendar of the Mayans remains a mystery although there are a number of speculations as to why 260 days were picked. The most obvious is that 20 is basic to the Mayan system of counting—it is the total of our fingers and toes—and 13 is the number of moons (or months) in the year. Thus, two cycles of 20 and 13 seem perfectly natural in their origin.

Another theory relates the 260-day rotation to the interval of days between the two times each year in which the sun is vertically overhead in the land of the Mayas. On other days of the year the sun does not climb so high in the sky and a stick standing vertically at noon will always cast a shadow. But on two special days alone this shadow will vanish. An important Mayan observatory, which could well have been used in making a measurement of this interval, was located in the exact region where the number of days between the two occurrences each year is exactly 260!

Practical Calendar

In addition to the sacred calendar, the Mayans employed yet another time cycle—the practical calendar. Based upon the sacred counting unit of twenty, the practical calendar consisted of 18 of these twenty-day cycles. The rotation of the rotation within the practical calendar happens after 18 × 20 = 360 days have elapsed. This period of 360 days is exactly the same time interval used by the ancient Sumerians, and survives today in the fact that we divide the circle into 360 degrees!

This practical calendar was used to count the year, which is the time taken for the earth to complete its own cycle around the sun and return to its starting point. It was a cycle in which each month and each day had its own deity.

Of course, we know that the year actually lasts 365 days and not 360. This fact was also known to the Mayans, who, like the Sumerians and Babylonians, preferred to work with a 360-day cycle to which were added an additional 5 days. In a sense these extra days lay outside time and were sometimes called "unlucky days."

We speak of the year as being 365 days long, but we must not forget that every leap year we add an extra day to the year. This is because at midnight on December 31 the earth has not yet quite caught up to the original position that it occupied at midnight on December 31 of the previous year. In fact, it takes it just over six more hours traveling through space to reach that starting point. Each leap year we add an extra day to our calendars (4 × 6 hours = 24 hours, or one day.) If we did not do this, then slowly the 365-day calendar would get out of phase with the seasons and the time when we celebrated our New Year's Day would slowly fall back in time so that after several centuries we would celebrate the New Year in the fall!

The Mayan astronomers took account of such movements within movements and computed the length of the year as 365.2420 days (as compared with the modern Western scientific estimate of 365.2422 days!). Using this value they made corrections to the practical calendar to ensure its precise correspondence to the earth's rotation for centuries, and indeed thousands of years, to come.

Even allowing for such corrections, the first day of a cycle is never exactly renewed, for every movement in nature is always partaking within a greater movement. At the end of each year the earth returns to its same point in relationship to the sun, yet the earth is only one part of the solar system. The planets Venus, Mercury, Jupiter, Saturn, Mars, and the rest are also turning their own cycles. Each January 1 on planet Earth, the other planets are in new relative positions with respect to each other, for their own cycles have not ended. The Earth's cycle is part of a much greater cycle of cycles of cycles. This was known to the ancient Mayan astronomers, who constructed yet more calendars based upon the cycles of the other planets and conceived of time and number in terms of great interlocking cycles.

Time and Astronomy

When we begin to examine the Mayan calendar system we are struck by the fact that the Mayans must have been remarkable astronomers who made accurate observations of the sun and moon and several of the planets. Indigenous peoples all over the world have paid great attention to the movements of the cosmos. Throughout North and South America we find medicine wheels, marked stones, apertures in buildings, temples, and observatories that testify to the importance of astronomical observations. But to what extent do the approaches of Native American astronomers differ from those who base themselves in Western science?

Thanks to Galileo, scientists adapted the terrestrial telescope (first used by mariners) to observe the heavens. How could Indigenous astronomers manage without such telescopes? While it is true that a telescope will magnify the appearance of the moon and the planets, when it comes to making observations of the positions and movements of stars and distant planets its main purpose is not to magnify an image but to collect light. Indeed, it is not possible to magnify the image of a star using an optical telescope—even through the word's largest telescopes a star still appears as a point of light. But what a telescope can do with its system of mirrors and lenses is to isolate a tiny portion of the night sky and to collect sufficient light so that even the faintest stars can be seen. Another use of a telescope is to make repeated and accurate measurements, day after day, in order to track the movements of bodies in the heavens.

It turns out that exactly the same principles were employed by Mayan astronomers. But because they did not have a system of lenses or mirrors to isolate and focus on a tiny portion of the sky, they did something else that was equally ingenious—they dug deep pits in the earth! Lying at the bottom of one of these shafts the Mayan astronomer could look up out of the sur- rounding blackness and into that tiny portion of the sky that could be seen at the end of the shaft. All extraneous light and other distractions would be blocked out and, in this way, consciousness could be focused upon a small group of stars.

At the physiological level the eye will accommodate itself to a very faint object—and remember that the human eye is capable of responding to a single photon of light, that is, a single atomic event that took place within a star eons ago. By this method Indigenous astronomers were able to make accu- rate measurements and keep records of the cosmos over days, weeks, years, decades, and even centuries.

I do not doubt that the precision and sensitivity of these operations far exceeded anything that could be achieved with the naked eye in our present civilization. For recall that Native people are all trained in a particular method of observation from childhood. This observation is not of an active, controll- ing, grasping sort that drives us to want to pick up the world and put it in our pocket. Neither does Indigenous observation seek to hold onto and retain what is "picturesque," "beauti- ful," or "striking"; rather, it is part of the general flux and process of nature.

Through the processes of coming-to-knowing, eye and brain become coordinated to a point where, I believe, the Native mind *itself* becomes a finely tuned instrument. One must never forget that, physiologically, the eye is part of the human brain. During the development of the embryo, the retina, with its rich carpet of receptor nerves, grows as a part of the brain which has been projected into the back of the eye sockets. In essence, therefore, eye and brain are a single organ. It is my speculation that, through training, tradition, and the ceremonies of renewal and alliance with the various spirits of the cosmos, the eye-consciousness of the Mayan astronomer became so sensitive that it was capable of making truly remarkable acts of observations—observations that would be considered physiologically impossible within the West. (There are anecdotal stories of how, in their legends and stories, Native Americans appeared to display certain elements of astronomical knowledge that were not known in the West prior to the invention of the telescope—for example, knowing that certain stars were double stars, and knowing the number of moons around certain of the planets.)

Let me try to justify this speculation using the language of contemporary science. Processes within the stars release energy in the form of photons that travel great distances through space until, by chance, some of them happen to enter the human eye. Within the retina of the eye other quantum processes take place, leading to an unfolding of activity within the brain. In a sense, therefore, the processes within the heart of a star enfold into the photon and, as it reaches the eye, photon activity unfolds into consciousness.

Curiously enough, Einstein's theory of relativity tells us, that with respect to the light ray, the time taken for the journey from star to eye is zero—no time at all. Suppose that you were to travel along a similar path and to measure the journey by your watch. The faster you go the more your watch would slow down until, at the speed of light, the watch would not tick at all, thus the time you would measure for this vast journey would be "no time." In an analogous fashion the distance that you would measure in this journey would also be zero. As far as the photon is concerned, the distant star and the eye-consciousness of the Mayan astronomer are in intimate contact.

The quantum mechanical version of this story tells us that between the star and the eye of the astronomer there is an irreducible link. Indeed, quantum theory emphasizes that this (photon-link eye-consciousness) and the star are an irreducible whole. Another way of thinking about this is that, according to quantum field theory, a photon cannot be emitted unless something is already there to receive the emission. Indeed, it is not so much that the photon leaves the star and enters the eye, but rather that eye-consciousness and star lose their separate distinctions within an overall quantum process.

Thus, the Mayan astronomers who carried out their observation from deep within those shafts in the earth may truly have been in direct communion with the processes of the cosmos, and these same processes may have been unfolded into their symbols, sacred numbers, cycles, and calendars.

The Calendar Round

As we have seen, the Mayan people possessed two basic calendar systems, a sacred system of 260 days and another that was based upon Earth's movement around the sun and consisted of 360 days, 5 "unlucky days," and a number of very accurate corrections.*

Indigenous science tells us that all movement is part of a greater movement. Thus, as the sacred calendar rotates, both number and time return back to themselves after 260 days. During this same time period the practical calendar will not yet have completed its own cycle. In other words, when the sacred cycle is complete the earth is only part way through its yearly astronomical movement.

Faced with two calendar systems, our first reaction may be to mesh them together and create yet another cycle of cycles of cycles—much in the same way that the cogs of the twenty-day

---

*We should be careful not to fall into the trap of fragmenting the sacred from the profane. This distinction between the two calendars is a non-Native one and implies that the Mayans partitioned time into two segments. But Indigenous societies do not work in this way, for everything is sacred and ceremony and prayer are inseparable from daily life.

uninal cycle were intermeshed with the thirteen-period cycle to produce the sacred calendar of 20 × 13, or 260 days.

But this is not the way that the Mayans chose to proceed. Even to me as an outsider it seems that these two calendars, the sacred and practical, should not be directly enmeshed by setting one inside the other. The reason is that these two great cycles belong to different orders of movement, or to two different relationships of spirits. One, the sacred, manifests an eternal cycle, while the other, the practical, is contingent upon the ever-changing flux of the heavens, for it requires periodic corrections to account for the earth's cycle around the sun. While the animating powers of spirits of each great calendar strike an alliance, they are never subservient one to the other. The cogs of one cycle do not drive the other, nor is one cycle enclosed within the other.

Rather, two animating principles exist, two "movements of movements" that extend from the earth to the heavens, from the people to the gods. Each set of cycles unfolds its own process and movement, but there are also those rare occasions oin which these independent cycles of movement happen to coincide when it comes to determining the date of the first day.

Think of these two calendars marking off the cyclic passage of days. The first of these is the sacred calendar.

Elapsed days	Number of cycle
260	1
510	2
1020	4
2040	8
4080	16
8160	32
16320	64
.	.
.	.
18980	73
.	.
.	.

The other way of marking time is using the secular cycle that renews every 365 days.

Elapsed days	Number of cycle or year
365	1
730	2
1095	3
1825	4
.	.
.	.
.	.
.	.
18980	52
.	.
.	.

Note that after 52 cycles of the secular calendar have been completed, the first days of the secular and of the sacred year coincide. In other words, exactly the same number of days have elapsed after 52 rotations of the secular calendar and 73 cycles of the sacred calendar have been recorded. After 18,980 days the two great cycles renew themselves on exactly the same day! (For the mathematically minded, 18,980 is the lowest common multiple of 260 and 365.)

No wonder that the completion of this period of fifty-two secular years was considered of great significance to the Mayans. It marked what they called the Great Calendar Round. Later on the Aztecs were also to celebrate this same Calendar Round. The end of this great cycle, also marks the rebirth of a new great cycle and so all fires were extinguished. It was as if time had come to an end and, with the symbolic relighting of the fires, the movement of time had begun again.

All over Turtle Island the ceremony of lighting a fire is used to begin a cycle. When people come together, to talk in a circle for example, they light a fire at their first meeting that is then kept burning, night and day, for the duration of their deliberations. Finally, when the circle is ended and the people are about to disperse, this fire is extinguished. The midwinter ceremonies of the Mohawk include the extinguishing of the fire and the raking of its ashes. Other peoples mark the ending of a cycle by breaking pottery.

Everything that comes into manifestation is part of a cycle of time and will flower and grow. Unless it is periodically renewed it will decay and die. This applies as much to societies as it does to the waxing and waning of the moon, the passage of the seasons, and the cycle of a person's life. At the ends of the great cycles the people must renew their alliances and contracts with the spirits and power and energies of the world. There may also be a time when the people acknowledge that their society is approaching its end and they should not enter into a further period of renewal.

Lunar and Venusian Calendars

In addition to the unfolding movements of the time cycles that make up the Great Calendar Round, the Mayans constructed a calendar based upon the movements of the morning star, or Venus.

The Venus calendar has a period of 584 days, which means the Earth and Venus return to their same relative positions around the sun every 2920 days. In other words, Venus and Earth assume the same relative positions every eight years. In the time taken for earth to make their eight journey, around the sun (eight years), Venus will have made five journeys. Thus five becomes the sacred number of Venus and Quetzalcoatl.

Besides the interlocking of the Venus and the practical calendar there is a correspondence with the sacred calendar cycle as well. According to Mayan cosmology, Venus appears as the morning star on the first day of the sacred calendar. It will appear in the same position again at the end of another sacred calendar round only after 37,960 days have elapsed. In other words, the cosmos contains a great movement that encompasses 146 cycles of the sacred calendar—the day called 1 *Ahau* becomes the start and finish of this great cycle of time.

We are only beginning to touch upon the complex movement of time and number. The Mayans also employed a calendar to compute the movements of the moon. Through their observations they were able to make highly accurate corrections necessary to predict lunar eclipses. Some Western commentators believe that the Mayans also constructed calendars that dealt with the cycles of the planets Mars, Mercury, Jupiter, and Saturn.

Cycles and Durations

Time and number were inseparable for the Mayans, and with their metaphysical understanding of the power of zero they were able to generate ever greater cycles of time and number. Some of these are listed below:

> *kin* = the day
> *uninal* = a period of 20 days
> *tun* = 360 days or 18 *uninals*
> 20 *tuns* = 1 *katun* (7200 days, or 20 years)
> 20 *katuns* = 1 *baktun* (144,000 days, or 400 years)
> 20 *baktuns* = 1 *pictun* (2,880,000 days, or around 8000 years)
> 20 *piktuns* = 1 *calabtun* (57,600,000 days, or 158,000 years)
> 20 *calabtuns* = 1 *kinchiltun* (1,520,000,000 days, or 3,200,000 years)
> 20 *kinchiltuns* = 1 *alatun* (23,040,000,000 days, or 64,000,000 years)
> 1 *hablatun* = 460,800,000,000 years.

These latter names refer to truly enormous numbers and to vast time periods that extend beyond recorded history into the time span of the human species and beyond that into the evolution of life on this planet, into geological time, into the sorts of astronomical time frames concerned with the creation of the earth and sun, and even right back to where Western scientists date the big bang origin of the universe at several tens of billions of years ago. Indeed, the greatest cycle—the Mayan *hablatun*—vastly exceeds the age of many universes, each one cycling from its big bang origin through a period of expansion and the building of stars, through the first evolution of life on certain planets, the flowering of consciousness, the decay of stars, the eventual heat death of the universe, its contraction taking it back to a point that becomes the origin of yet another big bang, and so on, on and on, universe after universe, cosmos after cosmos, all within the blink of a single *hablatun*.

The Sixth Sun

These vast cycles of time were not created simply for the exhilaration of expressing large numbers, but appear to be related to real dates that are very accurately expressed. Much of the Mayan civilization is veiled, but those who have examined a variety of its inscriptions have noted dates and recorded years that seem to have been measured from a common starting point—August 12, 3113 B.C.

It seems reasonable, therefore, to assume that this date marks the beginning of one of the great cycles of time. If this is true it means that the present time will come to an end on December 24, 2011! Indeed some Mayan people, like Hunbatz Men, are already speaking of the ending of the Fifth World and the coming of the Sixth Sun, a time of renewal and reconsecration. With the coming of the white man, they say, the Mayan people reached a point in their cycle where they needed to withdraw from their civilization, but now a time is coming when the Mayan alliance will be renewed again and there will be a second great flowering—not only in Central America but over all the Americas.

Such prophecies are being echoed by Elders and spiritual leaders all over North America. No matter the language they speak or the people from whom they originate, they all look to a time of great change. Some speak of it as the Great Purification when many living things will be destroyed and Mother Earth with enjoy a time of rest. Others say that it will be an inner purification or a change of consciousness. Some prophecies speak of the time when a new fire—the Seventh Fire—

will be lit by the red and white peoples to serve as a light to all the races of the world. Others say that the time has come to speak to the white man again, that five hundred years ago The People spoke and no one listened, but now the white brother is more willing to sit down and learn from the red brother before it is too late. And, at least for the Mayan people, the time of this great change is already written in the stars.

9

Language:
The Sacred Vibrations

Introduction

Language is the key to our culture. This is the message I have heard at so many of the circles, ceremonies, and meetings I have attended. Elders, traditional people, community leaders, and Native educators argue that the language they speak is an expression of their society, their history, and the world they live in. Language contains the story of their landscape, their great journeys and migrations, and the spiritual alliances that go back hundreds and even thousands of years. Songs, ceremonies, traditional ways, and all the trappings of Indigenous science can be found enfolded within the language.

To hear the Haida people speak is to listen to the sounds of waves on the shore and the cry of birds. Other languages carry the sounds of the winds; the sense of an overwhelming presence within the Eastern Woodlands; a dim memory of the slowly moving growl of a glacier from the last ice age; the sounds spoken to animals; the words whispered to the spirit world; the high pitched sounds sung softly by the Blackfoot as they ride at night so as not to frighten animals in their passing; and the vibrations that invoke the powerful energies of the cosmos.

The language of a people is their life, but in so many cases this life is endangered. Within several communities the traditional language is spoken by only a handful of Elders. In other cases the last speakers of some languages passed away earlier this century and, in a deep sense, this may also mean the end of those societies. A people can no more live without its language than a tree can grow without roots.

The Languages of Dominance

But how can a language be that important? Most of us take it for granted that anything we say in English can be equally well expressed in Spanish, French, or German. People who have attended business meetings in Europe and have experienced simultaneous translations are amazed at the speed with which their sentences can be switched from one language to another. If ideas can be translated so rapidly between English and German, Italian and French, what can be so special about Huron, Mohawk, or Haida?

But suppose, instead of dealing with European languages, you were to go into a law court with a Native American witness. Your experience would be quite different. Natives love to joke about those situations in which a judge makes a brief remark and waits while the translator begins a long oration in an Indigenous language. The judge asks in surprise, "Did I really say that?" The translator replies "Yes,... more or less." "But," the judge will say, "I only spoke a couple of sentences and you went on for about twenty minutes!" A little later, when asked a question, a Native witness will begin a long speech, at the end of which the translator may simply report, "The witness says, 'No'."

What is going on is not simply a matter of moving between two different languages but of translating between profoundly different worldviews. What to the judge was a single sentence may have contained words that are related to concepts, that touch on issues, that are never found within the traditional Indigenous worldview. The translator will have to set the scene, as it were, and provide the context in which the judge's brief remarks can be understood. Likewise, the act of saying no, within some cultures, may depend upon a variety of factors that are not thought to be relevant in ours.

These issues do not arise when we translate between English, Spanish, French, and German because Europeans and North Americans share a common worldview. Our notions of reality, time, space, and causality are more or less identical, so there is no need for a translator to deal with radically new concepts when discussing a land deal. A similar ease of movement between English and Mohawk, Cree, Hopi, or Haida is not possible.

Not only do Europeans share a common worldview, but their languages are very closely related. Therefore, what we take as a measure of "foreignness" is somewhat of an illusion, for the European languages (Germanic and Italic) are very close, being part of an even larger family, called Indo-European, which includes the Celtic, Slavic, Albanian, Greek, and Iranian languages, as well as the vast family of Indo-Aryan languages such as Hindi, Bengali, Sinhalese, Panjabi, and the sacred Sanskrit language. (Finnish and Hungarian are not members of this great family.)

All these languages have their origins in a single proto-Indo-European that was spoken before 3000 B.C. This may have been the language spoken by the nomadic Kurgan peoples who moved from southern Russia to the Danube area of Europe around 3500 B.C. Indeed, proto-Indo-European may have originated several thousand years before in an even earlier language that had something in common with the Uralic languages like Finnish and Hungarian. Thus, when we hear a language that is totally foreign to us, we may nevertheless be within our own language family, dealing with peoples who share some of our values, culture, worldview, and science. Native American languages, however, are profoundly different from Indo-European, and within the North American continent there are several language families as different from each other as English is from Chinese.

Historically, the Western scientific vision has come to dominate large regions of the earth through its economic and technological power. All over the world people watch movies and television programs, read textbooks, and operate computer programs, many of which were originally developed in English. Much scientific research is written and published in English and even the study of linguistics is dominated by academics, books, and research articles that use English or one of the other European languages. Hence, even language itself is viewed through the perspective of European languages and worldview.

Our technological world is so remarkably uniform that what we take to be differences of attitude and culture are generally nothing more than variations upon one particular theme. When we enter the world of Indigenous American languages, however, we encounter profoundly different concepts and worldviews. Indeed, not only are the concepts enfolded within the languages radically different, but even the meaning of language itself and the function of the sounds people make is profoundly different.

Language, so traditional Indigenous people say, is the door into their world. When I speak with Leroy Little Bear or Sa'ke'j Henderson I sense their struggle to find the right words in English for the sound-vibrations within their own languages; for these sounds relate to a very different system of thought. As Sa'ke'j says, "Some mornings I wake up with my head full of rhythms, and rhythms of rhythms, and rhythms of rhythms of rhythms. And to have to speak English is like having to put on a straitjacket."

When I get into a deep question with Leroy he will remark, "Well, in Blackfoot we say..." and produce a pattern of sound for me. Or he may pause and sing to himself very softly as he tries to discover a way of putting the vibrations, and all that they convey, into the particular linguistic structures demanded by English.

The Algonquin peoples are concerned with the animation of all things within their process-vision of the cosmos; verbs are therefore the dominant feature of their language, some of them having well over one thousand different endings. For the Iroquois peoples, relationships are important, as they are for all Indigenous peoples, and thus well over one hundred different kinship terms are used in the Mohawk language.

Learning Mohawk is not simply a matter of picking up a

vocabulary of unfamiliar words along with the rules of grammar and syntax. It means being able to understand the meaning and nature of different kinship relationships, realizing why they are important, and understanding the whole worldview in which they are embedded.

The way a language differentiates between various relationships reflects the way a society chooses to structure itself. In societies like the Iroquois, many important decisions are made by women. In other societies men may play an important role. In some groups the responsibility of a boy's growth to manhood belongs to father's brother. The blanket term *uncle* would clearly be inadequate in such a case, for it does not distinguish this privileged role from the less important one of the mother's brother. This is a rather obvious case in which it is important for the language to make a distinction between different forms of what Westerners see as one relationship. Other cases are far more subtle and can only be understood by a person who grows up and lives within a particular society.

Chomsky and Structure

One reason we find it so hard to grasp the significance Indigenous people give to their languages is that we generally take language to be simply a medium in which to express our thoughts and feelings. It is as if a person were to pick up a news bulletin on a variety of different receivers—a car radio, an expensive stereo system, and a cheap transistor. In each case the sound quality would be different, but there would be absolutely no difference between the information contained in the news; the values of certain stocks, traffic conditions on a given highway, and the current temperature would remain the same. We tend to think that the languages we speak are like different radio sets—the passive vehicles for our ideas. Within Indigenous science, however, language has a power all its own, and to speak it is to enter into an alliance with the vibrations of the universe.

Noam Chomsky, the MIT linguist, has proposed that there are deep linguistic structures within the brain that are common to human beings irrespective of the language they happen to speak. Particular languages—English, Spanish, Mohawk, Haida, or Japanese—are only surface phenomenon, forms we happened to pick up in childhood, but the deep structure of language is something we are born with.

Computer engineers who set up the functioning of word processors use a machine language that is closer to algebra and mathematics than to English, yet what you see on your screen are sentences in your own language. Each time you hit a key on your keyboard, processes within your computer's brain take place in machine language. The messages that appear on your screen are determined by the fact that your particular word-processing package happens to be in English, French, or some other language. It is a simple matter to switch between an English, French, Spanish, or German word-processing package and the underlying machine language remains the same.

In an analogous way, Chomsky has hypothesized that there is something like a machine language deep within our brains. When we speak, this deep language gets transformed at the surface into the particular language we happen to have learned. Within Chomsky's picture, the world's languages are surface structures, vehicles for expressing what is being generated at a much deeper level within the brain.

Indigenous people do not, I think, see things in the same way as Noam Chomsky. Within Indigenous science, thoughts are inseparable from language. The language that is spoken is not simply a medium, or a vehicle for communication, rather it is a living thing, an actual physical power within the universe. The vibrations of its words are energies that act within the transforming processes we call reality. Moreover, each language is a link with the particular landscape in which a people live.

Manifesting Words

When people sit in a circle "popping wind"—as the Mic Maqs say—they are creating physical vibrations within the universe, and these vibrations evoke and bring into direct manifestation other vibrations, powers, or energies. Speaking is a positive action that can bring about change, for what is said can come into actuality.

Within the layers of an Indigenous language there are ways of speaking that will only be used on ceremonial occasions. Linguists have noted, for example, that the size of the vocabulary of what they call a shaman is considerably larger than the vocabularies used by other people within the same society. Certain words have great power and should never be spoken unless the right people are present in a circle to contain the energies that circulate, evoked by that particular sound vibration.

Sa'ke'j Henderson has told me that within Mic Maq society, when traditional people have had a quarrel they do not curse. Rather, when they meet they quietly say harsh words to each other over the shoulder at the moment of their passing. The reason is that this quarrel is purely personal and neither party would wish to alert the powers and energies that are always around them and involve them in their dispute.

Indigenous hunters do not refer directly to the animal they are seeking by speaking its name. It is not so much that the particular animal would hear them and keep away, but that the energy vibrations of the name would alert the Keeper of that particular animal.

Hunting takes place not simply on the immediate physical plane but through dreams, visions, and the sweat lodge, for the hunters must enter into a negotiation with the Keepers of the animals and request that a particular animal should sacrifice itself so that the people can eat. In return the Keeper will demand certain obligations from The People. It is said that during these negotiations a person may trick the Keeper. Indeed, the Keepers of the animals are often amused if they can be fooled by a clever trick. One of the things that must be done is never to refer to an animal directly by the sound of its name, but rather to use speech in an oblique way.

The use of euphemisms is never more important than when speaking about the Bear—for this is one of the most powerful animals, the one who showed and taught The People about the plants and medicine ways. The Bear is referred to as Old

Grandfather, or by means of some other honorific. Likewise, after a kill the bear's bones and skull are treated with great ceremony and respect.

The Vibrations of Nature

Within Indigenous science the word itself has power. Conventional linguistics holds that the connection between a word and its referent is purely arbitrary. Thus, one of the fathers of modern linguistics, Ferdinand de Saussure, distinguished between what he called *signifiant* ("the thing that signifies," or "the sound image") and *signifié* (the concept or thing that is being signified).

This question of the arbitrary nature of words goes back to the disputes of the Greek philosophers. Aristotle, for example, felt that names had no intrinsic existence and were no more than symbols for objects and concepts. On the other hand, Plato suggested that a certain intrinsic relationship existed between the name and the thing signified. This echoes the tradition that comes from several of the world's esoteric and mystical practices that certain names in themselves have power and significance.

In many traditions the name of God is considered to be so sacred that it is never pronounced, but referred to obliquely. In the Christian tradition the Gospel of St. John equates the beginning of all things with the *logos*, the word. The cabala claims that certain truths can be uncovered by examination of the form of particular words. There are also traditions of sacred languages—the languages in which the gods spoke to humans—in which each word has a perfect correspondence to the inner nature of the universe.

Within Indigenous science, to say something is to create an objective event and release a process of energetic vibrations that enter into relationships with the other powers and energies of nature. Thus, since every sound is an event of significance, a person must take responsibility for whatever he or she says.

Language was created by the Ancestors as a direct connection to nature. Words link man to the inner meaning of things. There are stories of a time when humans and animals spoke freely together. One sometimes gains the impression that deep within the hidden recesses of Indigenous languages the words of power can still be found that will enable people to communicate with the life around them.

Sa'ke'j Henderson has explained how in Mic Maq the names of trees are the sound that the wind makes as it moves through their leaves in the fall. The name of a tree is therefore far from arbitrary. It is based upon the direct experience of listening to a specific sound that refers to a particular tree—for each of the different species of trees makes a different sound. It is, moreover, a sound made at that time of the year when the leaves begin to dry, a sound specific to a particular area of Turtle Island as the salt-laden wind blows in from the Atlantic Ocean.

Trees process, the manifestations of animating energies in a particular environment. Move to a different part of the world and the tree, in its deeper sense, is no longer the same. While the word dog changes in a purely arbitrary fashion as we drive across the frontier between the United States and Mexico, the sound vibration of the word for tree and the material manifestation of the process are all tied to the changing context of an actual landscape.

Categories of Thought

Another significant difference between Indigenous and European languages lies in what they reveal to us about the nature of thought. Within our European languages and thinking we have a tendency to group things together into categories. Thus, we have generic words like *birds, fish, trees, rocks, mountains, particles, people, thoughts, feelings* and *emotions*. Yet this form of categorizing is not an inevitable feature of the human mind, for Indigenous languages support totally different forms of logic and reasoning.

A wide variety of creatures swim in water. Some come to the surface to take a fly, others prefer to feed near the bottom, yet despite their many differences we classify them all within the category of fish, as opposed to other creatures that live in the water.

This concept of "fish" does not exist within the Algonquin languages. The Cree do not have a word in their own language that corresponds to our *fish*, rather they refer to the processes of animation that take place in rivers and lakes. Likewise, they do not have a concept of "bone," instead they use words that refer to particular animals, or to parts of an animal's body, or to something that is in a medicine bag.

It isn't that these languages have not properly developed, or that the thought processes of the Cree people area "primitive" because they do not categorize the world. They have chosen to work within the world in a very different way from us.

"What is inside that drawer?" we ask.

"Knives and forks," we are told.

When we open the drawer we are not surprised to see sets of fish and steak knives, a bread knife, a carving knife, a paring knife, a chopping knife, and a knife for cutting cheese. To us, knives are knives, things used for cutting. We may use adjectives to distinguish between fish and steak knives, but we would never go as far as to ask our language to differentiate between the individual steak knives in a particular set.

But in a hunter's world all knives are individual. Each knife was made by a particular person. Not only will it differ from other knives in the way it looks, works, and handles, but it will share the spirit of the person who made it. In English we say, "This is my knife, and that one is yours." But within the Indigenous world you may be able to put my knife to a different use and thus place your spirit into my knife and animate it. Thus, the sense of "possession" or "ownership" of a knife would be more fluid. Categories in the natural world always have fluid boundaries.

Indigenous languages reflect this transforming ability of objects. If there were to be categories, they would have to be categories that are always in a state of flux and transforming. Objects exist not so much in themselves but through interrelationships.

To create a category is to set a boundary within thought. It is to place a conceptual circumference around something. But, again, we must recall what the Blackfoot people say about their circles—they are always open, always ready to accept something new. Thus, if Indigenous science were to erect a category of thought, it would just be inviting the trickster to enter and transcend any boundaries that had been erected.

Take another example: If a caribou has been killed and its meat is to be divided, does it make sense to talk about proportions in terms of categories of thought such as half a caribou, or one quarter; or of weights such as two pounds? An animal like a caribou, moose, bear, or salmon is never divided according to abstract geometrical proportions such as shape; neither is it divided by weight. Rather, it divides naturally and physiologically according to the joints between its bones and its muscle structure. Neither can the food from different parts of its body be compared according to its weight. For how can cheeks, lungs, brains, tongue, stomach, and rump be placed on the same set of scales and evaluated? And when it comes to the division of food, should an old man's portion weigh the same as a young hunter's? Or should people be given to according to their needs and requirements? Fixed categories and abstractions simply could not work in such a situation. Instead, division must always be done within the context of the situation and with respect to each person.

Another set of categories common in Western thought that dates from the time of the ancient Greeks is the notion of mentally categorizing objects in terms of regular shapes. Old-fashioned books on drawing divide the human figure into cylinders, cubes, spheres, and cones. And, at least until the recent fashion for fractals and chaos theory came along, the world itself was viewed as being composed of shapes belonging to the classifications of linear, circular, square, elliptical, polygonal, cubical, and spherical.

Aboriginal peoples have no need for these idealistic classifications, for the tools they make—canoes, arrows, moccasins, snowshoes, knives, mittens, and so on—are always irregularly and individually shaped. Objects are made to be used; they follow the demands of the natural forms of materials and of the uses to which they are to be put. Where shape categories do exist, within the Ojibwaj language, say, they tend to be of the form of "somewhat round," "repeatedly right angled," "flexibly cylindrical," and "two-dimensional." Thus, language and perception is geared to the relationships of irregular, natural forms.

Animation

Some Indigenous languages do employ general classifications. These are used to differentiate between the animate and inanimate. But if anyone thought that this was going to be without complexity, he or she had not reckoned with the transforming power of Indigenous thought.

As we have already seen, the worldview of many of the Indigenous peoples of Turtle Island is based upon ideas of process, animation, and flux. Therefore, the important distinctions that are made within their languages are between the animate and the inanimate. Just as chairs and tables have gender in French and Spanish, what we would normally consider to be nonliving is spoken of in Cree for example, as being animate or inanimate. But discovering what exactly is animate becomes a different matter.

As an example, the Algonquin languages are rich in verbs, and the verbs themselves are similarly rich in their structure, with an intransitive verb having as many as 350 endings, while a transitive verb can have over 1200. These verbs, or rather the vibrations of their sounds and the "poppings" of their winds, comprise many of the sounds that Algonquin people make when they meet. They are an aspect of a complex music, a counterpoint of vibrations, a weaving of powers of animation that reflects, in a very direct way, the powers, energies, and alliances of the universe.

A people who can speak to rocks, and hear their voices, must clearly treat rocks as being animate in their language. But things are not that simple, for we, with our logical minds always want to put things into their Aristotelian categories: If a thing does not belong within the category A, then it must be a member of the category non-A. What is not inanimate must therefore be animate, and all things must fit nicely within a particular, uniform classification.

Indigenous science does not work this way. I can remember a Choctaw Elder, Mary Jones, speaking of her vision and telling me how she would speak to the rocks near her home. "The rocks are alive," she told me. Mary must have seen my scientist's mind starting to buzz because she looked at me for a moment and added, "But not every rock is alive."

A non-Native friend of mine had been told that while rocks are animate, not all of them are alive. "Well, which ones aren't alive?" he asked. "The ones that don't breathe," was the reply. Another non-native, when asking if trees could speak was told, "Yes...er...that one can speak. And...er...that one, and...er...that one over there."

Our problem is that we are used to living in a world of objects, so when the question of animation comes up we immediately look at the rock, or try to discover whether it has special characteristics that make it alive. But in the Algonquin world, animation is the primary reality and the particular manifestations, the rocks, are less important. Like young children excited with a birthday gift, we focus on the wrapping paper and forget about the present inside.

Sa'ke'j Henderson told me that the Mic Maq language is not really designed for talking about objects but for entering more deeply into the realities of the world. We have perfectly good eyes, he said, and if we want to discourse about chairs and tables we can simply point to them—or if, like many Native peoples, you think that pointing is impolite you can "point" with the lips of your mouth.

English, Sa'ke'j says, is a language for the eye, while an Algonquin language is a language for the ear. When he has to speak English instead of Mic Maq, Sa'ke'j feels that he is being forced to interact with a world of objects, things, rigid boundaries and categories in place of a more familiar world of flows, processes, activities, transformations, and energies. For Sa'ke'j, the Mic Maq language is itself a world of sounds that echoes and reflects the vibrations of the physical world. While the surface world of objects and material things can easily be identified by the eye, it is the ear that must deal with the more

subtle levels of flux, transformation, and reality behind appearances. The English language, in his opinion, does little
more than mimic what the eye can do far better by giving
emphasis to names and objects, while the Algonquin family of
languages complements the eye's abilities by addressing a
world of sounds and energies. In speaking English Sa'ke'j is
also struck by the many metaphors that refer to seeing. We say
"Yes, I see that" or speak of an "illuminating idea." Mic Maq,
by contrast, places less emphasis upon this world of visual
appearances.

The problem with English is that when it tries to grapple
with abstractions and categories it tends to trap the mind into
believing that such categories have an equal status with
tangible objects. Algonquin languages, being for the ear, deal
in vibrations in which each word is related directly, not only to
a process of thought, but also to the animating energies of the
universe. To the Algonquin people, language is not a duplica-
tion of sight, but a complement to it. Thus, "popping wind" is
not a representation of reality, or something separate from it;
rather it is an integral part.

Logic and Language

This very different understanding of the role played by categories has important consequences for the way Indigenous people reason and employ logic. When we think of that word *logic*
we tend to assume that one particular cultural approach to
thought is the arbiter for all. *Logic* has its origin in the
philosophers of ancient Greece, most notably Aristotle. In his
Logic Aristotle examined the different ways in which language
actually works within the domain of reasoned argument and
focused attention on categories, propositions, and the formal
ways that patterns of language are used to approach truth. In
essence Aristotle was not so much surveying the range of
human reason as modifying what was inherent in the Greek
language.

On into the Middle Ages philosophers cataloged the
various language patterns that ensure that a given argument,
or series of deductions is rational and "logical." These include

the famous law of the excluded middle, "A thing must either be so and so or not be so and so" and the law of contradiction, "A thing cannot both be so and so and not be so and so." These may seem necessarily true to us, but there are many cultures, such as that of classical India, in which such a logic does not apply.

Another example of reason based upon language forms is deduction:

If: All men are mortal
And: Socrates is a man
Then: Socrates is mortal

But it does not follow that

If: Some things that glitter are gold
And: This ring glitters
Then: This ring is gold

Such logic exists within a world of thought that operates using a structure of categories, something our own language does very well. This logic and language tells us that an object cannot simultaneously be a member of two mutually exclusive categories: An action cannot be both bad and good, something cannot be both subjective and objective, an electron cannot be both a wave and a particle.

Today we know that indeed an electron *is* both a wave and a particle. Niels Bohr suggested that within the quantum world science had to adopt what he called complementary descriptions—rather than having a single description that exhausts the phenomenon in question, science has to employ complementary, mutually contradictory, accounts. The world, at the subatomic level, does not accord with the traditional way our English-Latin-Greek language structures reality.

As soon as we begin to drop our obsession with categories and boundaries in thought many of these problems and paradoxes fall away. Quantum theory constantly emphasizes that the context in which events occur is of key importance. Set up an experiment in one way and the result is particles. Do it another way and it must be interpreted in terms of waves. It is impossible to separate a phenomenon from the context in which it is observed. Categories no longer exist in the absence of contexts.

Within Indigenous science, context is always important. Nothing is abstract since all things happen within a landscape and by virtue of a web of interrelationships. The tendency to collect things into categories does not exist within the thought and language of, for example, Algonquin speakers.

This leads to a profoundly different way of approaching and thinking about the world. For, in the absence of categories, each thing is mentally experienced on its own merits, and for what it actually is. Rather than indulging in comparison or judgment, Indigenous speakers attempt to enter into relationship with them.

In English we have the general category of "fish," which is the result of classifying, in terms of differences and similarities, the various creatures that live in the water. It therefore becomes convenient within our minds to gather together objects of different shapes, sizes and colors and treat them all as members of the one category "fish." The Algonquin family of languages, for example, does not make use of such categories or boundaries in thought. Rather, it is concerned with processes that are happening in the water and with the peoples' relationships to such processes. Iroquois languages for their part would tend to picture the world in terms of a complex web of relationships. Instead of using logic to reach a single truth, an Indigenous scientist is more concerned with achieving balance and harmony.

Language, Culture, and Thought

Within Indigenous science, language is irreducibly tied to landscape, culture, and thought. A non-Native linguist, Benjamin Lee Whorf, came to similar conclusions. As a result of his study of the language of the Hopi people, he found that their language reflects the non-Newtonian universe in which they live.

Whorf tried to understand the way the Hopi people saw the world around them and how this perception was expressed in the language they spoke. Their concept of time, for example, was not of a smoothly running stream that moved from past to present, and on into the future. Likewise, in their language there is no talk of duration, or of a past, a future, or the present.

Whorf concluded that, just as it is possible for mathematicians and physicists to have perfectly consistent descriptions of geometries that are not Euclidian, so, too, societies can have radically different, yet perfectly consistent, accounts of the universe. In the case of the Hopi this was a worldview in which separable time and space, as we know them in the Newtonian universe, do not exist. What Whorf called the "manifest," or objective, and the "manifesting," or subjective take their place.

The term *manifest* refers to all things that are accessible to the senses, and this means what is experienced without division or distinction between past and present—for all lie within the field of the manifest.

The term *manifesting*, on the other hand, includes what we in our worldview would refer to as being "mental" as well as what lies in the future. According to Whorf, the Hopi make no distinction between the mental and the future. Such categories simply do not exist within their language. Within Hopi, the manifesting refers to those things that exist in the heart, and not only in the hearts of The People but also in the hearts of animals, trees, plants, and rocks.*

The Hopi worldview, according to Whorf, does not contain a sense of movement or advancement of time. Rather, there is a notion of process whereby the manifesting enters the manifest and, at the edge of this process, the Hopi language is able to talk about things that are on the verge of coming into manifestation.

Possibly this leading edge of manifesting could be compared to that split second of no return when you are about to sneeze, or when the words within your mind are about to enter into physical speech. Although we in the West have a perception of our intention to act, this is not reflected in our language. Imagine what it would be like to think and speak

---

*These opinions on how the Hopi see the world are from Benjamin Lee Whorf's writings, and I am taking them at face value.

within a language that focused upon the movements of your thoughts, feelings, desires, will, and intentions; on the way intentions move into physical action, the ways in which things come into physical existence around you, and the movement between subjective and objective reality. Using the forms Whorf called "expective" and "inceptive," this is exactly what the Hopi are able to do. A complex and highly subtle world-view is enfolded within the Hopi language. If a person does not speak the Hopi language, there would be a considerable barrier to understanding and to experiencing this reality.

Linguists do, of course, learn Native languages, but usually as adults and from within their powerful Western scientific worldview. Thus, Natives smile and say, Oh, so-and-so thinks he can speak our language but he really doesn't know how to say very much. An amusing story told of a linguist who spent a long time trying to master a language only to have Elders smile when he spoke. He later found out, the reason was that he had been taught the first version of the language, the one used when teaching children.

The same difficulties can also be faced by Natives, for to learn a new Indigenous language is to put on a different way of thinking and is not at all the same as an English speaker's learning French or Spanish. Sa'ke'j Henderson grew up speaking Cheyenne and only later moved into the Mic Maq community. Mic Maq and Cheyenne are both members of the Algonquin family of languages; nevertheless, after many years of speaking Mic Maq Sa'ke'j says that he is still discovering the extreme subtleties of the language and attempting to enter those special areas of the language that are used when speaking of powerful matters.

I have been told that the most extreme punishment within an Indigenous society is that of banishment. In such a position people are not only cut off from relations and land, but from the language they have always spoken. To take up life in a new society is to begin, like a child, to learn its language and, in the process, take on new ways of thinking and being. If a person did not learn to behave in one society and world, he or she had to enter and learn another.

Shakespeare understood the true meaning of banishment. When Thomas Mowbray, Duke of Norfolk, is banished by the king in *Richard the II* his major concern is his loss of language.

And now my tongue's use is to me no more,
    Than an unstring'd viol, or a harp, . . .
    What is thy sentence then, but speechless death,
    Which robs my tongue from breathing native breath?

A Language of Process

One of the recurring themes of this book has been the role of chance, flux, and process within Indigenous science. This worldview is perfectly reflected in many Native languages, in particular that of the Algonquin family (Cree, Ojibwaj, Mic Maq, Blackfoot, Cheyenne, and several others). With its emphasis upon verbs it perfectly reflects a reality of transformation and change. Sa'ke'j Henderson has said that he can go a whole day without ever speaking a noun, just dealing in the rhythms and vibrations of process. Nouns do exist within the language but, like the vortex that forms in a fast flowing river, the nouns are not primary in themselves but are temporary aspects of the ever-flowing process.

What is interesting about this language-worldview is the way it has been reflected in modern physics. Niels Bohr, one of the creators of quantum theory, pointed out the way in which our language disposes us to employ concepts that are entirely inappropriate for the quantum world. David Bohm took this further. Bohm rejected the idea of a reality composed of objects in interaction in favor of processes and activities in a continuous movement of unfolding and enfolding. Moreover, this reality is not confined to matter but extends to thoughts, feelings, and emotions unfolding within the brain and body.

To Bohm there was no dichotomy between inner and outer, mental and physical, subjective and objective, for all are aspects of one underlying movement. The English language, however, keeps bringing us back to a world of objects. "The apple is attracted to the earth," "The girl catches the ball," and "The cat sat on the mat" are all examples of the ways in which our noun-dominated language lends itself so naturally to a worldview composed of objects in interaction.

What is needed, Bohm argued in his book *Wholeness and the Implicate Order*, is a new sort of language, one based upon processes and activity, transformation and change, rather than on the interaction of stable objects. Bohm called this hypothetical language the "rheomode." It is based primarily on verbs and on grammatical structures deriving from verbs. Such a language, Bohm argued, is perfectly adapted to a reality of enfolding and unfolding matter and thought.

David Bohm had not known when he wrote of that concept that such a language is not just a physicist's hypothesis. It actually exists. The language of the Algonquin peoples was developed by the ancestors specifically to deal with subtle matters of reality, society, thought, and spirituality.

A few months before his death, Bohm met with a number of Algonkian speakers and was struck by the perfect bridge between their language and worldview and his own exploratory philosophy. What to Bohm had been a major breakthroughs in human thought—quantum theory, relativity, his implicate order and rheomode—were part of the everyday life and speech of the Blackfoot, Mic Maq, Cree, and Ojibwaj.

Indigenous Science

Science Defined

In claiming that The People do not have anything that could remotely be called a science, what most people would have in mind for science is something that comes close to what Aldous Huxley writes about in his essay "Beliefs" when he refers to the scientist as selecting "from the whole of experience only those elements which can be weighed, measured, numbered, or which lend themselves in any other way to mathematical treatment." Huxley goes on to point out that by this technique of simplification and abstraction from experience, science has succeeded in understanding and dominating the physical environment.

When it comes to the notion that reality lies in what can be "weighed, measured, and numbered" the uncompromising scientific attitude is best expressed by an autobiographical remark attributed to the psychologist Hans Eysenck: "The fact that my mother did not love me is not important, because such a thing cannot be measured. It is very difficult to see how a mother affects her child. If it cannot be tested, it does not exist."

The point of Huxley's essay happens to be that within this act of abstraction, science does not consider "the intuitions of value and significance,...love, beauty, mystical ecstasy..."

found in reality. The problem arises when the scientific picture of the world is taken for the whole of reality.

If Huxley's definition is what most people mean by science, then it is probably true that Indigenous people do not possess a science. After all, why should people whose philosophy speaks of relationship, the primacy of direct experience, and the interconnectedness of all things ever wish to divorce themselves from their world and fragment their experience though such acts of abstraction? If there were to be an Indigenous science then it would deal not in abstraction, weighing, and measuring; but in relationship, holism, quality, and value.

Huxley's definition of science captures, I believe, what many scientists think that their discipline should be. But there are other definitions. The *Oxford English Dictionary*, for example, employs a wider scope:

> 1. (a) "the state of fact of knowing." Knowledge (in the sense as opposed to belief or opinion).
>
> (b) "...the distinction to be drawn between the theoretical perception of a truth and moral conviction.
>
> 2. knowledge acquired by study...mastery...trained skill
>
> 3. a recognized department of learning...contradistinguished from art.
>
> 4. In a more restricted sense: a branch of study which is concerned either with a connected body of demonstrated truths or with observed facts systematically classified and more or less colligated by being brought under general laws, and which includes trustworthy methods for the discovery of new truths within its own domain.

These definitions do come closer to the spirit of Indigenous science even if that shade of fragmentation and abstraction remains, with science being distinguished as a "branch," or separable part, of a much greater tree of knowledge, or in that one should take pains to distinguish science from moral convictions. Nevertheless, it seems reasonable to assume that any science must be concerned with "truths" that form a "body," and that it should deal in "observed facts" and their systematic classification. Without integration and cohesion, what would distinguish science from a random collection of facts, observations, and recipes? Furthermore, a science also demands general laws and trustworthy methods for discovering truths.

I believe that Indigenous science does, to a greater and lesser extent, conform to the various aspects of these definitions—if not to all of them. As a science, it is a disciplined approach to understanding and knowing, or rather, to the processes of coming to understanding and knowing. It has supporting metaphysics about the nature of reality, deals in systems of relationship, is concerned with the energies and processes within the universe, and provides a coherent scheme and basis for action. On the other hand, it is not possible to separate Indigenous science from other areas of life such as ethics, spirituality, metaphysics, social order, ceremony, and a variety of other aspects of daily existence. Thus it can never be a "branch" or a "department" of knowledge, but rather remains inseparable from the cohesive whole, from a way of being and of coming-to-knowing.

Changing the Yardstick

Until now I have been asking if Indigenous science is truly a science, and in so doing I have assumed that only one yardstick exists that provides a standard set of definitions—Western science. But this is not to question whether Indigenous science exists in its own right, but to enquire how it measures up to Western science. As far as Indigenous people are concerned, there is no need for them to justify their spirituality, their traditions, or their science by reference to anything external to their society. Indigenous science does not need to explain itself to anyone. It has no need to compare or authenticate itself against the standard of Western science. Because it may not always accord with the dictionary definitions of science does not mean that it is not a valid discipline and way of knowing in its own right.

This book is intended to be a bridge and to provide people with a way of seeing things slightly differently. It may be that after reading it people will begin to look at their own culture from a new perspective and, in turn, develop a new sensitivity to the traditions and worldviews of Native Americans. While Indigenous science needs no justification outside itself, there may be some value in comparing the two sciences. Let us explore where their similarities and differences actually lie.

Western Science: A Cold Topic Turns Hot

A good starting point for this comparison would be to begin with Western science and see to what extent it actually measures up to some of those definitions given above, as an objective, dispassionate, systematic, and integrated discipline. Over the past few decades historians and philosophers of science have been trying to sort out what scientists actually do as opposed to what they claim to do. Well-known names in this field include the philosophers of science Sir Karl Popper, Paul Feyerabend, and Thomas Kuhn.

It is generally accepted that the major difference between science and superstitions or folktales is that the former is based upon reason, objective observation, and well-designed experimentation. In superstition, or pseudoscience, practitioners can believe more or less in anything they want to; while a true science is guided and arbitrated by nature. For example, a scientific theory is supposed to stand or fall according to the results of a single critical experiment, and no amount of belief or wishing can ever change this state of affairs. Scientists pride themselves on their honesty, integrity, and courage in facing new facts, even when they challenge their most cherished theories.

All this sounds very noble, and there are a number of instances in science—or at least there are supposed to be—where a theory has indeed stood or fallen on the basis of a crucial experiment. Generally, however, things are not that dramatic, or that clear-cut, for experiments and interpretations always take place within a context of assumptions, ideas, and beliefs, and there are strong personal and social motivations that influence what a person does and sees.

To take an extreme example, go back to the announcement of the discovery of cold fusion made on March 28, 1989. On that day Martin Fleischman and B. Stanley Pons of the University of Utah in Salt Lake City, and, quite independently, Steven Jones of Brigham Young University, also in Utah, claimed that they had discovered a way of creating nuclear fusion at room temperature—fusion in a test-tube. While Steven Jones did not measure any energy output during the supposed fusion—the reaction itself was identified by the detection of elementary particles—Pons and Fleischman spoke of producing a considerable quantity of heat and hailed their discovery as promising cheap and manageable energy for the whole world.

For the purposes of this chapter, the interesting thing about cold fusion is not whether it works, but the sociological upheaval its announcement produced within the scientific community, an upheaval in which scientists on both sides exhibited their true colors, which were far from being those of calm, dispassionate, detached, and rational investigators.

To begin with, the majority of scientists, without really taking time to investigate the claims in detail, rejected them out of hand; some heaped scorn on the putative discoverers. The reasons for this reaction are fairly complex. To begin with, the idea of cold fusion seemed absurd, for it totally violated the directions in which conventional fusion experts had been working for decades. Nuclear fusion, most scientists believed, must involve very high temperatures and tricky problems of containment, and this spells elaborate equipment, massive budgets, and large international teams. It was supposedly impossible to create fusion with a minimal budget and inside a test-tube.

The initial scientific reaction therefore was based not so much upon the objective examination of the experimental evidence but on the conviction that cold fusion simply could not happen. There was really no need to examine the claims in detail, for no one was willing to take them seriously.

To be fair, very few people had a chance to examine Pons and Fleischman's evidence firsthand, for rather than being willing to disseminate their results freely and allow other scientists to visit their laboratory, as the orthodox model of science suggests, Fleischman and Pons became reclusive, and, with the exception of a few scientific friends, most people found it increasingly difficult to discover exactly how the two scientists had done their experiments. Thus began the rather ludicrous process of scientists trying to guess what had happened in Fleischman and Pons's test-tube, and then, based on these guesses, setting up careful experiments to prove that these guesses would not work!

There were other reasons why the scientific community rejected this claim so rapidly, including the fact that the announcement came from the Midwest and appeared to fly in the face of the authority of the great eastern universities. While it was perfectly all right to do science in a minor university, properly speaking, this should only be done by following the lead of one of the major U.S. teams. If you were going to challenge the authority of some of the big names in the field— and their grant-pulling ability—then you had to expect them to band together and slap you down.

Other researchers felt that the purity of science had been contaminated by Pons and Fleischman, and to a lesser extent by Steven Jones, particularly by the very public way in which the announcements had been made. Because of this, the players involved had to be publicly discredited, and so words like "charlatans" and "liars" were heard at scientific conventions in connection with Pons and Fleischman.

Yet there were two other smaller camps. One consisted of supporters who were willing to believe the claim, and another was made up of those who were prepared to remain open-minded. It is hard to guess the motives of the strongest supporters. Some may have felt that they had genuine scientific insights about what was going on; others may have had a need to believe in something like cold fusion and what it promised for the world; and still others may have wanted to defy the authority of big names, organized science, and the power of the major universities, to associate themselves with the scientific underdogs, or to simply enjoy a good fight.

On all sides the motivations that underlay the early reactions to cold fusion—the flurry of announcements, press releases, lectures, meetings, conferences, and scientific papers—were personal and emotional based upon the beliefs and value systems of the players.

An initial reason for rejecting cold fusion had been its apparent theoretical impossibility. If this were so then the phenomenon simply could not take place and therefore the experimental results that had been reported had to be either mistaken or possibly even faked. However, as the days went on, the logic of this argument became particularly confusing. Theoreticians love a challenge, and some of them adopt the maxim that whatever can be conceived of in the imagination will probably occur. So pretty soon several of them, some of them quite competent, began to play around with novel ideas and generated theories that showed that cold fusion was not only perfectly possible but seemingly inevitable! What had been a scientific absurdity one day became, a few weeks later, a theoretical commonplace. So experimental scientists were faced with theoreticians who had proved that, under the correct experimental conditions, cold fusion must inevitably follow from the nature of certain collective and cooperative effects, while others, equally categorically, demonstrated that it was a physical impossibility.

And as to the experiments themselves? They proved to be extraordinarily difficult to carry out, with some experimenters confirming cold fusion and others discrediting the whole affair. One thing the affair did make clear, to me at least, was that in the age of space travel, virtual reality, and the supercomputer one of the most common devices in everyone's life— the electrolytic battery (generically the same thing we have in our cars)—is far from being well understood. Indeed, getting one to run through its paces in the laboratory remains a black art. Since many of the processes involved in cold fusion are analogous to what happens in a car battery, getting them to work, or getting them not to work, as the case may be—

required more of art and intuition than all those definitions about dispassionate quantitative investigation would lead us to believe.

But this is something that many organic chemists have always known, that performing experiments involves a craft and art of careful observation, sensitivity, intuition, experience, and a sixth-sense "feel" for the materials involved. At times, being an experimenter is closer to being a master chef than to a mechanic or a dispassionate computer. And, far from all experiments being reproducible, as the definitions of science suggest, it is well known that some individuals can get a particular experiment to work, while others never will. Hence, the very basis of science, its objective, repeatable, quantitative observations and experiments, is an unattainable ideal, for the way scientists are able to design experiments and carry them out is influenced in so many subtle ways by their feelings and sensitivity to the complex universe around them.

The sociological lessons of cold fusion tell us that if a new phenomenon falls within the current scientific paradigm, then it becomes relatively easy for it to be considered objectively, but when it falls outside, or in some way offends the beliefs and values of influential scientists, it becomes very difficult for anyone to take it seriously. The real issue is not so much whether a particular observation is valid but how it accords with the beliefs, values, aspirations, and worldview of the influential majority of scientists.

If this is true, then the ground becomes shaky under science's appeal to objectivity and its stance in opposition to the mere beliefs of superstitions and pseudosciences. And what about a truly scientific theory standing or falling by a single experiment? The very fact that such a crucial experiment would be performed in the first place is the result of our current scientific paradigm; one that suggests that we should be looking at nature in that particular way in the first place. The experiment asks a precise kind of question, one that assumes only a limited number of possible answers. In other words, the very context in which the experiment is devised presupposes to some extent the range of answers that will be given, each of these answers having meaning within the current scientific context. What a specific experiment will never do is to produce results that are totally out of context or point in radically different directions. If we dangle a fishing line from a boat we may or may not catch fish, but we certainly can't expect to pull in eagles, butterflies, or squirrels!

In other words, observations, experiments, and interpretations are always made from within the confines of a particular paradigm. And while a crucial experiment may help science to decide between two rival theories within that particular paradigm, it will never be able, by itself, to overturn that paradigm. An experiment can never do this because the very motivation to do the experiment in the first place and the language in which its results will be discussed are all aspects of the paradigm itself.

The only way paradigms can be overthrown is not through a particular crucial experiment but by an overall change of thinking, and by the accumulation of new possibilities and puzzling anomalies. Only then, when the time is right and people's thinking has already begun to change, will a crucial experiment be possible. Newton's physics, for example, was never overturned by any experiment. The anomalies that had been discovered at the end of the last century, such as in the motion of the planet Mercury and the failure to detect the effects of the ether on the velocity of light, could all be explained from within Newtonian physics. It was not a crucial experiment that overthrew Newton in favor of Einstein, or, for that matter Ptolemy in favor of Copernicus. Rather, new ways of thinking seemed more in tune with the times and therefore more attractive, aesthetic, unifying, and appealing. It was only then, when the scientific community was willing to entertain a radically different form of thinking, that crucial experiments became possible.

The Human Face of Science

The discussion above seems to indicate that the way science is practiced does not really conform to either the dictionary definitions or the popular conception of an abstract, idealized, and value-free pursuit of pure truth. The fact is that Western science, and the way we pursue it, is a product of our value-system and our worldview. Societies with other values and other worldviews may choose to carry out their science in radically different ways.

Of course, the criticism could be leveled that in choosing to base my discussion around the example of cold fusion I have deliberately picked out an example of poor science or bad scientists; and that to criticize the goals and ethics of science in terms of its deficient practitioners is like condemning the values of a religion on the basis of the prejudices and excesses of some of its followers.

But the fact remains that, for us in the West, science is not a religion and lays no claim to transcendental truth. It has been established as a strictly human enterprise and does not exist apart from the scientists who practice it—with all their idiosyncrasies, values, beliefs, shortcomings, and fallings from grace. The fact of the matter is that a pure, "ideal" science no more exists than does a pure, ideal human being. If we accept the abstract ideals and dictionary definitions of *science* as the yardstick against which true sciences are to be measured, then Western science in its day-to-day operations does not always measure up to its own exemplar.

And this, I think, is how it should be. For it is the way of the West to constantly abstract and idealize, to seek to compare and to measure, to look at things in terms of good and bad, better or worse. Thus, what had its origins in a desire to understand, acknowledge, and seek a relationship with all of nature became transformed into a monolithic search for objective truths. In this transformation Western science began to lose its individual, human face and became swept up into the vast, expensive, and complicated bureaucracy of knowledge.

Western and Indigenous Sciences

The point of this chapter is not so much to criticize Western science for not measuring up to its abstract and rather grandiose ideals, but rather to drop our obsession with these ideals and comparisons and suggest that Indigenous science presents a valid understanding of nature in its own right. It may be profitable to explore the differences and similarities of these two scientific approaches—Western and Indigenous. While in many cases there is a direct correspondence, some things are emphasized in one science that seem to be missing in the other. The chart below outlines what I take to be the characteristics of Western and of Indigenous science.

Comparison of Western and Indigenous Science
Western Science

Experimentation	Instrumentation	Observation
Prediction	Mathematics	Representation
Control	Objectivity	Distancing
Freedom		Uniformity
of external social		
values		
Models	Causality	Technology
Progress	Fragmentation	Explanation
Authority	Truth	Transformation

Indigenous Science

Spirituality	Location	Observation
Initiation	Cosmology	Causality
Role of humanity	Harmony	Ceremony
Elders	Artifact	Practice
Spirit	Dreams	Visions
History	Maps	Symbols
Subjectivity	Relatedness	Understanding
Sanction	Transformation	Path
Sacred mathematics	Sacred space	Representation
Technology		

Let us now explore some of the similarities and differences in greater detail.

Observation

Keeping in mind that what people do in practice does not always measure up to their ideals, the fact remains that Western science is generally characterized by careful, repeated observation and the collection of data. This, in turn, requires a high degree of technology and the development of a conceptual framework that allows scientists to identify and isolate what is to be observed and studied.

Very careful and painstaking observation is also emphasized in Native science and is part of the coming-to-knowing process of every Indigenous person. One can think of the careful observations made of birds, animals, insects, plants, roots, fungi, etc. A study of rocks, crystals, wood, and other materials has enabled Indigenous people to use them in the construction of various tools and objects. In the case of ancient astronomical observations, even though the telescope had not been developed, the building of observatories and the recording of observations reached a high degree of sophistication.

For observations to be of use they must be recorded and passed on. In the case of Western science this is done through textbooks, scientific papers, lectures, and student apprenticeships. While many Indigenous peoples do use writing systems, knowledge is generally passed on through markings on rocks, mnemonics, songs, ceremonies, practices, artifacts, and such things as earthworks. In particular, much knowledge about the world is enfolded within traditional stories.

Experiment

Physical science in the West is associated with the birth of the experiment at the hands of Galileo. Galileo's first experiments are seen as having transformed the scientist from a passive observer into one involved in an active engagement of nature, an engagement in which the scientist selects and isolates an aspect of the world which can then be observed in a repeatable way. Experiments are designed to exclude or control external influences and to emphasize a few key variables, or conditions, which can then be studied in a repeatable fashion. In its extreme form one finds echoes of Hans Eysenck's dictum "if it cannot be measured, it does not exist."

Recently, this experimental philosophy has come under attack for its association with a certain dominant or even "paternalistic" attitude toward nature, the sort of thing that is contained in Francis Bacon's dictum that we should put nature on the rack and force her to reveal her secrets. The poet and philosopher Goethe had pointed out the artificial nature of scientific experiments for, in their retreat from the fullness of phenomena, they have the effect of isolating and tricking nature. So while experiment is the key to Western science it has also been criticized as being artificial, as increasing our sense of distance from nature, and possibly even leading to a fundamental distortion in the way we relate to the world.

Within Indigenous science there does not seem to be that same deliberate attempt to move beyond observation by setting constraints on nature. Indeed, from within its holistic viewpoint in which everything is connected to everything else, experiment would have to take on a new role. In this sense, Indigenous science fails to meet one of the most important criteria within the current Western definition of science.

However, there may be a sort of experimentation that is of an inward nature—an experimentation of the mind, so to speak. In a holistic world in which each part enfolds the whole, it becomes possible to enter into the inscape of the smallest insect, plant, or leaf and zoom outward into the whole universe. Sa'ke'j Henderson has suggested that the People's relationship with plants, animals, rocks, and trees serves them as a sort of electron microscope. By entering into direct relationship with the animals and the Keepers of the animals, The People were able to gain access to the knowledge they have about the world. Native people, Henderson would say, not only have knowledge that comes from direct experience, but access to the knowledge of the birds, insects, animals, rocks, and trees. This sort of process of knowing allows one to enter directly into the perception of nature at many scales and levels.

The mystical traditions of the East stress the employment of instrumentation, experimentation, and observation in their meditative and mystical practices. Within the mystical traditions these disciplines are considered to be scientific precisely because they are disciplined and reproducible. There is a codified body of practices that will lead to predictable and well-defined results. In this approach, internal observation is used in an objective way to gain direct insights into the ways we engage the world and the nature of its realities.

I believe that analogies can be drawn between these contemplative practices of the East and the observational/experimental approaches of Indigenous science. So, while Indigenous science does not employ experiment in the Western scientific sense, it does employ a disciplined approach to merging horizons with the inner reality of the world and revealing its different levels of process.

Prediction

Prediction is given the highest value in the physical sciences. Indeed, it has become the crucial test of any theory; for it is not sufficient to explain a wide range of phenomena—one must also be able to predict some new effect that can then be tested. Prediction is also tied to the philosopher Karl Popper's notion of falsifiability as being the ultimate test of a proper scientific theory. According to Popper, to be called scientific a theory must be constructed in such a way that its predictions are capable of being falsified in a crucial experiment. Theories that cannot be falsified in any direct way belong to superstitions and pseudoscience. (Followers of Popper include psychoanalysis and astrology as examples of such nonfalsifiable pseudosciences.)

However, other thinkers, such as Paul Feyerabend and David Bohm, do not go along with this current fashion for predictability and suggest that understanding is the true criterion of science. The current emphasis on prediction, in their opinion, has become an obsession and, by itself, does not lead to understanding. Indeed, in some cases it simply confirms what is in effect a closed system of thought.

While Native scientists have concerned themselves with prediction, this comes about within a different metaphysics. Prediction does not so much involve something new in the future but a celebration of return and renewal. What we take for prediction could, in the case of Indigenous science, be closer to an expression of the harmonies and relationships between things. Within Mayan science, for example, great emphasis was placed upon the wheels of time and upon the exact dates of eclipses and planetary movements.

The concept of what, within Western science, would be

called prediction is profoundly different within a metaphysics that is not based upon the notion of causality. Indigenous science deals with connection, harmony, and relationship rather than with the mechanical influence of forces on bodies. Thus, if we try to apply that concept of prediction, it would be something arising out of pattern and relationship, out of one thing being contained within another.

There is also a sense in which dreams can have a predictive quality or, to put it another way, in which the dreamer is not confined to a single present but can move back and forth along the curve of time. A dreamer may see the strangers who will arrive at camp several days into the future, or may discover where game is to be found on the following day. This ability to anticipate the future does not arise, as within Western science, from casual deductions based upon knowledge of the present—for example, applying the laws of planetary motion to predict the occurrence of an eclipse—rather, it appears to be a form of direct connection to knowledge. Such a connection can be made in many ways; in dreams, ceremonies, or by means of a bone held in the hand, for that bone connects to the Keeper of that particular animal.

The idea of prediction within the West is based upon the premise of the linear flow of time and upon the absolute separation of present from future; thus, the very notion of prediction arises from the Western ability to separate or abstract itself from events and project them into an imaginary future. But in a society that views time as a circle there is never that sense of separation, nor is there a need to seek control over the world through scientific prediction. To use the example of the Hopi worldview, future events exist within the realm of the manifesting, that realm of subjectivity that includes the mental as well. Thus, prediction would not so much mean the ability to see into the future from the past, but rather a concern with that edge of manifesting where things pass from one world into another.

Control

As we saw above, our scientific obsession with prediction is ultimately based on the illusion of control. The dream goes that if science can describe a system according to some theory or model, and if it can predict the outcome of particular effects, then it becomes possible to control nature. This desire for control has come under particular attack from feminists who see it as the direct outcome of a paternalistic attitude toward nature. Ecologists are also uneasy with the belief that more and more science can be used to solve the world's outstanding problems by exerting ever more control.

Native science, for its part, is concerned with relationship, harmony, and balance in the movement of the sun, moon, and planets; the sequence of seasons; the arrival of the Thunder Birds in spring; the Four Winds; the movements of game; and the fertility of the land. Scientific control of these phenomena would imply a distancing and separation from them. The use of ceremony and renewal within Native tradition involves a different metaphysics. Ceremonies are held to ensure success in hunting, or in planting corn. In these ceremonies direct participation within natural processes is called for, along with acts of obligation and sacrifice. To hold a ceremony in order that the sun will rise tomorrow is different from the desire to seek a way of controlling, or exerting force, over the sun's movements.

Although it could not be said to be a form of control in the Western sense of the word, Indigenous peoples are also able to make use of certain processes in order to bring about desired effects. Indeed, the bringing about of effects, or entering into relationship with them, is very important. Examples include the ability to heal and to extract diseases from the body, or to negotiate with clouds in order to produce rain. Songs could also be thought of as processes, or scientific instruments, that bring about certain effects. And if Indigenous science is not so concerned with control, it is definitely occupied with the idea of power or energy. For, in order for a person to move within a world of powers, spirits, and energies, it is very important to have a map, to be able to enter into relationships with the surrounding energies and to have knowledge of the sources of power.

Objectivity

Western science is strongly associated with the search for objective, independent truth, while, at the same time placing a lower value on subjective experience. Science aims to be value-free in this regard; that is, it seeks eternal truths that are independent of particular social and religious contexts.

In Native science, however, stress is laid upon direct subjective experience and upon closeness to nature. The powers, energies, and spirits of the world are personified to the extent that it is possible to enter into direct relationship with these elements and negotiate pacts, compacts, and ways of living together with them. If objectivity implies the ability to abstract and distance oneself from nature, then this is definitely missing within Indigenous science. In its place, however, stand consistency, integration, harmony, and balance.

Uniformity

The vision of Western science rests on the notion of the uniformity of nature and its law. The current perception of the universe occurs in terms of a hierarchy of laws built on the foundation at the most fundamental level. Mathematical elegance, simplicity, and beauty are considered to be a feature of the universe and its laws. Complexity is a secondary effect that emerged out of the primordial simplicity of the big bang through a series of chance processes called "symmetry breaking." What is considered to be preeminent about the univerrse could perhaps be classified as the general, the abstract, the repeatable, the context-independent, and the all-embracing. By contrast the individual, the idiosyncratic, and the singular event are considered to be of less importance, or as being particular and superficial cases of something deeper and more embracing.

While Native science also stresses harmony and balance, it nevertheless gives importance to diversity, as well as to the particular event—to the dream and vision, to a unique phenomenon, and to the experience of each individual. Indigenous science accepts the rich complexity of life and the natural world as being the essence of the cosmos. Relationships and renewable alliances take the place of fixed laws, and Indigenous science accepts the possibility that chance and the unexpected can enter and disturb any scheme. Thus, the circle is left open and chance, as represented by the clown, the trickster, and gambling games, occupies an important role.

Models

Western science emphasizes theoretical models, simplified conceptual frameworks in which one particular aspect of natural phenomena can be studied through reason and experiment. By means of experiments, scientists seek to test their models against the behavior of the natural world. To take one example, a gas such as oxygen is assumed to be composed of an enormous number of rapidly moving molecules. One of the earliest models of a gas pictured the molecules as moving dots, independent, structureless, and of negligible volume. Based upon this model, scientists worked out relationships between the temperature of a gas and its volume, and could also predict how a change of pressure would effect the volume of a gas. These relationships and predictions were confirmed experimentally. With more accurate experiments, small deviations between experiment and the model were discovered, and it became necessary to add refinements to the model to allow for the actual, very small, size of the molecules and their weak interactions. In this way, by progressively refining its model, science pictures itself as moving even closer to the truth about a particular aspect of nature.

While approaching nature through conceptual models involves simplification, abstraction, fragmentation, objectivity, and distancing, it also allows the power of abstract mental representation, logic, reason, and focused application to be brought to bear upon particular phenomena.

Although Indigenous science is not normally concerned with abstraction and simplification, it nevertheless, possesses a strong component of representation. Thus, traditional prac-

tices and teachings revolve around symbols, numbers, geometric shapes, special objects, etc., that evoke the flavor of a
mental model. As an example, the circle of the tepee and the
sacred hoop becomes a model for the earth, for the life of a
person, and for the movement of time. Other symbols, or
"models" deal with the heavens and with various forces of
nature. However, the relationship between the symbol and
nature is quite different from that between a Western scientific
model and nature.

Within Indigenous science a particular symbol is not an
abstraction or a reflection of reality, that a model within
Western science is. Rather, it is something that permits direct
connection with the energies, spirits, and animating power of
nature. There is the sense that, like a holograph, a symbol and
object can enfold the whole of reality. Thus, the sacred hoop
does not have a single interpretation, or level of meaning, as
does the molecular model of a gas; instead, it contains and
reflects a multiplicity of meanings.

Many of the symbols found in the Indigenous science of the
Americas (the tree, four sacred directions, fire, serpent, bear,
rock, sacred plants, sacred animals, worlds within worlds,
etc.), are shared by Indigenous peoples across the earth and
are found in records left by the peoples of prehistoric times.
The psychologist Carl Jung associated these with archetypes of
the collective unconscious, but to the Native mind they are not
metaphors, images, representations, or archetypes. Rather,
they *are* the reality itself. There really *is* a bear, a rock, a sacred
direction. Their reality is undeniable and can be experienced
directly within the world. Jung's archetypes are too limited,
too literal, and too impoverished to account for the vitality of
Native American imagery.

Indigenous symbols act to unify, for they correlate whole
groups of experiences and practices. In this light it is interesting to ask to what extent concepts like space, time, causality,
force, matter, and energy provide the integrating features of
our own thought and could be taken to be the symbols or
archetypes of the Western mind.

Within the science of the Middle Ages, as within certain
Eastern philosophies, one can find the idea of "as above, so

below," that is, the universe repeating and enfolding itself at every level. A human being is a "model" or representation of the entire cosmos. But this should not be taken to mean that a human being is a model of the cosmos in the sense that a plastic toy is a model of an airplane. Rather, the human being enfolds the cosmos and within the order of body and mind can be found the cosmic order. Likewise, as human beings work at transformation and coming-to-knowing they are affecting the entire universe.

Similar ideas exist within the science of Indigenous peoples. A striking example comes from the Maori people of what is today called New Zealand. Their *marai*, or community dwelling house, is a microcosm of the cosmos. To our eyes the house is packed with symbolism; in terms of the numbers of wooden supports, location of windows, decoration, and so on. But it might be truer to say that these are not representations or metaphors of the universe, but rather that the universe is contained within the *marai*.

In a similar way, the wooden houses of the Haida people with their special arrangements of seats are a model, in the deepest sense, of the structure of their society, which to our eyes appears to be extremely hierarchical. Other models, or microcosms within the macrocosm, would be the longhouses of the Iroquoian people, the hogans of the Navahos, and the tepees of the plains peoples. In each case the dwelling place becomes an expression or a manifestation or a place of containment for a whole cosmology that includes society and the individual.

Causality

Western science is firmly based in the belief of causality—the idea that everything that takes place is the direct result of particular causes, and that a given cause will produce a specific effect. While Newton himself was willing to accept the possibility of "occult forces" and a mysterious action-at-a-distance, the science that bears his name is wedded to the notion that all causes are of physical origin—involving impacts, pushes, pulls, or the action of electrical, mechanical, and gravitational fields and forces. A science that is not based upon causality appears unthinkable.

But not all the world's philosophies view causality in the same way. The notion of causation is a cornerstone of Buddhist thought, for the second of the Four Noble Truths is the understanding of the origin of suffering that lies in causation. But this Buddhist notion of causation transcends the more limited scientific notions involving the outcome of a purely mechanical applications of force. Similarly, Carl Jung and the physicist Wolfgang Pauli introduced the notion of patterns within the universe arising from what they called synchronicity or "an acausal connecting principle."

Native science also acknowledges the importance of cause, but the inner nature of these causes appears to be substantially different from those considered in the West. Some causes involve the action of spirits or energies, an idea that has no counterpart in modern physics but may well be closer to the ideas of Newton, Kepler, and the alchemists. Jung's idea of synchronicity may also have some resonance in Native science, as does the medieval notion of correspondences, and "as above, so below."

Instrumentation

Western science is characterized by its reliance on instruments such as telescopes, microscopes, thermometers, and X-rays to extend the normal human senses. However, Anab White-house, the Sufi scholar, has pointed out to me that instruments and their careful preparation are also spoken of in the esoteric or mystical sciences. Thus, the Sufis teach that "the mirror of the heart" is an instrument that must be carefully cleaned and polished if it is to reflect Allah's light. The Buddhists seek to prepare the mind as an instrument of scientific investigation by freeing it from confusion and attachment. The instruments of mind and body can then be used for careful, disciplined and repeatable experimentation and observation.

Something similar may apply in Native science. We have already seen how knowledge goes beyond what can be ap-prehended through the normal senses by entering into alliances with the various plants and animals. In addition, ceremonies and practices such as fasting, acts of sacrifice, dancing, ingestion of various preparations, dreams, and visions all serve to refine the instruments of perception and allow direct contact with extended realms of reality. During certain healing ceremonies it seems to be possible to obtain direct perception of the nature and location of a disease within the body.

Indigenous science also makes use of technological instruments. For example, the Cherokee people utilize crystals in many different ways. One is in the preparation of medicine where sunlight is guided through the crystal and onto the preparation to potentiate its power.

The Blackfoot people have their medicine wheels, which are treated with great respect and importance. Archaeologists have advanced a variety of theories as to the purpose of these patterns of rocks but their true meaning can probably only be found in the heads and hearts of the Blackfoot people. Certainly it seems that a single explanation—that they are astronomical devices, for example—is far too simplistic. However, in their arrangements of stones many of them do acknowledge the patterns and harmonies of earth and sky. Medicine wheels are built at powerful sites and seem to have the power to focus or concentrate. In other words, they have a technological role to play within the Blackfoot application of Indigenous science. Indeed, Leroy Little Bear and I have half-joked that just as Western physicists build gigantic circles in the landscape— elementary particle accelerators—to carry out experiments on the ultimate nature of matter, so can cosmological investigations can be performed with the Blackfoot medicine wheels. So maybe we should apply for a major scientific grant to build an even larger medicine wheel!

Technology and Progress

Technology is not simply the offshoot of Western science, it is often the spur that pushes science forward, for each new technological advance provides the means for further experimentation. Pure research in solid state physics gave rise to the transistor, which, through further refinements, made high-speed computers a possibility. In turn, the computer's ability to carry out complex simulations and solve complicated nonlinear differential equations made possible the new scientific approaches known as chaos theory and fractals.

In the West, technology is tied to notions of progress and the belief that "more is better." Some scientists contend that the difficulties we face today involving energy, sickness, social violence, and ecological damage will eventually be solved by better science and improved technologies. The psychologist Hans Eysenck takes this belief in the power of science to extremes:

> We know quite enough about botany, agriculture, and physics to make sure of a very good living for everybody who is on earth at the moment, but what stands in our way is our lack of knowledge of psychology. Why are there warring factions in Yugoslavia? Why is the Russian communist experiment failing. Why do we have strikes? These are all real problems which we are incapable of solving because we lack scientific knowledge of them. I hope that in two hundred years' time psychology will be an adequate science to deal with these difficulties.

A belief in the need for constant progress and change, along with the accumulation of wealth and material resources, is generally absent from Indigenous societies, which place more emphasis upon balance, harmony, and the circular passage of time. Social value and personal prestige are gained in other ways, and people sometimes appear conservative about adopting new technologies. In addition, those technologies that have been developed, or adopted, generally tend to be used in ways that do not disrupt the particular environment and way of life.

This is not to say that there have not been striking technological advances within Turtle Island. The Clovis spear point was one of the first and most far-reaching pieces of advanced technology in the prehistoric world. The Olmec people appear to have used compasses one thousand years before the Chinese. Haida and birchbark canoes indicate deep knowledge of materials and design. Systems of farming, the working of artifacts, the design and building of great earthworks in the southeastern United States, as well as the temples and cities of Central America all imply considerable technological support. But these changes have generally come about within an environment of balance and do not represent "advances" in the sense of being a forward movement and a split and separation from tradition.

Spirituality

At one level, Western science has struggled to free itself from the confines of established religion. Nevertheless, the writings of the greatest scientists from Newton and Kepler to Einstein and Planck are all profoundly spiritual. God is constantly invoked as the final arbiter of nature and scientific truth. Important notions of beauty, elegance, simplicity, harmony, and uniformity within scientific descriptions of the universe may have similar religious roots. Science's goal of ultimate law and ultimate level also reflects the prevailing notion in the West of a single, unified deity.

Native science is also profoundly spiritual. Indeed, there is no division between science and spirituality for every act and every plant and animal is sacred. Yet this is a spirituality, that is capable of supporting the diversity, subtlety, and complexity within nature. Rather than seeking a single, most fundamental ground, the Native mind prefers to dance among the ever-changing movements of a living, subtle nature. Harmony and balance must accommodate change and the activities of the trickster.

Fragmentation

In seeking its objectivity and freedom from subjective values Western science has cut itself free from pursuits such as art, religion, etc. In this way Western thought has become profoundly fragmented. Scientists also feel that their discoveries are, in a sense, absolute truths that are beyond moral values. They are neither good nor bad and their potential use lies outside the province of science. The result of this fragmentation is a knowledge that is divided into a number of specialized compartments, along with such by-products as an accelerating technology, ecological damage, alienation, high-tech medicine, etc. Science itself has become divided into a number of specialized branches of study. By contrast, Native science cannot be separated from spirituality, art, ceremony, and the whole social order. Every action is a spiritual act and has its effect on nature and the individual.

Fragmentation also arises through the power of analysis. In Western science, systems are understood by taking them apart in the laboratory, separating them into their various components, and then studying these individual components. In turn, these components are broken down into yet smaller entities. Just as natural systems can be physically analyzed, they are similarly analyzed in thought. They are abstracted and broken down into relationships between logically simpler parts.

Contrast this view with the importance of context within Indigenous science. For example, in Indigenous science the healing power of a plant should not be studied simply in terms of some molecular component that acts on cells in the human body according to a particular mechanism; rather, the plant becomes enveloped within ceremony and story: The plant possesses a spirit. It may only be collected and used in a certain way. Within Indigenous science the whole meaning of the plant, and of healing, can only be understood within a wide, multilevel context. Meaning is always context-dependent, rather than absolute and context-free as in Western science. However, the idea of a context-dependent meaning and interpretation is now being forced on Western science as well by the quantum theory.

Explanation

Western science seeks understanding through a clear, consistent, and unique explanation, with reference to models and systems of laws. In turn this explanation should be reducible to laws that operate at an even more fundamental level. By contrast, Native science works with a multiplicity of symbols, images, and stories. There is no single, unique reading to a story, but rather many enfolded and interpenetrating levels, none of which needs be thought of as being more fundamental than any other. Understanding comes from a direct experience of the dance between these levels of meaning.

In this sense, understanding within Indigenous science has something in common with Niels Bohr's notion of complementarity. Bohr's complementarity states that a single consistent description will never exhaust the meaning of what is happening at the quantum level. Rather, what is required are a number of complementary, mutually contradictory descriptions. An electron is described as being both delocalized and wavelike, but also localized and particlelike. Likewise, the meaning of a traditional story depends upon a variety of contexts and can be unfolded in a variety of ways.

Authority

Western science prides itself on having gained its freedom from the authority that was once held by the church and the ancient philosophers. Nature is said to be the final arbiter of truth. As the physicist Richard Feynman put it, "Nature cannot be fooled." But in practice the scientific establishment is itself highly authoritarian in that it determines what is considered an acceptable and proper topic for study, and what lies outside the pale. The scientific establishment carries tremendous weight, and while theories can be overthrown and replaced within the range of a particular paradigm, it is very difficult for any approach that seriously challenges the limits of the current paradigm to get a fair hearing.

Native science gains its authority partly through the society and its Elders and partly through direct experience, dreams, visions, and the voices of animals and plants. But really, *authority* is the wrong word to use, for it is alien to most Indigenous American societies for any person or office to set rules, give orders, direct the lives of others, or claim that authority personified by an individual speaks for the society as a whole. *Authority*, if we are to use that word in the context of Native science, resides in individuals and their direct experience rather than in some social establishment.

Truth

Western science seeks ultimate truth, for it believes in a rational universe that can be understood by experimentation and reason. The truths of this science are founded upon observation and experimentation carried out within the context of particular theories and hypotheses using the methods of induction and deduction. While the metaphysics of this approach has been much debated, as far as the everyday working scientist is concerned, scientific truth can be reached through careful experimentation.

Truth in Native science is of a very different order. Truths are not value-free but depend upon tradition and social and spiritual sanctions. Dreams and visions are systems of validation. Truth is contained within origin and migration stories, songs and ceremonies. And the source of truth is found in nature and in the direct experience of individuals through dreams and visions; conversations with rocks, trees, and animals; and patient observation of the world around them.

Location

Unlike Western science, the importance of the landscape, and specific places in it, is a characteristic of all Indigenous science. A mound, rock, medicine wheel, river, or tree may be of deep significance to a people. Even the language spoken by a people arises out of the land they live in and and of the "map in the head" they all carry.

Within Indigenous science there is an association of spirit or energy with particular places, and it is important to visit these places and carry out ceremonies there. Fasts and vision quests are carried out on particular hilltops. At other locations, medicine wheels can be found whose alignments connect to movements and harmonies within the sky. There are rock markings and paintings all over the Americas. The Ojibwaj people, for example, appear to have taken young people to these sites in order to impart their sacred teachings. In some places the rock teachings were protected by a layer of grass or moss that was removed only during the period of teaching. There may also be a connection between the power of certain sites and the historical voyages and migrations carried out by The People.

This idea of the significance of place and the energies associated with it is common to Indigenous sciences all over the world. Certainly it must have been present in megalithic Europe. In Australia one finds the dream tracks, or songlines, made by the Ancestors when they walked the land. And, recalling that time is neither linear nor an arrow, we should realize that this time of the dreaming of the Australian Aborigines is not something that exists only in an absolute past, nor should dreaming be associated with our Western sense of what a dream is.

The notions of landscape have also been explored by René Dubois. Paul Devereux has told me that in his own recent book *Symbolic Landscapes: The Dreamtime Earth and Avebury's Open Secret.* He maintains that the landscape of Avebury in England was created in megalithic times as a sort of dream landscape, or expression of numinous power.

Within Turtle Island something similar may lie in the creation of the straight roads, that can be found all over the continent, particularly in Chaco Canyon. Chaco Canyon also contains a host of observation points, containing worked rocks whereby, at certain significant times of the year, sunlight or moonlight is channeled through the rocks, into a cavern, and onto a geometrical marking on a wall. Anna Sofaer, who discovered the first of these channels—associated with the Sun Dagger markings in the Chaco Canyon—has since formed the Solstice Project to carry out careful research into this phenomenon, involving, among other things, computer simulations of orientations of buildings and sites within the canyon and their correlation with astronomical events.

Sofaer pointed out to me how not only observation stations but whole towns and important buildings were laid out to correspond to the orientation of the rising sun on these significant dates. Minute by minute the sun's light would move across the canyon, touching these markings in turn. "It must have been like a great fireworks display," she said.

Indigenous science often expresses the deep connection between the landscape and the whole cosmos. The People's role in this connection is to maintain a sense of harmony and balance. Thus, I have heard it said that some of the great migrations and voyages were undertaken to maintain balance within the earth.

Western science does not appear to have a corresponding concept. Certainly there are universities and research centers where initiation and coming-to-knowing is practiced, but these learning centers could have been built almost anywhere, and their locations were determined more by economic considerations—nearness to cities, the presence of outstanding researchers, etc.—than by consideration of the land itself. There are, however, major pieces of scientific equipment, such as observatories and elementary particle accelerators—our megalithic records for the distant future, as it were—that are built at specific geographical locations. But the notion of sacred space and the significance of the earth in sacred terms is missing in Western science.

Initiation

In several Native traditions a person is pictured as walking on a road through life. Certain steps along that path are marked by ceremonies, visions, dreams, fasts, or initiations. In the Midewiwin society of the Ojibwaj, coming-to-knowing involves a series of degrees of initiation, with each of the four Earth Degrees involving extensive training and the knowledge of special ceremonies. So while coming-to-knowing is generally based upon personal experience and dreams and visions, it can also come, in particular with the Ojibwaj people, though special training and learning of songs, ceremonies, stories, and the interpretation of the meaning of scrolls, petroglyphs, and so on. And following each stage of initiation there are ceremonies of acknowledgment and recognition.

The preparation for knowledge in Western science follows a similar rigorous system of learning, grades, initiation, and ceremonial acceptance. Reaching the higher, graduate grades generally requires special study under a professor and the production of a special piece of work such as a thesis.

In addition to the formal degrees of Western initiation there is also a more subtle and informal process in which a special vocabulary, formal language, practices, and paradigms are acquired. The scientifically initiated are immediately recognized by the special language they speak!

A special vocabulary of verb tenses and/or other language forms are also a feature of Indigenous languages. However, a Western initiate is judged competent simply on the basis of accumulated knowledge and practice, for there is no need for sanction to come independently from dreams, visions, or spirits.

Cosmology and Calendar

Cosmology—the study of the nature and origin of the universe, of "all that is"—is one of the foundation stones of Western science. Cosmological conceptions also play a vital role within Native science. Cosmology is intimately connected to the origins and the great migrations of peoples; to calendars, sacred cycles, sacred mathematics, and Indigenous notions of time. Cosmology is not abstracted as a particular branch of Indigenous science but is fully integrated into the unity of nature and of all living things, the harmony between the world of spirits and the manifest, the special names and roles of plants and animals and the life-path of each individual. Indigenous cosmology provides a set of values, social integration, and validation for The People. It is a way of life, a relationship to the natural world, a deeper reason for ceremonies and daily practice, a foundation for song, art, and artifact.

Mathematics

It is difficult to imagine a branch of science not leaning in some way on mathematics. In the nineteenth century it was said that "mathematics is the handmaid of science" and, in the context of quantum theory, Heisenberg claimed that "the truth lies in the mathematics." It has also been maintained that mathematical beauty is connected to mathematical truth and that "God is a mathematician." Today's scientific theories have reached such a high degree of abstraction that they are guided as much by mathematical considerations as they are by physical intuition.

Sacred mathematics is an important part of Indigenous science, and this has been discussed in previous chapters. Sacred mathematics revolves around the importance of number and its relation to spirit and cosmology, special symbols and shapes, and the ability to carry out surveying measurements and the laying out of buildings in particular geometrical arrangements. Sacred mathematics is concerned with the renewal of harmony between earth and sky.

Representations

A system of mathematics generally presupposes some form of symbolic, abstract representation. Indeed, representation is essential in Western science with its formulas, chemical equations, symbolic models, and computer simulations.

It is often assumed that, leaving aside the Mayans and Aztecs of Central America, writing did not exist in North America until the advent of the Europeans. There is, however, evidence of elaborate and very early representational systems, including those of the Ojibwaj, Mic Maq, and many other groups, that can be found recorded on rocks, birchbark, wood panels, talking sticks, as well as in other systems such as wampum belts. In the case of the Mic Maq writing, I have been told that it did not attempt to represent the spoken language but served more in the nature of formulas of thought.

The Role of Life and Humanity

In Native science The People have a strong personal connection and relationship to every aspect of the natural world—to rocks, plants, animals, and stars. In a cosmology in which every human action has repercussions within the natural world, The People learn to treat everything with respect and accept their obligations to renew the harmony of the cosmos and maintain the balance of nature.

The traditional Western view of science is that life had its origins as an accident on a particular planet, at the edge of a star system, within a vast, impersonal universe.* Human consciousness together with our perception of the cosmos represents the end result of fortuitous chance processes related to evolution. At the official level, the scientist's first duty is to truth, and considerations of the nature and value of life enter only at the realm of what can be observed and measured. However, it is certainly true to say that many individual scientists often have a mystical sense of direct connection and communion with nature.

Ceremony

Ceremony plays a significant role in Native science. Ceremonies are associated with acts of renewal, healing, and relationship to particular forms of knowledge. The use of ceremony focuses the mind and creates a sacred space in which knowledge can be discussed.

There is little evidence of ceremonies in Western science, other than the superficial formality of thesis defense, seminars, and the conferring of degrees and awards. However, ceremony is of central significance within Western religion which, many centuries ago, separated from the sciences and arts.

Today many people in the West who feel a sense of loss and lack of connection with the earth and cosmos are attempting to invent or revive ceremonies. Following the writings of Joseph Campbell and Carl Jung there has been an attempt to "invent" a mythology for the end of the twentieth century. To my mind at least, these attempts feel artificial, unconvincing, and are sometimes downright embarrassing. Our technological, industrial society is truly without tradition. In so many ways we

---

*More recent theories suggest that the molecules of life were originally formed on the surfaces of interstellar dust that fills our galaxy.

have lost our connection to the earth, and, for many people, contemporary drama, art, literature, and music simply do not speak to the need for meaning. It is difficult to know where we, as a people, can walk, since we do not know where we stand.

Elders

Elders are held in high regard within Native science as the repositories of wisdom and special knowledge. Older Western scientists may also be respected, but more for their reputation and charismatic aura than for their present abilities. Indeed, in the West, scientists are generally regarded as being in their prime between their late twenties and thirties. Older scientists are sometimes judged as fit only for philosophical musing and popular public lectures. They are also often seen as a barrier to advancement by the young.

While Native science respects the wisdom of its Elders, Western science seeks to overthrow the ideas of the previous generation, although this is generally done in limited ways so that the major paradigms of science persist from generation to generation. Nevertheless, the battle between father and son continues with every generation. It will be interesting to see if, and how, this social paradigm changes as more women enter into the scientific mainstream.

Spirit and Energies

The animation of nature and the energies or spirits that reside in plants, animals, rocks, and trees are characteristic of Native science. The acknowledgment of powers and the renewal of alliances through a variety of ceremonies also play a key role in Native science.

This notion of spirit, or numinous energy, is missing in Western science. However, the studies of alchemy, astrology, and natural magic were taken quite seriously by a number of scientists at the time of Newton. Their origins can be traced partly to Arabic mystics, scientists, and alchemists. Within this framework are found notions similar to those within

Indigenous science, such as hidden forces, animate nature, and the parallel reflections between the purification of the individual and the harmonious workings of nature.

Dreams and Visions

Dreams and visions are held to be of key importance in Native science. A young person may go on a vision quest. A healer may receive sanction through a vision. In many groups knowledge and initiation come through dreams. The world of dreams is particularly real and of deep significance. Initiation by dreams is also characteristic of some Eastern traditions and ways to knowledge.

At first sight there is no parallel to this belief within Western science. However, in the lives of many scientists the dream or vision has played a major role in leading to a significant discovery. The self-taught mathematician S. Ramanujan, who astounded the mathematical world in the 1910s with his brilliant and original theorems, spoke of receiving them directly from a goddess without the need for intervening steps of reason and proof. In many other instances a theorem or scientific advance has appeared directly in dreams, visions, or through sudden acts of insight without the need for mathematical and logical reasoning. Within the Western worldview, such dreams are interpreted on a psychological basis as arising within the unconscious and as having nothing to do with external spirits or direct contact with a transcendent reality.

Maps

The idea of "a map in the head" is often spoken of by Native people. This map is more than a mere geographical representation of a given area, for it is a multidimensional combination of time and space, the sacred and profane, history and origin, animals and spirits. It is richly textured, both as the physical actuality of the land and as a living metaphor.

While the notion of a theory as being a "map of the world" is used in Western science, our maps tend to be relatively impoverished in their connotations and hold little in the way of social value. By contrast, Native maps contain spiritual and social values. They bind people to each other and to their past and they are magical and sacred. The world of Native maps is endless and its connection to Native science is profound. Indeed, one could hazard the speculation that to a great extent the map is the science, while, by contrast, within the West it is said by philosophers that "the map is not the territory."

Paths

The notion of a path is present in both Western physics and Native science. Indeed, within the context of the theory of relativity, paths have an almost numinous quality for the physicist. The idea of a path is also important in Native science, where it is pictured as the Earth Walk, the Good Red Road, the trail through a landscape, and an ancient journey undertaken by The People. To the Australian Aborigines, paths begin in Dream Time; they are synonymous with the creation of the landscape and species, they are eternally present, they are songs and stories, and they are the physical and spiritual links between different groups of people.

In Western physics, the path, or trajectory, of a body through space and time is a key concept. To Aristotle each body strove along its path to attain its own special place. Galileo and Newton, however, introduced the notion of inertia, whereby an undisturbed body persists in moving along its own trajectory. Deviation from that path was always the result of a force or field. With Einstein the notion of a trajectory, now called a geodesic, became even more subtle, for the force of gravity had been eliminated in favor of a curved geometry. His notion was that every star and planet moved along its own special geodesic, essentially because *there was no other way it could possibly move*. This now stands as the dominant concept in relativity. Thus, the idea of the "right path" becomes the image in which the motions of bodies are to be understood. Indeed, it is almost possible to remove all mention of forces and think of physics only in terms of paths.

Native science resonates with this notion of a "right path," yet the idea of necessity or inevitability is missing in Native science; or rather, it has a different flavor. All that happens is the result of the operation and alliances of spirits, or as some peoples would put it, the Creator. Moreover, it is necessary to perpetuate these relationships and alliances through ceremonies, songs, and personal sacrifice. So the path in Native science is not mechanically predetermined but is a path of participation, in which all living things must play their role.

Reality and Transformation

The whole field of transformation and reality in Indigenous science is so subtle that it is again given a chapter to itself, chapter 11.

Conclusion

Indigenous science must be judged on its own grounds. It offers a valuable way of coming-to-knowing, and one that represents a tradition of disciplined thought, observation, and experience that stretches back hundreds and thousands of years. While it is true that a number of striking similarities exist between Indigenous and Western science, what is perhaps more interesting is their differences. Each society can approach the world in its own way, for the cosmos has unending richness and subtlety. We need a new spirit of openness and tolerance so that the peoples of the world can come together to listen and dialogue, each respecting the other's way of living and envisioning a new and harmonious relationship for the cosmos, the planet, and all of its creatures.

Realities

Science is an attempt to understand reality, discover our relationship to the cosmos, and provide a rationale for our actions and the structure of our society that satisfies all levels of our being. Taken to its limit, science merges into drama, dance, music, art, poetry, literature, philosophy, ceremony, religion, and all the other forms the human race uses to acknowledge and celebrate the universe. Western and Indigenous sciences meet because both are concerned with the nature of reality and the place of human beings in the cosmos. It is in the ways these sciences approach their common meeting point that their differences lie.

A Science of Perception

Western science is dominated by visual and tactile perception. What we take for reality is what we can see around us—what is real is defined by the evidence of our eyes, that have become prehensile so that sight can reach out, touch, and move over the surface of the world; eyes that have been extended with telescopes and microscopes. Our minds imitate the faculty of sight as thought reaches out to grasp, explore, and caress ideas and concepts. Objects of perception revealed by our inner and outer eyes become the objects of reason and abstraction. This is the essence of the reality Western science serves and seeks to understand.

Western science is a triumph of understanding the surfaces of things. The prehensile power of eye, hand, and mind gives us the sense of reaching to the inner essence of things by breaking them apart, dissecting the parts, exposing ever smaller entities and ever more detailed surfaces. At the same time, theories and abstract models of these new domains are created in the mind and are served by beautiful and powerful mathematical systems.

By contrast, Indigenous people do not seem to live with such a visual obsession. It is true that from an early age Native children are encouraged to observe and preserve an alert watchfulness, but the eye is not such an exclusively dominant instrument of perception. The People also rely upon the ear to reveal a world of energies and vibrations. I have spoken to Indigenous people, from the Americas and elsewhere, who have commented on how impoverished the "Western" sense of smell is. The Maori, Polynesian, and Inuit greetings do not involve "rubbing noses," but rather taking in the smell of another person and offering one's own. To such people, smells are an important dimension in which reality is expressed.

The Indigenous instruments of perception also involve the heart and the whole being and allow people to move beyond what we would term "rational thought" in ways that touch the inner essences of things. While Western thought grasps at the surface, the Indigenous heart, mind, and being seeks the "inscape"; that inner voice and authenticity that lies within each experience and aspect of nature. In engaging the inscape a person is not preoccupied with measuring, comparing, classifying, categorizing, or fitting things into a logical scheme, but rather with seeking a relationship that involves the whole of one's being.

Touching the Inscape

The realities inhabited by Western and Indigenous scientists differ and, in turn, each seeks to serve its own particular reality. If one truly believes that the presence of the world is accurately reflected by Western science then Indigenous science will simply not measure up to this power. But if one entertains the possibility that reality is not exhausted by our Western "rational" scientific investigations, then one becomes open to the possibility of other forms of science, and other levels of experience.

It is, for example, difficult to account for the experiences of artists, poets, and mystics on the basis of a purely "Western scientific" vision of reality. On one occasion, while talking to a friend, the poet William Blake stared into a part of the room and said that he had just seen the soul of a flea, which he later attempted to sketch. While looking at the sunlight reflected from a pewter dish, Jacob Boehm felt that he had entered into the heart of nature, an experience that persisted when he walked outside and saw the inner light of the grass and trees.

Spontaneous and direct experiences of the inscape of nature have been granted to poets and mystics alike. I do not believe that anyone who has spent time with a still life by Paul Cezanne has not experienced the sense that the painter had been taken into the heart of things, and had learned how to move between surface (or landscape) and inscape.

Western reality, with its focus on material surface, does not have room for spirits, angels, flea's souls, or the inner nature of apples. Cezanne, however, like all great painters, shows that the inner vision of the reality of things is not simply an elusive, intangible experience, but can go hand in hand with discipline, training, and intention.

The importance of the connection between the numinous inscape and an ordered and disciplined mind and heart was appreciated by the poet William Wordsworth. One thinks of his famous definition of poetry as "the spontaneous overflow of powerful feelings: it takes its origin from emotions recollected in tranquility." Less quoted, but making even a closer connection to this question of science and reality, is a further definition from the same letter, written by Wordsworth to Lady Margaret Beaumont, May 21, 1807, "Poetry is the breath and finer spirit of all knowledge; it is the impassioned expression which is in the countenance of all science." So, to Wordsworth and his friend Coleridge, the poetic spirit was itself a way of coming to know both the inscape and landscape world and an expression of its true countenance and appearance.

For the Sufis, members of the mystical, or esoteric, dimension of Islam, the instruments of perception and contemplation include not only the mind but also the heart. The inner glory of the world and the light of the names of Allah is reflected within this mirror, provided that it is polished and kept free from tarnish. Sufism is a science devoted to the disciplines of cleansing and perfecting the instruments of perception so that they reveal the nature of reality in an undistorted fashion.

Transformation

Within Indigenous science this inner world, this essence of each thing, is in a state of flux, for reality is the domain of animating spirits, energies, and powers. Indigenous science and Indigenous languages do not seek to control or to hold on to stability within this flux with analytic ideas, laws, and concepts. Instead they seek balance, harmony, and relationship.

One of the most persistent aspects of Western reality is the prominence given to the individual in society. We, our egos, and everything that is represented by the name we carry from birth to death are free, purposeful, and autonomous within the world. Likewise, our names are permanent things and fix us within our family and society. The situation is quite different within a Native American culture where a person's name is not fixed, but, according to circumstances and contexts, changes throughout life. A child may be renamed as certain characteristics become apparent. The name will change again when the child carries out some extraordinary deed or is associated with an unusual encounter. New names are also given during important ceremonies, and in some groups a transition in life is represented by reversing a former name.

Names, like the things they represent, are always in a state of flux and transformation. The name of a bird or animal may change with the seasons as it alters its coat or plumage. Coyote, Raven, Napi, Nanabush, and the other trickster figures of Turtle Island are also transforming; now appearing as an animal, then as a person.

The ability to transform and metamorphose also comes with increasing knowledge. Within Ojibwaj society, for example, certain people have the power to change themselves into animals, and there are stories of how these powers were occasionally used for selfish personal ends. In our society we would probably classify such people as "evil." But such dualities as good and evil do not really exist within Indigenous metaphysics, and it is probably better to say that a desire for purely personal power created an imbalance that would eventually act back on the practitioners. There are cases, for example, in which threatening animals have been shot in the night and, on the following day, a person has been discovered nearby with a bullet wound. In one case, a father, suspicious that a "bearwalker" was going to rob his children's grave, concealed himself nearby. During the night a bear appeared and was shot. The next morning a dead man was discovered by the grave. There has even been a murder trial in which the defense argued that the killing had been done while the murdered man was metamorphosed into a bear.

Masks and Beings

Transformation of form and name is an essential element within Indigenous science. A particular case involves the so-called False Face Societies of the Iroquoian peoples. The Mohawk Elder Ernie Benedict has told me that the commonly used term *False Face* is really incorrect, for these masks are not in any sense "false."

The masks are employed in many different ways, including in ceremonies of healing. The various Face societies could be said to be "secret" in the sense that the masks contain and connect them with exceptionally powerful forces within the universe. Such matters are treated with great respect, and persons would only seek to enter into relationship with a mask after they had acquired a certain degree of knowledge and undergone the necessary stages of preparation.

Knowledge could be said to be "secret" not because initiates wish to preserve their own exclusivity, but because of the danger that lies in attaining only partial or casual knowledge. Certain objects contain great power and even to speak about them would involve the use of names and words that connect a person to potent forces and energies. Secrecy is therefore common to cultures in which powerful matters are contained. It ensures that powers are not needlessly evoked and that those who finally reach a source of knowledge will have gone through the necessary degree of preparation.

A self-imposed silence also allows a person to contain and focus the powers that are associated with the attainment of that certain degree of knowledge. Thus, the medieval alchemists were cautioned not to speak about their work to the uninitiated. While this secrecy served to prevent alchemical knowledge from falling into idle hands, it also concentrated the work within the alchemist's life, for casual talk can dissipate power. In a similar fashion, while a Native person may talk about an important dream or vision, he or she will hold something back in order to contain the power within the dream. It is for these reasons that the true meaning of the Iroquoian masks remains a mystery to us.

The Importance of Sanction and Containment

At this point I want to emphasize yet again the importance within Indigenous science, of the need for social sanction. Individuals may need to come into contact with great powers, or use exceptional healing energies, but this is always done, so I have been told, through the sanction of the society. A society possesses the necessary ceremonies to contain the powers and energies, that may be released. Thus, Sa'ke'j Henderson has told me how, among the Mic Maq and other peoples, certain powers are only summoned when the right number of people are present.

This idea of an official sanctioning of special powers appears to be true of other societies as well. Dr. Setha Al-Dargazelli of the Physics Department of Durham University has written about the ability of the Sufi dervish school known as Tariqa Casnazainyyah. Its practitioners appear to be able to sustain a variety of body traumas, such as piercing with skewers, without producing wounds or subsequent infection. Dr. Al-Dargazelli writes that no special training or discipline is required beyond a ceremony of initiation from one of a distinguished group of dervishes called Califas, a procedure which need only last for a few minutes and ends with a vow and ritualistic handshake. Dr. Al-Dargazelli argues (and I have no knowledge or experience of such practices) that special powers can be passed on directly through the sanction of a school and its masters without the need for any special training on the past of the initiate.

Masks as Incarnations

Masks could be thought of as incarnations of the power of transformation. They are endowed with the ability to speak, albeit with a limited range of sounds, and must be handled with great respect. It is said that an older mask can instruct newly completed ones and may demand to be placed with them. Masks show powers of animation such as sweating, bleeding, or moving from the location in which they have been placed.

Masks are living beings, and this is why traditional people are particularly distressed to see them on display in museums and gift shops. They caution people not to buy such masks or exhibit them in their houses. No one would think of displaying radioactive isotopes in their living rooms, yet people quite happily put Iroquoian masks on walls and Hopi kachina "dolls" in display cabinets. But these masks and "dolls" are replete with powers to transform themselves into different forms. To leave one hanging on a wall could have a considerably disturbing effect on the occupants of that house.

One sees Iroquois masks and Hopi kachinas being sold alongside ceremonial pipes, eagle feathers, crystals, and tobacco. Sometimes the excuse is made that the eagle feathers are dyed hen feathers and the masks and kachinas are "not real," but only copies. But as my Mohawk friend Kim Hathaway-Carr told me quite forcefully, when people make masks they put something of themselves into them. If they are making masks to be used in certain traditional ceremonies, while the masks are being carved they will conduct their lives in a proper way, refrain from drugs and alcohol, and focus their minds on what they are doing. But suppose a person is "only making a copy"; in such a case a mind may wander and other thoughts and forces may be allowed to enter. As the person works on what is essentially a traditional form, all these extraneous things enter into the mask, animate it, and give it their power. So a mask that is "only a copy of the real thing" may become the container for a variety of unwanted forces, all of which people then take into their homes.

The origin of the Iroquois masks seems to lie in the stories of creation. After the Creator had finished making the world, he came across a being who asked him what he was doing. The Creator said that he was looking at his handiwork, but the being replied that this was actually *his* world and had belonged to him ever since it had existed. To demonstrate his power the being commanded a mountain to move. However, while the being looked away the Creator also caused a mountain to move with great rapidity. "Turn around," said the Creator, and at that instant the mountain moved so fast that, as the being turned, he struck his face against the mountain and became disfigured. The being then begged for forgiveness, but the Creator banished him and placed on his people the obligation that, whenever humans should wear the masks and call for help, the beings with the twisted faces should return and teach their knowledge and healing powers.

In another story, a hunter, hearing strange sounds from a cave, discovered a giant with a twisted face. The monster showed the hunter how to construct a mask from a living tree and gave instructions on how the mask was to be fed, purified, and used. The hunter was told to spread that knowledge among his people.

Traditional masks are carved from the wood of living trees. It is said that when a mask was required for a special occasion a tree of exceptionally balanced growth was selected. Following tobacco offerings and acknowledgments of respect, the tree was requested to share its life spirit. The mask was then carved into the tree and, after further ceremonies and tobacco offerings, it was split away and removed. To wear a mask is to come in contact with the powers it contains. Some of the energies contained within the mask are very potent and, unless treated with respect and made the subject of tobacco offerings, their powers can shift a person's life out of balance.

Although the true meaning of the masks is known only to certain traditional Elders, it seems that they are manifestations of the way forms and beings transform themselves, the manner in which powers can enter into things, and the way living objects act as containers of energy.

Reality and Transformation

Spirits, powers, and beings can manifest themselves in a variety of different forms. Masks, rocks, knives, canoes, animals, and humans can act as containers for these energies. Thus, reality, as it is experienced by The People, goes far beyond surface forms and involves a much deeper level of processes and transformation.

In our current Western attempts to come to grips with reality, it seems that, in some ways at least, we have begun to think along similar lines. Physicists ask if the nature of quantum reality lies within the elementary particles themselves, or if these are not merely the material representations of something deeper. This was the approach favored by Werner Heisenberg in his old age. I can remember talking to the distinguished physicist a year or two before his death. He said that speaking about electrons and protons as "the building blocks of matter" was a confused misrepresentation of the nature of quantum reality. Rather, they were the surface manifestations of underlying quantum processes. What was more fundamental, Heisenberg had suggested, were symmetries rather than particles.

Maybe we could translate Heisenberg as saying that reality lies not with the elementary particles, nor in the surface forms we see around us, but with the relationships that exist within the flux of energy and processes of quantum nature.

Elementary particles are always in a state of flux; some transforming spontaneously one into another, others transforming when they collide and interact together. Thanks to Einstein's famous equation, $E = MC^2$ (E stands for energy, M for mass, and C for the speed of light), we know that an electron can be thought of as concentrated energy. The transformation of elementary particles one into the other changes in the surface manifestations of this underlying energy flux.

In the Blackfoot stories, Napi is always manifesting himself in a different form; sometimes he's an old man, at others times he's an animal or baby. This sense of fluidity of form that occurs again and again in trickster stories and is also found with the elementary particles. The electron is constantly switching back and forth and manifesting new forms. Since matter is a form of frozen energy, all energy has to do is to manifest itself as different particles.

But some of these particles are associated with a greater energy than the electron itself contains—more energy than is given by $E = MC^2$ where M is the mass of the electron. How are such transformations possible when not enough energy is available? It turns out that the electron, or rather the processes of which the electron is a manifestation, can borrow a little energy from the universe. Using this energy, the electron transforms into a different particle. But this new particle can only exist for a short time, for the universe demands that energy should always balance, and what has been borrowed must be paid back. The new particle dies back into the processes that gave birth to it, and as it pays back the energy it has borrowed the electron is born.

This image is analogous to that of balance within Indigenous science. When sweetgrass, or the sacred pipe, is passed around the circle, it is possible for some people to take a little energy from it, and for others to give up some of their energy. However, when a person needs to take energy there must always be, as the circle is completed, a final balance. Western scientists picture the transformational dance of the elementary particles in a similar way. Energy must, in the long term, balance, although, in the short term, it is possible to borrow energy provided that it is paid back later.

The electron's continuous exchange of energy with the universe means that it can never be isolated as an independent individual. Just as Indigenous science teaches that all things connect and everything is relation, so, too, the electron is in relationship to the entire cosmos.

Observer-Created Reality

The transforming, animating energies of Western science are strictly impersonal and move according to the objective laws of physics. These laws are pictured as being totally indifferent to human wishes and desires. Even movement of energy and the transforming manifestations of the elementary particles never acknowledge the existence of human beings or other living things.

By contrast, the Indigenous world is alive. Not only do humans, animals, birds, and insects partake in life and mind, but so do trees and rocks and stars. Far from being indifferent to the existence of humans, it is possible for The People to negotiate with the world of spirits and form alliances with the powers that animate the universe.

As an example, when drought occurs The People may carry out a rain dance. This is not so much designed to "cause" rain to fall as to restore balance within the environment, thereby allowing food to grow and The People to live. The People do not seek to bind nature to their will: Allowing rain to fall involves negotiations and exchanges with the clouds. Certain sacrifices or obligations are demanded of The People, in return the clouds transform and rain falls—a balance being kept in the total cycle of relationships.

It is sometimes said that Native people pray upon a hilltop so that the sun will rise on the following day. To anyone who believes that the movements of Earth and the other planets are the blind results of gravity and Newton's laws of motion this is pure nonsense, or wishful thinking. Indigenous science, however, does not talk in terms of causal influences. The sun, Earth, and The People are not separate actors, mechanically and mindlessly obeying impersonal laws. Rather, all things connect and are the manifestations of underlying powers and beings. The rising of the sun is one expression of the harmony of all things, a harmony that extends from sky to earth and can never be fragmented into separate domains.

Harmony involves the relationship of the various powers, energies, and beings of the cosmos—"all my relations." "All my relations" means humans, animals, insects, birds, plants, rocks, trees, Mother Earth, Sky People, and all the animating powers of the universe. "All my relations" means that The People have entered into alliances and contracts, have obligations to fulfill, and must at times make sacrifices. Harmony is present when everyone, human, animal, plant, and planet, fulfills their obligations and goes about their proper business. For The People these include the various ceremonies that must be carried out according to each group and nation.

A Native person does not will the sun to rise, rather, the harmony of earth and heavens, including the rising of the sun each morning, is a manifestation of the relatedness of all things and of the way in which all living things carry out their obligations. The continued harmony and the renewal of these relationships is a responsibility of The People, along with the birds, rocks, trees, and insects. All have their role to play in renewing and ensuring those alliances and relationships that lie behind the movement of the seasons and the rising of the sun.

Visions of Reality

Why can't *we* talk to rocks? With the exception of a few mystics, artists, and poets, the rest of us, unlike Native Americans, never feel direct access to the underlying movements of nature.

Our society firmly hangs on to the view that reality consists of what we can immediately see and touch. When people experience other modes of perception and being, these experiences are talked about in terms of "altered states of consciousness" (ASC). The underlying assumption is that altered states of consciousness are in some way bizarre or disordered. This division between normal and abnormal is not the case within Indigenous society where it is acceptable for a person to perceive reality in a wider and fuller sense, receive visions, go on strange journeys, fly in the air, converse with rocks and trees, and enter into negotiations with energies and spirits.

Our attitude toward such an extension of reality is nowhere put better than in the *Diagnostic and Statistical Manual of Mental Disorders* (DSM), which is published by the American Psychiatric Association and is the standard diagnostic manual used by psychiatrists and in hospitals throughout North America. In defining "illogical thinking," as one of the indicators of mental disturbance, *DSM-III* gives the following example of a psychopathological utterance:

> Parents are the people that raise you. Parents can be anything—material, vegetable, or mineral—that has taught you something. A person can look at a rock and learn something from it, so a rock is a parent.

What a fascinating example to have chosen, considering that all over the world Indigenous peoples have special relationships to rocks and stones. Native Americans talk to rocks; rocks appear in their dreams and visions. In Australia the Aboriginal peoples speak of The Dreaming, a reality in which the Ancestors walked on the land and special resting points created certain features. Some Ancestors turned into rocks. But this does not mean that the Ancestor stopped being and metamorphosed into an inanimate rock. Rather, the Ancestor still exists, for Dream Time is different from our linear arrow of time, in which the past is gone forever. Dream Time coexists and interpenetrates the here and now—the Ancestor and the rock enfold one another.

Rather than being an example of "illogical thinking," the idea that rocks can teach and act as parents is a direct experience within Indigenous reality. Instead of speaking of people having access to "alternative" or "nonnormal" realities, it is probably more accurate to simply say that Indigenous people live their lives in a wider reality.

Pam Colorado said to me, "You know, David, we all have weak minds." Her perception of Westerners was that their minds are hard, logical, and forceful; and that they confine themselves to what they consider to be the practical, concrete reality. It is difficult to shake such a mind and move it from its predetermined path, for it immediately rejects all experience that appears out of the ordinary. Only under conditions of extreme stress may such a person begin to see beyond the limits of "daily reality." For Pam Colorado, however, the Native mind needs to be weak, for it does not erect barriers to an extended reality.

Native people talk of speaking to animals, trees, and rocks. As Leroy Little Bear puts it, "Trees talk to you, but you don't expect them to speak in English or Blackfoot." Part of me senses—in a very fragile and dim way—what Pam and Leroy are getting at. I think that part of our difficulty may be that our society, with all the intense drama of television and film, has conditioned us to think of the voice of a rock as something that will boom and reverberate into our minds like God in a biblical spectacular.

But what if this voice is very quiet and subtle, a gentle movement unlike the normal chattering of our thoughts; something closer to a gentle breeze than to a hurricane, to a sixth sense rather than a confrontation, a feeling rather than a thought, an emotion rather than a sentence? Silence surrounds Indigenous people. Could it be that the voices of trees and rocks can only be heard within such a silence? Maybe the voices are always present, but we in the West have forgotten what it is like to be still. As Therese Schroeder-Sheker put it, the angels want to sing to us, if we could only be silent long enough to hear them.

Creating the Inner Ear

Indigenous science has developed a variety of ways in which the wider reality can be experienced even more directly. Looked on from the Western scientific tradition they appear to be techniques designed to break down the mind's resistance and cause it to release its hold on everyday reality. They include fasting, purging, going without sleep for long periods, vision quests, placing the body in conditions of extreme danger, drumming and dancing, long ceremonies, and the ingesting of various substances.

In this manner people meet the Keepers of the animals, guardian spirits, and other beings, but, being a science, the approaches are disciplined and reproducible. Visions are neither personal nor haphazard. A Native person who attends a particular ceremony, or who ingests a particular substance, will see a specific spirit being. I have been told these beings, are quite objective so that several people sitting in a circle will see the being at the same time and agree on the details of what they have experienced.

Some of these ceremonies involve eating or drinking a variety of substances. It is easy to equate these with the "psychedelics" taken in the West. Indeed, it is sometimes felt by Westerners that using a variety of drugs will bring them closer to the experience of shamans. But these analogies can only be taken so far. What is essential within Indigenous science is not so much the molecular composition of a substance, but the spirit it contains. The ceremony is not really about taking a psychedelic but about preparing a person to come into relationship with a powerful spirit in such a way that he or she can speak and negotiate with the energies it controls. Such ceremonies are not engaged in lightly but always in a disciplined, scientific way, for knowledge is to be gained and powers obtained on behalf of the entire group.

Dick Katz, author of *Boiling Energy: Community Healing Amongst the Kalahari Kung* and *The Straight Path: A Story of Healing and Transformation in Fiji*, told me that in his experience it was relatively easy for any one person to enter into so-called altered states of consciousness. Altering consciousness was, to him, a rather trivial matter; what was more important was what a person did with this experience and how it was integrated into the life of the community. As Dick pointed out, a person would only perform a ceremony or enter into an experience when there was a specific reason for doing so.

Shamanism

It is inevitable in any talk of altered states of consciousness that the topic of shamanism should come up. This is one of those particularly touchy areas in which traditional people and those casually attracted to Native American ideas part company.

Shamanism, with all its associations of visions, special powers, and contact with other worlds, holds a tremendous interest for non-Natives. They sign up for "shamanic courses," and announcements are placed in New Age magazines for Shamanic Weekends; to "contact your power animal"; and for supervised vision quests. I have even seen ads selling shamanic drums, sacred pipes, spirit rattles, didjeridoos, Tibetan bowls, "sacred Native American plants," "skulls, claws, teeth, etc.," and "a genuine shaman's shirt." A series of international conferences on the "Study of Shamanism and Alternative Modes of Healing" shows how shamanism has found its way into the laboratory. One paper, presented at the third international conference, has the exotic title "The Integration of Shamanic Practice Into the Ongoing Life of an Accredited Academic Institution"!

The word *samân* is found in the Tungusian language spoken by Indigenous peoples of Northern Siberia. Within this culture it is a perfectly legitimate name given to people who perform certain spiritual and healing ceremonies. Anthropologists, noticing similarities in religious and healing practices across the Arctic regions, applied the same term to the Inuit (also referred to as Eskimos) of Alaska, Northern Canada, and Greenland. Gradually *shamanism* become a catch-all term for all manner of exotic practices and occult knowledge.

I have only once talked to Native people about so-called shamanism, and that was to an Inuit friend, Gideon Qaunaq, who spoke with great feeling about his grandfather. A very traditional person in his nineties, his grandfather was probably the oldest Inuit living in the eastern part of North America. Gideon explained that his grandfather was a healer, but emphasized that he was not a shaman. I was told that healers care for sickness in each community, but occasionally a very special sickness occurs. Only then, when something exceptional is needed, would the shaman appear. It seemed to me that people did not care to speak about shamanism or necessarily know who the shaman was, yet in a time of crisis the shaman would come forward. With the rise of Christianity in such communities, people were less willing to discuss the survival of certain traditional ways.

Shamanism, with its emphasis on trances, visions, and altered states of consciousness, has become synonymous with Native American spirituality and Indigenous science in the popular mind. This particularly angers traditional people, for nothing could be further from the truth. They are disturbed about the casual way in which non-Natives make an easy amalgam of their wisdom and seek quick effects in cheap ways.

I can remember being at a gathering where Native Elders talked about their traditional ways. A few non-Natives like myself happened to be present, and one evening I asked the non-Natives to tell me about their particular interest.

"We're all training to be shamans," one replied.

"Really! How do you do that?"

They told me that they met in a motel on weekends to contact spirit helpers, totem animals, and to go on vision quests.

"Vision quests?" I asked in surprise.

"Yes, and we go on fasts as well...but not very long ones."

To me that just about sums it all up, for it suggests that we can get in touch with the powers of the universe as a sort of hobby and that ancient spiritual disciplines can be learned on spare weekends.

The Anthropologists' Account

Anthropologists who have studied Siberian shamanism suggest that it evolved in the birch forests of Eurasia some six to ten thousand years ago. They associate the sensations of "flying" with the ingestion of a psychedelic substance—fly-agaric—that grows on trees there. Thus, shamanism also becomes associated with the idea of the tree in its various forms—the World Tree, or the Cosmic Axis—that stands at the center of the earth and forms a ladder or pathway between earth and sky. The roots of the tree penetrate to the underworld, its branches rise to the sky, a serpent lies at its base, and a bird perches at its crown. It is the ladder that allows the shaman to travel and conduct traffic between the two worlds, or realities.

Healing From Another World

All over the world, from Australia to the Kalahari Desert, from Siberia to Northern Canada, drawings can be found of skeletons, or bodies in which the bones are showing. Anthropologist have interpreted the drawings as portraying the ability to see directly into another person's body and diagnose diseases during some visionary state. Other explanations suggests that these X-ray drawings are supposed to be a portrayal of the "shamanic experience" in which a person is stripped down to the essence—to the bones. Anthropologists suggest that after ingesting mind-altering substances shamans enter into a visionary state where they identify with "first shaman," journey to the moon, talk with spirits, and see into human bodies.

I suppose, since this book is an attempt to bridge two sciences and two worldviews, I should try to put things another way. It does not seem to me so much the case that shamans visit another world as that they partake in reality in a much fuller way, and that this reality transcends the normal limits of matter, space, time, and causality.

When non-Natives take mind-altering drugs they tend to enter into distorted states of perception in an uncontrolled way. For the Indigenous healer, however, the whole thing seems to be an intentional business. Thus I have heard stories about how, while a person was talking to the voices of spirits, he or she was also keeping an eye on the fire and ensuring that those nearby did not harm themselves. Unlike us, the shaman—if you want to use that word—is occupying, in a perfectly alert way, an extended reality that includes the worlds of matter and of energy, power, and spirit.

It is also said that the vocabulary of a traditional shaman is much larger than the vocabulary of the rest of the members of a society. Most non-Native North Americas use an average of fifteen hundred words in their daily discourse. The Yakut of Siberia use around four thousand but what is truly surprising is that their shamans use some twelve thousand words. The same is true of many Native American groups in which a rich vocabulary is associated with certain spiritual states and practices. People say that "old worlds," and lost languages, only dimly recognized in normal life, are regularly used during important ceremonies.

I believe that this expanded language is an objective manifestation of a much larger reality. Language enfolds reality. We need maps if we are to navigate within a world of energies and powers. We need the power inherent in sacred languages if we are to meet the Keepers of the animals; come into contact with the beings that animate rocks, trees, and stars; and enter the ancient times when alliances and relationships were established by the Grandfathers. This also explains why certain traditional people must undergo such a long training. They are learning the science and the language that enables them to move in a landscape that extends far beyond our normal, practical life.

This could also explain why people in the West who spontaneously enter such states experience such great distress. Unable to function effectively in this world, and not knowing the techniques of return, they are considered mad. Such people have wandered into unexplored realms of reality without the maps and language that would help them to contain their experiences. They are devoid of any social context in which to undertake their journey and have never gained the discipline of mind and body that derives from a long process of coming-to-knowing.

Dick Katz told me of an Elder who had taken some young Native men from a mental hospital fishing. He spent the day simply being with them and afterward said that if they had been living in traditional ways they could have become great healers. The young men had spontaneously broken the limited bounds of our everyday reality but no longer had the support of their society, nor did they possess the language, songs, and ceremonies that would help them navigate. They were lost, confused, and frightened to find themselves in a disorienting world of voices, beings, powers, and energies with no access to the Indigenous science of navigation.

Contrast this view with the fact that shamans and Native healers are judged psychotic according to Western psychological tests. Could it be that our own society, with its rigid, compulsive grip upon a single dimension of reality, is the one that has become abnormal?

Wounded Healers

It has also become something of a cliché within Western psychology to refer to shamans and others as "wounded healers." The reason for this is that in many cases traditional healers have suffered some great physical or mental trauma that brought them close to death. Such experiences, anthropologists suggest, open the doors to special powers and an extended reality. This is one explanation. Another is that in order to attain great powers for use in a society, an individual also has to make a great sacrifice. People may, for the needs of the society, take upon themselves the role of healer, but in every act of healing there is always great danger, for the balance of nature must be preserved and sicknesses that are plucked out of one body may enter another. I have been told of people who have been called upon to conduct arduous ceremonies in the sweat lodge that may have hastened their deaths.

Equating great sickness with the onset of special powers and visions is not confined to the Native world. Carl Jung made his most far-reaching breakthroughs following a personal crisis that, to outsiders, had all the appearance of a psychotic episode. Jung had the sensation of literally falling into madness and of walking and conversing with different beings. In the midst of one of these episodes a voice dictated an important piece of writing, *VII Sermones ad Mortuos*. This crisis recalls the knowledge that was given to Black Elk and to Handsome Lake when they lay near death.

Shaking Tent

One system of navigation into the world of powers and energies takes place within the Shaking Tent. Although it is used in the far northern part of the North American continent as well as in Siberia and other parts of the Arctic Circle it is not generally spoken about, for it involves the manipulation of very great power. The tent is only used when an exceptional healing is required, to locate people who have been lost or drowned, or to journey in order to find lost souls. As with other forms of healing, it must only be employed when specifically requested out of great need—for the tent makes considerable demands upon the healer.

The person who has the power to use the tent is approached with a gift; tobacco or blankets, for example. The tent itself is quite small—generally only large enough for one person to enter—and its poles are anchored into the ground.

People who enter the Shaking Tent without proper training could lose their reason. They are about to take their lives into their hands on behalf of their people. There is a sort of "madness" that affects people who, without proper training and containment, have come into contact with great powers. It is not so much an irrational form of insanity, but rather that such people return to the world with a sense of some vital part missing. They are unable to reengage in life and appear disconnected and forever lost. Yet those who have been properly trained are able to move within the greater reality of the spirit world again and again and return unharmed.

The operator enters the tent and after a time those who wait outside hear noises and different voices. It is as if the person inside the tent were speaking to a variety of powers and beings. At this point the tent begins to shake and in some cases, although well anchored into the ground, rotates and even spins rapidly.

I have been told that the tent acts as a sort of antenna, or meeting point, of great energies from the sky and earth; that a gulf opens under the tent and extends to the center of the earth and that a column of energy reaches up into the sky. Within the tent the practitioner is able to call upon and use considerable powers. They may make long journeys across the earth, fly into the sky, or visit the land of lost souls; they may be given new eyes to see the exact location within a lake where the body of a drowned person lies.

The Shaking Tent is found in particular regions of the north, but in other parts of Turtle Island there are other ceremonies and techniques through which people can come into alliance with great powers. Whenever people sit in a circle, sing their songs, and speak their traditional language, they have the ability to draw upon the energies of the universe and strike alliances. It is said that it is possible to bring a person back from the dead and converse with him or her for a short time. But such an action should only be undertaken with the consensus of the whole group, for it involves the expenditure of considerable energy and, as with any experiment, it has an implication for the balance of the whole environment.

When Western scientists carry out an experiment they are essentially constraining the universe to work in a particular way within their laboratory. They do not consider that the local ordering demands that chaos should appear elsewhere in the environment. Every experiment has a global effect. In a similar way, the Shaking Tent and other ceremonies that involve the utilization of energy within the cosmos imply that balances and rearrangements must take place on a much wider scale. Therefore ceremonies can only be conducted through consensus and with the support of the whole society, for all things are connected and no experiment can be isolated from the rest of nature.

Flying

All over the world Indigenous peoples speak of their ability to undertake great voyages and travel long distances during particular ceremonies. Strangers may arrive at a village unannounced to find a meal prepared and their exact number anticipated. I have heard it said that a person does not hunt an animal, in the sense of tracking and following it, rather the hunter must arrive at the correct spot at exactly the right time to meet the animal by agreement. I have also heard it said that Native people possess the ability to look down on the land as if they are seeing it from a great height. Sometimes people indicate that they fly through the air, others seem to suggest that it is their vision, or ability to see, that makes the journey; some even speak of being given special eyes when in this state.

I have been particularly struck by these images of flying, which at first sight seem so alien to our Western scientific worldview, yet are so pervasive and vivid among the world's cultures. It is almost universal that spiritual and elevated persons and beings have the ability to fly. It was even said that Saint Thomas Aquinas, a man of great weight, hovered in the air while celebrating mass.

Over the last few years I have been on the faculty of Antioch College's annual conferences on Jungian ideas, held in Assisi, Italy. What struck me there were the reports of flying during dreams or periods of active imagination. Michael Conforti, a Jungian analyst and organizer of the meetings, feels that such fantasies are danger signals that indicate a person is retreating from actuality—for by the laws of nature human beings cannot fly.

While I agree in part, I was still nagged by the importance Western therapists, artists, and other creative people were placing on such experiences and how at times they were associated with knowledge and insight. This led me to think of the very many ways in which our culture seeks to simulate this sensation of flying through such sports as hang gliding, parachuting, skiing, skating, and skin diving, and how much the sensation of free flight is created in films through sweeping camera movements. One thinks, for example, of the opening scene of Alfred Hitchcock's *Psycho*, in which the camera moves across the city, sweeps down, and enters a bedroom window. It is as if we, the viewers, were in a dreamlike trance and flying into the events of the film. Federico Fellini's last film, *Intervista*, opens with a simulation of a dream of flying.

The more I looked into this the more I became convinced that we all have the intuition that human consciousness is not confined to the material space-time location of the physical body, but that there are times, or were times, in our distant past, when consciousness and perception could move freely and purposefully.

Have you ever taken a walk in the bush? You notice the natural paths created by the animals that use the forest. Imagine that you are part of a group walking along that path on a hunting expedition. The forest is alive, all around you are sounds and odors and sights; there are signs to be read, and somewhere, ahead on the path, is the game you seek. It does not take much intuition to begin to see how consciousness begins to focus and broaden, moving outward, extending a little along the path.

A non-Native person who is very alert soon begins to see some distance ahead. But imagine people whose whole culture is spent hunting in the woods. How much easier it would be for their consciousness to stretch out, like a laser, along the path and begin to see and read the signs that indicate the presence of animals or strangers.

It is my conjecture that human consciousness has the ability not so much to radiate outward but to focus and travel along paths that are shared with the animals of the forest, that may be the conduits of energy and allow one to gather information of what lies hours or even days ahead. Such a direct and vivid perception could indeed be very similar to that of flying. It may also be possible to share in the perceptions of birds and animals so that as consciousness moved along the path it could make use of the perceptual faculties of birds that circle high in the air, or animals that move close to the ground.

The idea that consciousness and perception can move along the guide tracks of paths ties into other considerations. All over the world the idea of a road or path is of great importance in ceremony and mythology. England has its "leys," straight tracks that apparently traversed parts of Britain and Europe in prehistoric times. Although the subject is controversial, it is claimed that the more important prehistoric sights align perfectly along these leys. Similar paths are found all over the Americas, the most famous being the roads of Chaco Canyon, which were, for no apparent reason, built perfectly straight even though they do not appear to link anything of significance. Add to this the various markings and earthworks that can only be seen from the air, such as the white horses carved on the chalk hills of the south of England or the curious patterns of lines in Peru that depict birds and animals.

My conjecture, and here I am not supported by anything I have been told from Indigenous science, is that these roads are tracks of power along which could travel both energies and human consciousness. The residual memories of these abilities, I believe, remain with us in our dreams.

Society and the Individual

A particularly significant way in which the Western and Native American visions of reality differ is in the idea of the individual. My most vivid experience of the world is myself, my ego, identity, and personal history—that which differentiates me from the buzzing confusion of the outer world. Reality begins within our own minds and radiates outward into our relationships.

A great deal of modern psychology is devoted to the primacy of the self and the strengthening of its identity. As never before, our society is stressing individual rights and seeking to protect them through legislation. In a sense this is simply an extension of Western metaphysics with its focus upon the object, on the importance of boundaries, and on the Western mind's preoccupation with concepts and categorization.

Nothing could be further from Native American metaphysics, with its insistence upon relationship rather than object as the primary reality, and the fluidity of its boundaries and constant transformation of its form. European social and political philosophy is based upon the concept of the isolated individual. To Thomas Hobbes, man "in a state of nature" desires to acquire domination over others while preserving his own liberty. The result is a brutish existence of constant conflict in which the higher concepts of justice and ownership of property have not evolved.

The resolution of this state of nature was for individuals to combine together into societies and acknowledge a social contract between them. This social contract, further discussed by John Locke and others, is the philosophical rationale for Western society. But if the individual is to sacrifice a measure of personal liberty within the social contract, then individual rights must be guaranteed by law. Thus, it has been said that, in law, rights are the fence an individual erects around himself for protection against his neighbors.

How absurd such a posture must seem from a worldview in which the individual emerges out of the society, rather than the other way around. The Indigenous worldview is one of relationship and out of that relationship, emerges the individual. In place of individual rights there are obligations and requirements of behavior. One does not so much sacrifice individual freedom by joining the group as achieve freedom by being a part of it.

This idea of collectivism and of an individual being defined through relationship within a wider context has much in common with the discoveries of modern physics.

Classical physics took the route of explaining complex systems in terms of the interactions of their components. It is a different story when quantum physicists study crystals, metals, and other solids and try to figure out how sound and other vibrations move through them, how heat is conducted, the way light penetrates and electrical currents flow. Scientists picture these flows in terms of the physical movement of particles. Curiously enough, however, these particles turn out to be "quasi-particles" or "elementary excitations," not so much particles in the traditional sense of the word (like miniature billiard balls) but rather the expression of the totality of the entire system.

Quasi-particles, with such exotic names as phonons, excitons, polarons, plasmons, and "dressed electrons," are in fact the collective expression of an astronomical number of entities that make up the solid. Out of this collectivity emerges something that appears just like a particle. It is localized in the sense that it exists within a particular small location and can move around, colliding with other excitations, bouncing off them and exchanging energy. The elementary excitation has all the attributes we associate with a particle, yet it is an expression of the whole. Thus it can never be removed from the totality. Indeed, if one attempted to remove a polaron or a phonon from a metal, then, like *Alice in Wonderland*'s Cheshire Cat, it would cease to exist. The elementary excitation manifests only by virtue of the totality of the system.

The notion that an elementary particle has no existence independent from the system finds an echo in that story, told in chapter 2, of the man who intended to leave his group: The further he rode away, the more was taken from him, for he had no existence apart from his group.

A Native person is always a part of a much greater entity and can never truly be separated from it. Each is an individual expression of the group, and, in turn, the group comes together in ceremonies to draw upon a much greater energy. Something analogous happens within a superconductor. Dressed electrons move through a metal wire and create an electrical current. Normally these dressed electrons bounce off objects in their path and, as a result, the flowing electrical current encounters resistance. Part of the electrical energy in a circuit is thereby dissipated into light and heat. This is the reason why a light bulb gives out illumination when it is switched on.

In a superconductor, however, it is possible for an electrical current to flow past obstructions without experiencing any resistance at all. This happens because the various excitations in the metal—the phonons and the dressed electrons—act in a coherent and cooperative fashion. It is as if there were a consensus to their movements so that all conspire to move in a coordinated dance.

Under normal circumstances, when an electron approached an obstruction in its path it does not possess sufficient energy to get past, so it bounces off—but now, thanks to the cooperative effects of the total system, it is smoothly guided around the obstacle. In the superconductor, electrical current flows as a unified whole, moving past all obstacles without experiencing any resistance and continuing to flow for decades, or even centuries.

The example of the superconductor also indicates the way in which a powerful new action can come about when people sit together, working through consensus and coherence. They are able to draw upon energies that vastly exceed those that are accessible to an isolated individual.

Conclusions:
Turning the Circle

Another winter has begun and almost passed since I began to write this book. The task has not been easy, for while I have at times been able to glimpse that other world, the world of Indigenous science, it has been difficult to set down its maps and contours in words. Previously words have served me for explaining such seemingly abstract concepts as superstrings and quantum reality, but as I entered the reality, of Indigenous America I realized how much my English words and "Western" viewpoints are inadequate to the task.

The best I can hope for is that this book is a start. If it has not opened a door into another world, at least it may have exposed a chink of light. If it has not built a bridge, then it may have showed the possibility of fording a river. Part of what is in this book relates to what I have been told and what I have sensed and experienced. Other parts of it appear as speculation, speculation in the sense of being about things that lie far beyond my experience, but also speculation in the way in which I have been forced to extend the boundaries of familiar images in order to convey what I only dimly perceive.

I hope that, now, at the end of the book the reader feels that reality is a bit wider than we had all assumed, that other valid worldviews are possible, and that there is much we can learn if only we take the space and time to listen. It is so difficult for us to change our ways. Ironically, we are all tainted with a history of struggle and heroism that does not dispose us to view the universe as a caring home.

The Hero's Quest

In the late sixteenth century an English clergyman, one Richard Hakluyt, began a three-volume series of books, *Principall Navigations, Voyages, and Discoveries of the English Nation*, which was to be "the prose epic of the modern English nation." Hakluyt had also written *Divers Voyages Touching the Discovery of America*, and for several hundred years these books were the inspirational reading of English-speaking schoolchildren. Hakluyt confirmed the heroic depiction of the early explorers. The first visitors to the New World became role models, larger-than-life figures who had followed their dreams and fought against appalling odds and privations in order to conquer new lands. The New World was virgin territory, ripe for conquest and exploitation.

This view of struggle and conquest did not originate with Hakluyt, for the hero's achievement is an ever-present theme in European thought and literature. In the legends of Greece and Rome, heroes are admired for their struggles against overwhelming opposition, adversity, the hostility of nature, and the force or foreign aggressors. Heroes symbolize the restless human spirit that led to the "Conquest of America," the "Conquest of the South Pole," the "Conquest of Everest," and now, the "Conquest of Space."

The heroic struggle between victory and defeat spills over into so much of that we do. We "fight crime," declare "war on want," and "wrestle" with inflation. Doctors must "conquer disease," use "aggressive" medical means, and develop the "magic bullets" of antibiotics. If street drugs become a problem, then we declare war upon them; and our organizations include the Salvation Army, Peace Corps, Boy and Girl Scouts, and, a century ago, the onward-marching Christian soldiers of the Victorian hymn. Joseph Campbell's popular books and television presentations on myth also speak of the "hero's journey."

I believe that this myth of the hero, while it has great value, must be kept in balance, for it is certainly not quite as universal as we assume. In the traditional stories of the Indigenous people of Turtle Island a variety of characters appear; some survived personal danger and performed acts of courage, yet they do not always fit conveniently into our heroic mold. Sitting Bull, for example, did not lead his people by riding into the thick of the Battle of the Little Big Horn. Rather, he led by remaining in his lodge, praying, and offering pieces of his own flesh as a sacrifice. Among the plains people it was considered more honorable to "count coup" on an enemy than to kill them outright. Counting coup consisted of riding into the thick of the enemy, symbolically striking a chosen opponent, and then riding away. The trickster, like Napi, is not cast in the Western heroic mold; rather, he performs foolish acts, turns things upside down, and makes the people laugh. It seems as if Native American culture has as much, or even more, respect for humor, comedy, and the absurd as it does for acts of heroism.

There is a story about how the Australian army wanted to test the endurance of its crack troops by arranging a race of several days' duration between a small group of soldiers and several Aboriginal people over particularly difficult terrain. Although the military group set a cracking pace, by the end of the first day the Aboriginal people were ahead. After making camp, they sat around the fire all night singing and telling stories. By the morning they had decided that they really did not have any particular reason for reaching their destination— a mere grid reference on a map—so, having had an enjoyable walk through the desert, they packed up and walked home.

This race between two cultures is also symbolized by the different attitude of Westerners and Tibetans to a mountain. If a Western mountaineer does not conquer a mountain and stand on its summit, the climb would be thought of as a failure. Tibetans, however, consider mountains to be sacred, and while they are willing to act as guides and climb them almost to the top, they will not normally set foot on their summits.

We interpret the lives of the Cree, Naskapi, Inuit, and others who live in the far North of Canada and Alaska as a heroic battle against an adverse, hostile environment. Yet the people of the North I have talked to love their land and way of life. I cannot forget how my Inuit friend Gideon Qaunaq, sitting in a city apartment, looked longingly at a photograph of a remote expanse of snow in the far North, saying "It would be very quiet there. There would be no one for miles."

Our Western minds see the wilderness as something to be tamed, shaped, and molded. In his essay "Wordsworth in the Tropics," Aldous Huxley argues that the Lake Country poet's identification with nature was confined to a gentle English countryside tamed by hundreds and thousands of years of human occupation. True nature, in all its wildness, Huxley argued, would have horrified Wordsworth. Huxley's assumption may be true. Yet, in a sense, Huxley himself is guilty of a similar blindness, for untamed nature appears to be associated in his mind with an intrinsic hostility and lawlessness, almost recalling Kurtz's dying cry in Joseph Conrad's *Heart of Darkness*, "The horror! The horror!" Many Indigenous forest dwellers, by contrast, would see the same forest as a nurturing provider of all that they need.

Brute nature is faced with human industry and an ingenuity that seeks to overcome its adversary. Science becomes the tool whereby change can be effected and nature controlled. Indigenous science, however, approaches the reality in a profoundly different way, for human society is not pictured as standing apart from the rest of nature. Animation and consciousness pervade all of nature from tree to plant and rock to star. Human beings are two-leggeds who have their role to play among the other beings of the world. Nature is not competitive, a battle for "the survival of the fittest," but a cooperative system of alliances. Even the plants grow though mutual relationship and support.

In a universe of animating spirits the heroic human individual cannot hope to control the world through brute force. Rather than seeking control, change, and progress, an Indigenous society prefers to live in harmony with the world.

Power certainly exists but it lies more within alliances and the ability to call upon external energies than it does in the human will or the unleashing of mechanical force.

Our world stands in need of renewal. So many difficulties face us: international tensions, poverty, starvation, economic instability, violence in the inner cities, the disappearance of species, and threats to the environment. Our worldview inclines us to perceive these as problems in search of solutions and crises in need of immediate and radical interventions. Yet so many different approaches have been attempted in the past and none of them has really worked. Over decades and centuries the same basic problems reappear and are never fully resolved. Even within the most revolutionary transformations of societies and governments so much remains unchanged and old problems surface in new guises.

Indigenous metaphysics offers us an alternative approach, a way of being within the world that does not analyze and categorize, control, and intervene, but rather admits the openness of the circle, accepts the unexpected, acknowledges obligations, and seeks harmony, balance, and equilibrium.

If we are willing to suspend our activity for a moment and listen to another way of being what can we hear and learn?

Farming Technology

Europeans came to the Americas in search of gold and discovered something far more valuable—vegetables and fruits. The Indigenous science of the Americas led to the development of a wide variety of crops that were taken back to the Old World. Today a large proportion of the food the world eats originated in the Americas. It has even been suggested that the Industrial Revolution would not have been possible without the cultivation of the crops that had been imported from the Americas. Ironically, these additional foodstuffs would ultimately lead to an explosive population increase along with the growth of dehumanizing cities and technologies.

Today scientists are beginning to study the remarkable farming methods practiced by Indigenous peoples in the Americas. Their aim is to discover techniques that could be transferred to the Third World and employed by ecologically minded farmers in the West. But this should be done in a cautious and watchful way, for Indigenous science was developed by people living in a particular landscape.

Biology

Recently a small number of biologists have begun to look critically at the foundations and ethical values of their subject. They have pointed out the respect that scientists should have for other species and, indeed, for all of life. Rather than biology remaining value-free, as is the case with the physical sciences, it should concern itself with ethics, responsibility, respect, relationship, and even love.

The biologist Brian Goodwin has called for a "reanimation of nature," while his colleague Mae-Wan Ho echoes Wolfgang Goethe's critique of the artificiality and ultimate distortions implied in the scientific experimentation of nature. It is their intention that the "new biology" should remain strictly scientific, in that is seeks to use reason and observation in order to come to an understanding of nature, but the same time they call into question the reductive and mechanistic approaches that are currently being employed in biology and, indeed, the whole way in which science approaches the phenomenon of life.

For thousands of years The People have supported ways of living in harmony with nature and of avoiding serious ecological disharmony. Their science of biology is rich, relying upon painstaking observations that are not exclusively objective but are the result of entering into relationship with each living thing. Indigenous biology also makes use of the knowledge and teachings of birds, animals, and insects. A dialogue between biology and Indigenous science could give Western scientists a new insight into gentle noninvasive observation, relationship, respect, and harmony with all of life.

Medicine

Modern medicine has in many ways been highly successful. Each year surgery becomes more skillful and less risky, infectious diseases that once ravaged certain areas of the world have been eliminated, and good sanitation and diet have helped to limit other forms of sickness. In the U.S. the death rate from heart attacks and heart failure dropped by 22 percent in the 1980s, while deaths from stroke dropped by 33 percent.

But Western medicine is not without its critics. To begin with, it represents the greatest cost that our society must bear. Increasing use of medical technologies has had the effect of alienating doctors from their patients to the point where many people feel that medicine now lacks a basic human touch. Indiscriminate use of antibiotics has had led to the evolution of drug-resistant bacterial strains, while modern life has created the very conditions that contribute to heart disease, cancer, and degenerative disorders. In addition, the whole area of mental health remains a cause for serious concern. Indeed, the act of simply living in our modern industrial world seems to create more medical, mental, and social problems than modern science can correct. Clearly medicine, as with all science, cannot be fragmented from society and human values.

Medicine is another one of those areas in which a productive dialogue could be held between the two worldviews. Indigenous science, as well as some forms of alternative medicine that are often based upon more ancient forms of healing, accents a profoundly different way of promoting health. Native medicine stresses relationship to the patient and the role of the whole society. It addresses the spiritual origins of disease and health and the way healing arises out of the patient's relationship to society and the cosmos. Within Indigenous medicine it is not possible to fragment an individual's sickness from the condition of society and the surrounding environment. A bridge between Native and Western medicine would be of importance to those who are concerned with the physical, mental, and spiritual health of society and the world at large.

The Physical Sciences

While medicine and biology seem natural avenues for dialogue, at first sight it would seem more difficult to contemplate a genuine exchange of knowledge between contemporary physics and Indigenous science. Indeed, what could be further apart—the one being concerned with the objective analysis of levels of inanimate matter, and the other, among other things, with the domain of the powers and animating processes of animals, plants, and rocks?

However, it is important that some sort of a bridge should be established between Western physics and Indigenous science and metaphysics, for physics is generally taken as the model and paradigm to which all the other sciences aspire. In addition, the concepts and attitudes of physics have had a profound effect upon our general worldview and the way we behave toward the world. In many subtle ways the worldview of physics has a dominating effect upon attitudes and, thus, if a dialogue can be established with Indigenous science, the door may be opened to something even broader.

I think that the most profitable discussions will come about as Indigenous and Western scientists explore their worldviews and underlying metaphysics. Investigations of the nature of time and space, causality, matter, and energy; and the connection between language, thought, and culture, and matter and consciousness are extremely valuable. It would also be salutary for physicists, who have now begun to deal within the flux of forms demanded by quantum theory, to talk with people whose whole worldview has been historically based upon process, animation, and flux. Indeed, it is my belief that a serious, sensitive, and extended dialogue between these two worlds would reveal surprising degrees of concordance and lead to insights about the whole meaning of theoretical speculation in modern physics.* I wonder if, at some time in the future, Leroy Little Bear's dream that one of the great theoretical physicists of the next century will be a Native American will be fulfilled.

Provided Western scientists remain sufficiently open and sensitive, I believe that the dialogues held with Indigenous scientists and Elders can be of considerable value to the West. But what could be the effects upon Indigenous societies in such

---

*Already these dialogues have begun, under the sponsorship of the Fetzer Institute.

bridge building? It may be presumptuous for me to answer this question, but I have outlined a few suggestions below.

Cultural Achievement and Revival

The First People of Turtle Island continue to suffer the prejudice of having their spirituality, social customs, arts, science, law, and government compared to the dominant standard of the West and dismissed as "primitive," "underdeveloped," "animistic," and "superstitious." In an age when political correctness has become the stick used to beat academics into impotence and submission it is ironic that so many of its norms simply do not apply, in practice at least, to the rights of Indigenous America.

So many of the cultural myths of North America exclude or devalue Native American culture and history. To take a somewhat extreme example, on Columbus Day 1992, Michael Berliner of the Ayn Rand Institute hailed the European conquest, describing the aboriginal culture as "a way of life dominated by fatalism, passivity, and magic." Western civilization, he claimed, brought "reason, science, self-reliance, individualism, ambition, and productive achievement" to a people who were based in "primitivism, mysticism, and collectivism" and to a land that was "sparsely inhabited, unused, and undeveloped." Ironically, despite his prejudice and factual ignorance, Berliner is correct when he contrasts Indigenous "collectivism" to Western "individualism, ambition, and productive achievement." These latter values are certainly alien to most Indigenous societies.

To take another example, in Quebec, Canada, plans are afoot to extend the massive James Bay Hydroelectric Project. This will involve flooding huge areas of traditional hunting lands and building roads into the far North. Such an enormous engineering project will have a profoundly disruptive effect on the lives of the Cree who continue to live in a traditional way by hunting and trapping. Officials of the Quebec government, however, welcome this enterprise, arguing that it will "bring the Cree into the twentieth century" and give them "new concepts of space and time." Again, there is the unconscious assumption that North American culture is superior and its imposition will benefit everyone.

On the other hand, dialogues are beginning between Western and Native American thinkers. Elders claim that they attempted to talk to the white people five hundred years ago but they did not know how to listen. Today they are willing to try again. A Blackfoot Elder said that the white race is the youngest race. It has great energy and potential, but, for the past few thousand years it has been playing like a child while it is watched by the black, yellow, and red peoples. Now the time has come for the white race to begin to learn, and assume its responsibilities along with the three other colors in the world.

As we Western thinkers listen and learn, we will begin to understand the achievements of Native American societies and acknowledge their worldviews as viable alternatives to our currently dominant industrial worldview. How will this affect the Indigenous people themselves?

I have been told that many young Native people are now obtaining their values from television, non-Native teachers, and other students in mixed schools. As a result, many yearn for the culture of the West. Others, angered by the prejudices of non-Natives, reject North American society out of hand, while at the same time cutting themselves off from their own roots.

If Native children come to see their traditions being accorded respect by non-Natives it may help them retain a balance within a torn and threatened society. They may realize that some Western thinkers look to Native American philosophy, ecology, social structures, and systems of justice and government for insights into the very problems that face them today.

Native science could also play an important role in recreating cultural connectedness across the globe. Within Indigenous science can be found a metaphysics, a way of being and of coming-to-knowing, that is quite different from the approaches that presently dominate the world. The Western scientific paradigm is tied to the ideals of advancing technology and unceasing progress. Its effect has been to create global cultural homogeneity based upon values that were originally

European. The idea of an Indigenous science could perhaps provide an antidote to a particular cultural dominance and could also assist in the survival and renewal of endangered cultures.

Five hundred years ago Europeans arrived on the American continent but did not listen. They did not understand the land and the people they sought to conquer. Today, in the light of so much that has taken place in world history, we can no longer feel such confidence in the rightness and inevitability of our position. Perhaps the time has at last come when we can simply sit down, listen, and come-to-knowing. Maybe, as the millennium reaches its close, we can all engage in a ceremony of renewal that will cleanse earth and sky. Maybe the time is right.

Afterword:
From the Blackfoot to Pari

During the 1960s the art historian, Sir Kenneth Clark, wrote and presented a highly successful and informative television series entitled "Civilization." To Clark, as to many other educated people, "civilization" meant frescoes and canvases, printed books, cathedrals, theatres, universities, and concert halls. "Civilization" began in ancient Greece, flourished during the Renaissance, and could now be presented, albeit in a somewhat diluted form, on television. By contrast, this book argues that the term "civilization" should also be applied to other forms of social organization and to worldviews.

At one level *Blackfoot Physics* is about an alternative vision of the cosmos. At another, it provides a way of looking back at our own culture and knowledge system. By making an effort to see, however fleetingly, the world through the eyes of Native America, we can then look back at our own world and in this way realize what we have been taking for granted. The more we learn other ways of understanding, the more we come to recognize the levels of cultural construction within our worldview. In this way we recognize that what we take for "reality" is, in part, the product of a cultural history, values, and set of beliefs.

Having said this, I am by no means arguing in favor of the sort of cultural relativism in which reality changes according to whatever a person or group happens to believe. As a scientist I believe in a level of objectivity to the cosmos. On the other hand, the way we structure our perceptions and understand this cosmos is influenced by the values we have and the questions we ask. These questions and values are, in turn, governed by the structure and history of our society.

Western science prides itself on its objectivity and freedom from cultural bias. A measurement of the force of gravity or the speed of light should yield the same result no matter how intense or diverse is the belief system of the particular scientist who carries out the experiment. However, societies and their belief systems deeply influence the questions we ask, the experiments we design, and the stories we create about the cosmos. By posing questions in different ways, other societies formulate quite different accounts of the world. It is not so much that one account, or one truth, opposes or contradicts another; the important thing is that they represent different but complementary ways of seeing the same universe. To say, as quantum mechanics does, that the electron is a wave does not deny its existence as a particle. Taken together both complementary approaches provide a more complete description of the electron's nature. Likewise, by respecting other knowledge systems, we temper, illuminate, and enrich our own.

There are many ways of approaching the world and different stories to be told. One truth should not deny and replace another; rather, we gain a richness of understanding when we embrace diverse ways of seeing.

Western science today is a dominant force underlying the way North Americans and Europeans structure and understand their world. A considerable enrichment of this understanding is therefore possible when Western science dialogues with indigenous worldviews. In fact contemporary science is already engaged in other dialogues. There is, for example, a fashion for dialogues on art and science and between science and spirituality. Schools of psychotherapy also wish to dialogue with the "new physics."

Indigenous worldviews, art, religion, psychotherapy, and theoretical physics are different ways of experiencing and structuring the world. While translation between them is therefore never easy, the rewards can be great. Yet a danger arises when, for example, psychotherapy seeks to gain greater credence by giving its theories a "more scientific" basis. There are attempts to explain the therapeutic process in terms of fields, non-local interactions, or the forces exerted by strange attractors. Sometimes, underlying such accounts is the hidden assumption that the descriptions given by physics are more "fundamental," "deeper," or "truer" than the experiments of artists, the visions of mystics, the intuitions of the human mind, or the experience of indigenous peoples. To be fully enriching, all positions in these conversations about worldviews should be equally authentic.

Centuries ago there would have been no need to establish dialogues between art, science, and religion because they were all one. They were all equal aspects of what it meant to be human. It was only after the Middle Ages that the "Western" world became fragmented and specialized. Is the same true for "Western" and "indigenous" worldviews? Were we once *all* indigenous peoples? Can the roots of our "Western" scientific and technological world be traced back to an earlier indigenous world? Some Native Americans say that the "Western" mind is "hard" and that we "Westerners" experience a restricted view of reality. Is this inevitably the case or simply an historical accident?

What I have been calling in this book "Western civilization" required an economic base and an infrastructure of support. This meant that "civilization" was only possible in towns with a relatively fixed population and a vigorous economy based on trade and production. Today more and more of the world's population lives in cities. This has changed our relationship with the natural world. Cities shield us from the fluctuations of nature. Street lighting makes it difficult to see the night sky, and the phases of the moon become less important than the fluctuations of the stock market or the particular time when a soap opera is aired. The affluent are able to maintain a summer cottage by a lake, on a seashore, or in the mountains and take a Sunday drive to a "natural" park—their experience of the natural world has become indirect and even painted over with a wash of romantic nostalgia.

The city presents a radically different environment from the Italian village in which I now live, or the Blackfoot camp I once visited. That is not to say that one is necessarily better than the other. They are simply different, and this difference affects our consciousness and thus the way we structure our world.

The Western mind has produced enormous triumphs with its technology. We can traverse the globe in hours or communicate instantly by telephone and the Internet. New materials have been created, and medicine has eliminated many diseases. All this was made possible through our constant desire for progress. But as we have come to understand in recent decades, "progress" has its shadow side. We have seriously disturbed the balance of nature, sometimes in irreversible ways, and we have a long history of imposing our values on other, less economically powerful societies. Is this an inevitable characteristic of the Western mind? Must technological improvements always be tied to a desire to dominate and control? Are the values associated with other, more gentle, societies forever lost to us? And will those societies, in turn, adopt the values of the West?

Questions like these came to my mind as I finished writing this book. In the end, I discovered some answers in the medieval hilltop village where I now live (although I may also have found it in other villages in Italy, Spain, France, Greece or Portugal, and maybe in small communities in North America).

I came to Pari by pure chance while taking a break from writing. Two years later I left the world of the city and returned to live here permanently. Maybe this decision was made in part because I was seeking a hint of that continuity that would link our Western civilization to the common origin of all cultures, an origin that stretches back to the Neolithic age, a time when people lived and celebrated together in small communities close to nature and her seasons.

The village of Pari is located about twenty-five kilometers south of Siena. Written records from at least a thousand years ago and a thirteenth-century century map shows Pari laid out exactly as it is today. The area itself was inhabited far earlier. Over two thousand years ago the Etruscans enjoyed the nearby hot springs, and their graves can be found in the valley below our village.

The land immediately around the village is not rich, but for centuries was sufficient to support a population of over two thousand in the village and surrounding farms. The olive oil is of highest quality for, as they say here, "the poorer the soil the better the oil." People have their vines for wine—we are on the border between the Chianti and Brunello regions. Many families still keep chickens and a pig. Wild boar, deer, hare, and game birds are hunted in the woods nearby.

Flour was ground from wheat grown further down in the valley, and at dawn people would take their loaves to the communal oven. Clothing was made from wool from the local sheep, which also supplied milk for the pecorino cheese. A type of linen was made from the ginestra or broom plant and mulberry trees fed silkworms. Shoes were studded with nails for durability, and in summer the local cobblers made sandals from snake skin. The village had its blacksmiths, tailors, dressmakers, carpenters, and builders—it even had a choir and orchestra. In those days everything worked on a barter system with the only money in circulation coming from the sale of wine to Siena and the smuggling of salt past a nearby customs post. In this manner Pari, like other small villages, could be totally self-sufficient for century upon century.

During the 1950s Pari suffered the major impact of Tuscany's industrial and economic revolution. People were lured away to the cities or to work in factories. Land was sold and houses stood empty. Today the population within the village itself stands at around two hundred. Yet because so much of value continues to be cherished and preserved, it makes me wonder if indigenous European roots were not unlike those of Native America and other indigenous societies.

The people of Pari do not live in tepees or hunt buffalo, but in summer you will find a circle of chairs in the main piazza. This is where the men sit and talk each evening. On the other side is a circle for women. It is in this piazza that decisions are made. What could be taken for gossip is constantly circling Pari. It takes only five to ten minutes to walk around the village, yet when people do this "giro" they are constantly stopping to talk to each other, and in this way news and information of a highly active nature is always being exchanged. People know what is going on and what has to be done. When the village holds the annual meeting of its association, Sette Colli, major decisions are debated and resolved in a handful of minutes. This is because, night after night, projects and proposals have already been discussed in the square to the point where everyone knows exactly what is going on. Lack of stress means that there is a very high proportion of people in their eighties and nineties—thus a continuity of history is preserved, and so the stories continue.

Even today most people in Pari do not live by the clock, but by the days and seasons. Those who work the land leave their homes at sunrise and return later in the morning, when the sun has become too hot. Work resumes in the cooler late afternoon and ends at twilight. Time in Pari is very much a circle. Everyone is aware of the phases of the moon and if a particular moon is early or late one month. Planting is done by the moon, and the moon brings about changes in the weather. People understand the winds, so that when the sky is particularly overcast and, to me at least, it looks like heavy rain, they will tell me, "It won't rain today." The year's round is marked by a cycle of the festivals beginning with the old witch, Befana, on January 6, and through communal lunches and dinners, village walks, picnics, the great festival of the spicy sausage at the end of September and, just before Christmas, a dinner, to celebrate the end of the year.

As with Native Americans, most men and women in Pari are generalists and their skills extend to farming, building, and general repairs, growing food, and so on. While total self-sufficiency ended half a century ago, and some people drive to nearby towns to work, people still have a strong attachment to the land. There is a sense of economy of means present in Pari. Articles are often repaired, rather than thrown out. Pillows and mattresses are periodically emptied, cleaned and restuffed. Linen is embroidered and clothing repaired. Until a year or two ago, when natural gas arrived, wood was still one of the major ways used to heat houses—it is still the only way mine is heated.

So much can be picked up in the woods and roadside. People know the locations of wild mushrooms, herbs, wild asparagus, and healing plants. Nuts and berries are picked along the roadside. Seeds are extracted from pinecones to make pesto sauce. A variety of medicinal plants can be found in the woods. Chestnuts are ground into sweet flour. If a pig is kept then, just as with the Buffalo of Native America in the last century, a use is found for every part of the animal. A small patch of land yields abundance—vegetables, tomatoes for sauce, a patch of artichokes, rows of vines to supply wine for the year, and there will be a grove of olive trees for oil, not to mention fruit trees and figs. Above all, food is of prime importance. It is something to be talked about all day and treated with great respect so that everyone in the family will sit around the table for the midday and evening meal.

The village itself is a containing place. Our three-year-old grandchild can wander from the main square, and we are confident that someone will look out for him and bring him back if he gets lost. Likewise, the one or two old people who have become confused are always contained within the village.

As I write this I can hear the chug-chug of Aladino's small three-wheel tractor as it comes up the hill from the fields. In summer you can almost set you clock by this sound. During my first weeks in Pari, Aladino would stop his tractor, point across to the land, and say to me, "Look." I'd look and nod but he would hold my arm and insist again: "No, look! Look!" as he was compelling me to see all that he saw. And what did he see? Beauty? Or is this a townsperson's romantic response to nature. Was it the spirit of land? Was it a "map in the head," a sense of belonging that stretches back a thousand years or more? The generations that had worked the land, picked olives, pruned the vines and cut wood for the fire?

Pari is only one of many villages that continues to preserve a traditional way of life. Its future is uncertain. In time the village may slowly die as young people leave to find work elsewhere, and the village becomes increasingly deserted. On the other hand, it could experience a revival as craftspeople move in set up new businesses, while others who respect the land and value a peaceful way of life decide to make it their permanent home. Or, as with other villages, it could become a parody of itself, a holiday village packed during the summer months with tourists on vacation taking photographs of the handful of remaining locals who sun themselves in the piazza.

The people of Pari and other such villages represent an increasingly smaller percentage of the world's population. But they are the containers of knowledge and a way of life that is of enormous value. Pari is as much a part of all that is valuable in Western civilization as the art treasures of Florence, the books in the Library of Congress, and the artifacts in the British museum. Only time will tell if villages like Pari, the history they preserve, and our own ancient roots will continue to survive into the twenty-first century.

—F. DAVID PEAT

To learn more about Pari see www.paricenter.com or David Peat's web site at www.fdavidpeat.com.

Bibliography

In recent years interest in Native America has begun to increase, and there are now many books being published about the First People of Turtle Island. In the past, most of these were written from a non-Native perspective and value system. Today, however, one can also find novels, plays, essays, and poetry written from a Native American point of view. Biographies and collections of interviews are also appearing. However, most academic works on Native American anthropology, sociology, art, spirituality, and linguistics still tend to be written by non-Natives. It will be interesting to see what changes occur when Native scholars begin to write about their own traditions and worldviews.

Most of the larger bookstores now have a section devoted to Native American studies where readers can browse while exercising a measure of discrimination. Firsthand accounts by Native people are the most valuable, and, of these, the recorded words of Black Elk, a spiritual leader of the Oglala Sioux, are particularly impressive. This material can be found in:

Black Elk. *The Sacred Pipe* (Recorded and edited by Joseph Epes Brown). New York: Penguin Books, 1971.

McLuhan, L. C., ed. *Touch the Earth: A Self Portrait of Indian Existence*. New York: Simon & Schuster, 1976.

Meili, Dianne. *Those Who Know: Profiles of Alberta's Native Elders*. Edmonton: NeWest Press, 1992.

Powers, Marla N. *Oglala Women*. Chicago: University of Chicago Press, 1988.

Taylor, Fraser. *Standing Alone: A Contemporary Blackfoot Indian.* Halfmoon Bay, B.C.: Arbutus Bay Publications (Box 12, Secret Cove, RR 1, Halfmoon Bay, B.C., Canada, VON 1YO), 1989.

Turner, Frederick W. III, ed. *The Portable North American Indian Reader.* New York: Penguin Books, 1974.

Wall, Steve, and Harvey Arden. *Wisdomkeepers: Meetings With Native American Spiritual Elders.* Hillsboro, Ore.: Beyond Worlds Publishing, 1990.

A variety of Native communities produce their own publications, newsletters, and newspapers—for example, Akwesasne Notes, published by the Mohawk Nation, Rooseveltown, New York. Such publications are invaluable, since they reflect the direct experience of Native communities. Native communities, school boards, and educational centers are also publishing their own collections of traditional stories and language primers.

For those who wish to visit Native America, an invaluable guidebook is:

Eagle/Walking Turtle. *Indian America: A Traveler's Companion.* Santa Fe: John Muir Publications, 1989.

As to additional readings, specific books and readings are referred to in the text and most of them are fully cited below, along with some other books for those who wish to explore ideas in greater detail. Their value is varied: While some of them appear to me to present their material in an honest and insightful way, others are inevitably tinged by worldviews and academic value systems that would be alien to many Native Americans.

Chapter 2

Bullchild, Percy. *The Sun Comes Down.* San Francisco: Harper Books, 1985.

Grinell, George Bird. *Blackfoot Lodge Tales.* Lincoln: University of Nebraska Press, 1962.

Napi Stories. Browning, Mont.: Blackfeet Heritage Program, 1979.

Chapter 3

Akwesasne Notes, ed. *Basic Call to Consciousness.* Summertown, Tenn.: Book Publishing Company, 1991.

Gidmark, David. *Birchbark Canoe.* Burnstown, Ont.: General Store Publishing House (1 Main Street, Burnstown, Ont., Canada, KOJ 1GO), 1989.

Griffin, Susan. *Woman and Nature.* New York: Harper & Row, 1978.

Huxley, Aldous. *Collected Essays.* New York: Harper and Brothers, 1958.

Katz, Richard. *Boiling Energy: Community Healing Amongst the Kalahari Kung.* Cambridge, Mass.: Harvard University Press, 1992.

———. *The Straight Path: A Story of Healing and Transformation in Fiji.* Reading, Mass.: Addison Wesley, 1993.

Lowes, Warren. *Indian Giver: A Legacy of North American Native People.* Penticton, B.C.: Theytus Books, 1986.

Ross, Rupert. *Dancing with a Ghost: Exploring Indian Reality.* Markham, Ont.: Octopus Publishing Group, 1992.

Taylor, Fraser. *Standing Alone.* Op. cit.

Chapter 4

Dewdeny, Selwin. "Dating Rock Art in the Canadian Shield." Toronto: Royal Ontario Museum Occasional Paper, No. 24, 1970.

_____. *The Sacred Scrolls of the Southern Ojibway.* Toronto: University of Toronto Press, 1975.

Dewdeny, Selwin, and K. E. Kidd. *Indian Rock Paintings of the Great Lakes.* Toronto: University of Toronto Press, 1967.

Johnston, Basil. *Ojibway Ceremonies.* Lincoln: University of Nebraska Press, 1990.

_____. *Ojibway Heritage.* Toronto: McClennand and Stewart, 1976.

Mysteries of the Ancient Americas. Pleasantville, N.Y.: Readers Digest Association, 1986.

Silverberg, Robert. *The Mound Builders.* Athens: Ohio University Press, 1970.

Swauger, James L. *Petroglyphs of Ohio.* Athens: Ohio University Press, 1984.

Chapter 5

Martin, Calvin. *Keepers of the Game: Indian-Animal Relationships and the Fur Trade.* California: University of California Press, 1978.

Nikiforuk, Andrew. *The Fourth Horseman: A Short History of Epidemics, Plagues and Other Scourges.* London: Fourth Estate, 1992.

Porter, Roy. "Bugged by Progress." *Sunday Times of London,* April 12, 1992.

Chapter 6

Frankl, Viktor E. *Man's Search for Meaning.* New York: Washington Square Press, 1965.

_____. *Psychotherapy and Existentialism: Selected Papers on Legotherapy.* New York: Penguin Books, 1973.

Katz, Richard. *Boiling Energy.* Op. cit.

_____. *The Straight Path.* Op. cit.

Chapter 7

Edmonson, Munro S. *The Book of the Year: Middle American Calendrical Systems.* Salt Lake City: University of Utah Press, 1988.

Maalville, J. McKim, and Claudia Putnam. *Prehistoric Astronomy of the Southwest.* Boulder, Colo.: Johnson Books, 1989.

Marcos, Joyce. *MesoAmerican Writing Systems.* Princeton: Princeton University Press, 1992.

Men, Hunbatz. *Secrets of Mayan Science/Religion.* Santa Fe: Bear and Company, 1990.

Morris, Ronald W. B. *The Prehistoric Rock Art of Calloway and the Isle of Mann.* Poole Dorset: Blandford Press, 1979.

The Place of Astronomy in the Ancient World. Proceedings of the Royal Society. Oxford: Oxford University Press, 1973.

Thom, Alexander. *Megalithic Lunar Observatories.* Oxford: Oxford University Press, 1971.

———. *Megalithic Sites in Britain.* Oxford: Oxford University Press, 1967.

Waters, Frank. *Mexico Mystique: The Coming of the Sixth World of Consciousness.* Chicago: Sage Books, 1975.

Chapter 9

Bohm, David. *Wholeness and the Implicate Order.* London, Boston: Routledge & Kegan Paul, 1981.

Carrol, J. M., ed. *Language, Thought and Reality: Selected Writings of Benjamin Lee Whorf.* Cambridge, Mass.: MIT Press, 1956.

Chapter 10

Devereux, Paul. *Symbolic Landscapes: The Dreamtime Earth and Avebury's Open Secret.* London: Blandford Press, 1992.

Eysenck, Hans. *Collected Essays.* Op cit.

Huxley, Aldous. *Collected Essays.* Op cit.

Chapter 11

Al-Dargazelli, Setha. "Doctor-Healer" *Newsletter* 7 (1993–94). 19 Fore Street, Bishopsteignton, South Devon, TQ14 9QR, England.

Grim, John A. *The Shaman: Patterns of Religious Healing Among the Ojibway Indians.* Norman: University of Oklahoma Press, 1987. (I know that the term *shaman* may be irritating to many traditional people. However, John Grim is a man of heart who has great respect for the Native American world.)

Jung, Carl. *VII Sermones ad Mortuos: The Seven Sermons to the Dead Written by Basilides in Alexandria the City Where the East Toucheth the West*, trans. H. G. Baynes. London: Stuart & Watkins, 1967.

Tedlock, Dennis, and Barbara Tedlock. *Teachings from the American Earth.* New York: Liveright, 1975.

Tooker, Elisabeth, ed. *An Iroquois Source Book: Vol. 3, Medicine Society Rituals.* New York: Garland, 1986.

———. *Native North American Spirituality of the Eastern Woodlands: The Classics of Western Spirituality.* Mahwah, N.J.: Paulist Press, 1979.

Index

325

An Alexandria Book

Phanes Press publishes quality books on
philosophy, mythology, ancient religions, the
humanities, cosmology, and culture.
To receive a copy of our catalogue and
information on conferences related
to the subject matter of
our titles, write:

Phanes Press
PO Box 6114
Grand Rapids, MI 49516
USA

www.phanes.com